THE WAY THINGS ARE

THE WAY

THINGS

ARE

conversations

with

HUSTON SMITH

on the

spiritual life

EDITED AND WITH A PREFACE

BY PHIL COUSINEAU

University of California Press   Berkeley   Los Angeles   London

University of California Press
Berkeley and Los Angeles, California

University of California Press, Ltd.
London, England

© 2003 by the Regents of the University of
California

Library of Congress Cataloging-in-Publication
Data

Smith, Huston.
    The way things are : conversations with
Huston Smith on the spiritual life / edited and
with a preface by Phil Cousineau.
        p.   cm.
    Includes bibliographical references and
index.
    ISBN 0-520-23816-8 (cloth : alk. paper).
    1. Smith, Huston—Interviews.
2. Religion historians—United States—
Interviews.   3. Religion.   4. Spiritual life.
5. Religion and science   I. Cousineau, Phil.
II. Title.

BL43.S64 A5   2003
200'.92—dc21   2003000592

Manufactured in the United States of America
11   10   09   08   07   06   05   04   03
10   9   8   7   6   5   4   3   2   1

The paper used in this publication meets the
minimum requirements of ANSI/NISO
Z39.48–1992 (R 1997) (*Permanence of Paper*).
♾

What is true is real,
but nothing more.

—SU CH'E

Lead us from the unreal to the Real,
lead us from darkness to Light,
lead us from death to immortal life.
Peace, peace, peace.

—*An ancient Hindu chant*

The elders told us that this is the road of life
that we're walking down. We're supposed to be
holding up one another, supporting each other,
having our arm underneath our brother's arms
while walking down the road of life.

—REUBEN SNAKE, *Winnebago medicine man*

CONTENTS

The Way Things Are for Huston Smith

In the summer of 1984, Huston Smith, the eminent historian of religion, arrived at the campus of the University of California at Berkeley, and like many a scholar before him, took a tour of the main library. The bountiful collection of books was a tantalizing sight, but as he followed the arrows and read the labels at the end of each shelf, such as History, Literature, and Chemistry, it occurred to him that something vital was missing.

"Where is the arrow that points to Importance?" he asked himself. "Where is the arrow toward Wisdom?"

In one form or another Huston Smith has been posing that question to himself—and the world—all his life. Where can we find what is ultimately meaningful? How can we discover what is truly worth knowing?

For Smith, the poet T. S. Eliot described the dilemma more precisely than anyone else in our time when he asked in his poem "The Rock," "Where is the wisdom we have lost in knowledge? / Where is the knowledge we have lost in information?" The modern debate about learning what matters most has ancient roots. When the Ptolemies founded the Library of Alexandria in the third century B.C.E., their dream was no less than to collect a copy of everything ever written. Eventually, the library accumulated an estimated five hundred thousand scrolls and manuscripts, but the library's motto, etched in the stone lintel above the entrance, hinted at its deeper purpose: "The Place of the Healing of the Soul."

For as long as he can remember, Huston Smith tells us, he has been trying to find a balance between the secular and the sacred dimensions of learning. In his avowed love of the spiritual life, he has always felt compelled to explore—and champion—the world's great religious traditions. When asked what he has gleaned from a lifetime of studying the religions of the world, he says it is "the winnowed wisdom of the human race." More important, he adds, he has gained access to "another world to live in," which he has variously described as the Eternal, the Timeless, the Ultimate, and the place where he encounters God.

Beyond the poetic descriptions of the seemingly ineffable lies a more elemental one. "Religion is for me the search for the Real," he told journalist Timothy Beneke in 1996, "and the effort to approximate one's life to it. Such approximation should be easy because the Real is so real, but in fact it is difficult because we are so unreal." Why we often feel unreal is at the core of his thinking: the dominant scientific—which Smith demotes to "scientistic"—worldview has shrunk our view of reality. Each time an eminent scientist, such as physicist Steven Weinberg, claims that "the more the universe seems comprehensible, the more it seems pointless," Smith fears that science, while banqueting us with technological gains, is starving our souls by eclipsing the Transcendent.

Defiant in the face of such nihilism, Smith has for decades communicated to his students and readers that this is *not* the way things are—life is *not* pointless, meaningless, purposeless. Instead, he admits to being driven to demonstrate the way things *are*, in fact—rich with purpose, value, and transcendental meaning. In the manner of one of his mentors, Aldous Huxley, he has cultivated "mystical empiricism" by compiling encounters with the Divine that saints, sages, and seers in every era have reported, a collection that makes a strong case for religion being the fundamental humanizing force in history.

PILGRIMAGE BETWEEN TWO WORLDS

Huston Smith's books are all still in print, his essays have been anthologized, and his documentary films are available on video, but the numerous interviews conducted with him over the years have not been collected until now. The twenty-two magazine and newspaper interviews and edited documentary film transcripts that compose this collection span three decades, from 1971 to 2002. I believe they provide a profound new source of insight into Smith's views on the world's religious heritage and its relevance for our times. Inevitably, the interviews cover some of the same ground as his books, essays, and articles, but these exchanges reveal a treasure trove of details about his long journey to discover the universal truths at the heart of humanity's search for the ultimate nature of things.

One of the richest discoveries for me came while I was poring through old clippings from Huston's file cabinets. So animated were the interviews that I found myself *listening* to them, as if sitting in on a series of enthralling conversations. Slowly it dawned on me that not only was the content invariably brilliant, but so was the form. What emerged was evidence of the venerable *art* of conversation. I was prompted to recall Caliph Ali Ben Ali's expression "A subtle conversation—Ah! That is the true Garden of Eden!" I thought of the time the transcendentalist philosopher Ralph Waldo Emerson confided to a friend that he would gladly walk a hundred miles through a snowstorm for one good conversation, and I remembered the incisive comment by the sociologist Peter Berger, who wrote that civilization advances by way of conversation.

These interviews may also be regarded as creative *dialogues,* in physicist David Bohm's sense of the "free flow of meaning" that is possible when people genuinely converse by listening to and sounding out each other. Writing and speaking are among the greatest pleasures we can cultivate in our lives, but there are vital distinctions between the two, which Huston respects and reflects on in his interview with educator Jeffrey Kane:

Writing can be disconnected from the writer. There it is in print, dead and frozen. Speech, on the other hand, is not only alive; it *is* life, because it cannot be separated from the living person in one mode of his or her own being. Exclusively oral cultures are unencumbered by dead knowledge, dead facts. Libraries, on the other hand, are full of them.

The liveliness of these conversations with journalists, scholars, editors, and filmmakers reveals a meandering path that embodies what the poet

John Keats had in mind when he wrote, "A man's life of any worth is a continual allegory." What unfolds in Huston Smith's life is often allegorical of the story played out by innumerable modern people who have encountered the alternately exhilarating and terrifying brave new world of our modern multicultural times—and attempted to respect, understand, and then tolerate it. If our culture has become any more knowledgeable and accepting of other people's religions, surely Huston has been in the vanguard of the movement.

"Let your life speak," say the Quakers, and Huston Smith's life has spoken, sometimes as quietly as a Quaker service, and at other times almost shouting, as when he sees religious freedom being threatened.

Born in 1919 as the son of missionary parents in rural China, Huston left when he was seventeen to venture off to America, where he planned to study for the ministry at Central Methodist College in Faytette, Missouri. By his junior year he had grown restive. One night during a feverish discussion with his fellow students on the meaning of life he had a realization he has described as "having the force of a conversion experience." What Smith discovered during his "night of fire," as Pascal called his own epiphany, was the world of philosophy—the study of wisdom itself—and the encounter shifted his vocation from preaching to teaching.

What began as an intellectual interest phased into a spiritual quest as well, which intensified during his graduate study at the Divinity School of the University of Chicago. It was there, in the early 1940s, that he vowed to devote the rest of his life to reconciling what Alfred North Whitehead has called the two most powerful forces in history—science and religion. His vision, as a callow young idealist, was to bring religion in line with science, because at the time he thought science had the Big Picture. That notion quickly collapsed. But he has remained a life-long teacher whose major appointments have been evenly divided between philosophy and religious studies (a distinction he blithely ignores) at Washington University in St. Louis, Massachusetts Institute of Technology, Syracuse University, and the University of California at Berkeley, from which he retired as Visiting Professor of Religious Studies at age seventy-seven.

With respect to the disciplinary distinctions between philosophy and religious studies, there is one point in regard to Huston's career that I do not find stated in these interviews or in his books, so I will state it here for the record. To my eyes, Huston Smith's top priority is not religion, but philosophy, and even more specifically, metaphysics. When push comes to shove, he will side with religion because he feels that today, when metaphysics has pretty much collapsed, religion is the chief custodian of the worldview that endorses Transcendence, the radiant reality that awaits us outside of Plato's cave. But in traditional times, which were not so much interdisciplinary as predisciplinary, the conceptual spine of the great religions comes closer to what we would now call metaphysics than theology. This is to say, Smith surely honors the contemporary world, even revels in the wonders of modern technology. But he honors *more* than the contemporary; he honors the timeless truths of the human adventure, what has been expressed by the perennial philosophy, the primordial tradition that is beyond the exigencies of the day.

That being said, long ago Huston stopped tilting at the windmills of reconciliation between science and religion, as they are positioned today. But his quixotic faith in reconciling ordinary people to their innate urge to find truth and Transcendence has never diminished. His six most important books chart the course of his attempt to communicate his essentially mystic vision of religion as the essential civilizing force in human affairs. Beginning with his classic text, *The World's Religions* (a revised version of *The Religions of Man*), and culminating in his recent international best-seller, *Why Religion Matters,* Smith has journeyed far in his intellectual pilgrim's progress. In the incisive words of M. Darroll Bryant, the editor of his *Essays on World Religion,* Smith has moved from "a naïve supernaturalism to theistic naturalism, and on to the mystical primordialism of the traditionalist outlook."

What distinguishes Huston's career has been his refusal to teach and write conventionally. Instead of clinging to the academic approach to religion, which aims for objective knowledge—such as historical facts, dates, and names—he has reached for what has touched him most deeply: the values and meaning that religions convey. His attitude toward pedagogy is also moral. He avidly believes that a teacher of religion has a responsibility to convey the *lived reality* of religious traditions. "My central object," he has said, "has been to offer my students another world to live in," and to do this he himself has tried to live up to the Platonic model of the well-examined and well-lived life. In the spirit of the Buddha, who told his followers, "Don't believe something merely because I tell you it's true—find out for yourself if it's true," Smith has striven to experience as much as possible of the traditions he has taught and written about.

To accomplish this task, he has ventured far beyond the libraries and books he reveres to specialize in what anthropologists call "participant observation." His ambition has led him to practice yoga with Hindu gurus in India, meditate with Zen masters in Japan, pray with Buddhist monks in Burma, dance with Sufi dervishes in Iran, practice tai chi with Taoist masters in China, observe Sabbath with his daughter and her Jewish husband, participate in sweats and peyote meetings with Huichol Indians in Mexico, take psychedelics with Timothy Leary and Ram Dass at Harvard, and discover polyphonic chanting among Tibetan monks in India, all the while worshiping regularly in his local Methodist church when he is home. In this way his religious life was more than born; it was awakened.

Huston has incorporated what he learned from many of these adventures into his own daily spiritual ritual, which to this day consists of morning readings of sacred literature, meditation, prayers in Arabic, hatha yoga, and composting. When asked how composting can be a spiritual discipline, he answers that philosophers tend to walk around with their heads in the clouds and that composting helps to "ground" him. His Native American friends tell him that he has learned to "walk his talk."

This sagacious synthesis of wisdom and method reminds me of the seven pieces of ancient Greek existential advice that greeted pilgrims at the Temple of Apollo at Delphi. Inscribed above the temple door was the renowned "Know thyself," and nearby was its twin inscription: "Nothing in excess." But some scholars speculate about five other maxims, including "Practice is everything." The oracular words suggest that one-sided wisdom is never enough; true wisdom is always two-sided. Self-knowledge is fleeting without discipline.

While Huston Smith's books and classes have been popular, his eclectic approach has turned many an academic apoplectic. The common criticisms are, first, that his interest in common denominators leads him to blur the boundaries between religions, and second, that he is proselytizing instead of teaching, prescribing rather than describing. His gnomic response is simply that sharing his love for his material is no different from a music teacher revealing her passion for Mozart through her teaching techniques.

If Huston has had a hidden agenda, it has been a noble one: to encourage his students and readers to study other religions so they might better enjoy the many splendid hues of the spiritual life. When Steve Reuys asked him in their 1972 interview for the MIT newsletter what someone might gain from learning about a religious tradition other than his or her own, Smith said: "What cross-cultural study can provide is a perspective on one's self, one's own condition. A single eye can give us up and down, and right and left, but it takes two eyes converging on an object from different angles to provide the dimension of depth."

As the painter Paul Cézanne chased the truth of light across the mountains of southern France, so has Huston Smith pursued the light of truth across time and space. This despite the fact that no one recognizes more than he the pitfalls of taking seriously the perennial quest for truth. This because he is so aware of Gandhi's assertion that "truth is the only religion; untruth is bondage."

The title of one of his books reveals this deeper concern. In *Forgotten Truth* Smith began the book by asking one of the fundamental questions of philosophy: "People have a profound need to believe that the truth they perceive is rooted in the unchanging depths of the universe, for were it not so, could the truth be really important?" Then he immediately personalizes the universal question by asking, "How can we hold our truth to be the Truth when others see the truth so differently?" Questioning the ultimate truth of one's deepest religious beliefs can be an agonizing problem for individuals and societies alike. The need to resolve it is at the core of his philosophy of religion, and it was his serendipitous discovery of the writings of Frithjof Schuon in the early 1970s, while on a year-long around-the-world seminar with his wife, Kendra, and thirty students, that helped break the impasse. In the book he co-authored with David Griffin, *Primordial Truth and Postmodern Theology*, Smith outlines the influence of Schuon's work on him:

I discovered that he situated the world's religious traditions in a framework that enabled me to honor their significant differences unreservedly while at the same time seeing them as expressions of a truth that, because it is single, I could absolutely affirm. In a single stroke, I was handed a way of honoring the world's diversity without falling prey to relativism, a resolution I had been seeking for more than thirty years.

Haunted by his original spiritual dilemma of the One and the Many, Smith finally realized that the perennial—or as he prefers, the primordial, since it includes space as well as time—tradition offered an ingenious third possibility. Instead of seeking the elusive universal essence that pervades every religious tradition, why not consider each one unique but still only one of the multiple expressions of the Absolute?

The Vedas said it best: "Truth is one; sages speak of it by many names."

THE LIGHT OUTSIDE THE CAVE

Invariably we find on the flip side of the *in*spiring aspects of religion what might be called the *con*spiring side. One side helps us to breathe in spiritual sustenance; the other suffocates it. If the former lifts our spirit, the latter yanks it down. Or as psychologist Carl Jung remarked, "The repressed god becomes a demon." At times it appears that Huston Smith has spent as much time defending the trustworthiness of religion as he has rhapsodizing about it. However, when confronted with its dark side, he is forthright about the horrors so often perpetrated in religion's name. "The full story of religion," he writes in the opening chapter to *The World's Religions,* "is not rose-colored; often it is crude. Wisdom and charity are intermittent, and the net result is profoundly ambiguous." All he claims to have attempted is to present the world religions at their best, and this has meant concentrating on their "empowering theological and metaphysical truth."

What Smith finds most troubling of all in our scientific age is the unbalanced relationship between science and religion, in which religion is cast in the role of the underdog. This patronizing disparagement derives from misunderstanding the strengths and weaknesses of each. "Between religion and science proper I see no conflict whatever," Smith told Steve Reuys. "On the contrary, I find in science all kinds of suggestive analogies as to what religion is up to and what it tries to say." He finds particularly gratifying the uncanny parallels between science's discovery of "other worlds" in the subatomic realm and the realm of distant space—the worlds of the incredibly small and of the incredibly large, neither of which can be described in everyday language without running into paradoxes at every turn and into the mystics' discoveries of the other, supermundane regions of reality.

At this point in his career, however, Smith sees those parallels doing little to level the playing field on which science and religion contend, because our public intellectuals are not willing to grant that the transcendental realities reported by mystics actually exist; rather, they dismiss those claimed realities as nothing more than projections of the human mind. What is needed is for both parties, while holding fast to what they do well, to realize that their methodologies are limited and that there are important gaps in the human experience—and in the objective world—that they should turn over to their partners to fill in. The posturing about science's limitless power, he feels, is risible because it makes us prisoners of its wizardry, not unlike the captives in Plato's cave.

The Allegory of the Cave, in Smith's view, is one of the central stories and richest metaphors in Western philosophy. As Plato tells the tale in *The Republic,* Socrates describes to him a group of prisoners who are chained to a bench in a dark cave where they watch passing shadows on the wall. The shadow play is cast by the light of a fire and by puppeteers they cannot see who are marching behind them and parading their cutouts. Hypnotized by the shadows, the enchained prisoners believe the flat, two-dimensional world they are shown is all there is to existence. Unknown to them, another world lies outside the cave's walls, ablaze with light, brightly colored, and three-dimensional. The moral of the story, for Smith, is that although another world of sunlight and dazzling color calls to us, we live in a world where people try to convince us that reality consists only of what we can see with our eyes or through their extensions, microscopes and telescopes.

We must have the courage to wake up, turn our heads, snap our chains, walk outside, and open our eyes to the larger world that includes things that are not sense based because they are not material, and then learn to return to the cave of our everyday world and tell the strangely redeeming tale. This is what Smith means by religion being the quest for ultimate reality, finding the light that allows us to see the way things are in their entirety—luminous, numinous, and glorious, including everything science has discovered and will go on to discover.

As the Sufis say, we need to see not only with our ordinary eyes, but also with "the eyes of the heart."

THE WISDOM JOURNEY

I first encountered Huston Smith in the winter of 1990, at a Christmas party given by our publisher, Harper San Francisco. Having just come out with my first book, I boldly introduced myself to him as the author of *The Hero's Journey*, the companion book to the documentary film I had co-written about his old friend, the mythologist Joseph Campbell. With a certain old-world elegance he bowed slightly, smiled warmly, and said he looked forward to reading the book. We shook hands, and then his eyes widened, as if he suddenly recalled something that he wanted to share with me. With no little charm, he told me of the time when Campbell tried to park his trusty old Volkswagen near his apartment in Greenwich Village. When he emerged from his vehicle he noticed a young boy standing on the curb, next to the car, with his arms akimbo. "You can't park there!" the boy said, defiantly. "Why not?" Campbell asked. "Because I am a fire hydrant, and it's illegal to park next to a fire hydrant!" Knowing a mythic moment when he saw one, Campbell moved his car. After sharing his little gem of a story with me, Huston told me he believed it exemplified Campbell's gift for recognizing the fugitive moments when the mythic imagination suddenly infuses everyday life. Somewhat wistfully, he added that Campbell had taught him that in their depths mythology and religion are indistinguishable, and that it is possible to unify the world's wisdom traditions in an existentially meaningful way.

Over the next few years Huston and I worked together in many venues. Our first collaboration was on a film project called *The Peyote Road*, which included a pilgrimage into the highlands of northern Mexico to participate in four consecutive nights of prayer meetings. Ultimately, the film was shown to members of Congress and played an instrumental part in passing the American Indian Religious Freedom Act Amendments of 1994. We also teamed up for an animated day-long seminar at UCLA entitled "Soul and Spirit" and a symposium at the Kanuga Conference

Center outside Asheville, North Carolina, in 1997, entitled "What Does It All Mean?" sponsored by the Journey into Wholeness Group. My first lecture for the Kanuga conference was based on the phenomenon of synchronicity—meaningful and sometimes life-changing coincidences—and afterward I joined Huston for lunch in the cafeteria. I was apprehensive because I wasn't sure how he would respond to the suggestion that synchronicity might be one of our royal roads to meaning. I needn't have worried. His eyes were dilated with delight, and he was beside himself with eagerness to share one of his own synchronistic experiences. With his hands weaving joyful mudras in the air, he told me the story of his 1969 academic year around the world with a group of graduate students.

"At that time," he said sotto voce, as if the university elders could have been listening, after all these years, "I hadn't yet run into the Native Americans and hadn't much knowledge of indigenous religions, and at our first stop I was scheduled to lecture on the indigenous religion of Japan, Shinto. You know how it is on the eve of departure. There are always a million loose ends to tie up, and I didn't have time to bone up on the subject, besides which I had never found a book that took me beyond the bare bones of Shinto and enabled me to understand its deep hold on the Japanese people. The day before we took off a book crossed my desk titled *In the Tracks of Buddhism* by Frithjof Schuon. An earlier book by him had sat half-read on my shelves for several years, but I noticed that this book included a short chapter on 'Shinto: Buddhism's Ally in Japan,' and being desperate, in the severe countdown decisions as to what to cram into my flight bag I managed to wedge it in for trans-Pacific reading. It proved to be the best decision of the year. It opened 'the way of the Gods' to me as nothing else ever had.

"Two months later," Huston continued, excitedly, "we arrived in India, and I found myself in the same predicament. I was to lecture on Vedanta, of which I knew the basic outlook, but was again feeling anxious about delivering an insightful talk. One afternoon I was browsing in a bookstore in Madras, and my eye fell upon a study of the Vedanta entitled *Language of the Self,* again by Frithjof Schuon. This time I didn't hesitate, and it proved to be another lifesaver!"

A raffish smile snuck across Huston's face. He said, "Would you believe a third episode? A few months later we were in Iran, where I was to lecture to my students on Islam. I asked the most respected Islamicist of the land if he could prescribe a book to ground me in the profundities of his faith. He pointed me to a book called *Understanding Islam,* describing it as 'the best work in English on the meaning of Islam and why Muslims believe in it.' And who do you think the author was? Frithjof Schuon! Three times I was stuck at the crossroads, and three times, as if by divine intervention, a book turned up in the nick of time to solve my problem, all written by same man." Recalling what has been called "serial synchronicity," Huston raised his right hand and jabbed his index finger into the air like the needle of a spire, then laughingly remarked to me, "Is there such a thing as *chance*? I don't think so. There's more, there's always more. Call it grace, call it synchronicity, but I think of it as God telling us that at the deepest level everything is scripted, of saying there are no accidents!"

One of the most moving moments I have experienced with Huston over the years we have been friends and colleagues took place on the last evening of the World Parliament of Religions that we attended together, in December 1999, in Cape Town, South Africa. We had traveled there with eight Native American spiritual leaders, as part of a delegation and film team, to allow them to share the story of the troubled state of religious freedom for native peoples. That evening had been cleared so that all the participants could attend the signature speech by the former freedom fighter and president of South Africa, Nelson Mandela. Dame Fortune smiled on us, and we were able to sit only a few rows from the stage, but in deference to Huston's hearing problem I tried repeating the opening words of Mandela's speech into his ear. After a few failed attempts to pick up my whispers, Huston raised his hand, signaling me to stop, and whispered, "It is enough for me to be within Mr. Mandela's *darshan.*"

I watched Huston out of the corner of my eye for the rest of the speech, in which Mandela credited his spiritual upbringing as the source of his indomitable courage in withstanding his twenty-seven years of imprisonment by the apartheid government. What struck me was the utter raptness of Huston's attention, the dignity of his bearing as he practiced the ancient Indian ritual of *darshan*, which means sitting quietly and humbly in the *presence* of someone whom you revere, growing simply from being there.

Thinking back on that evening, I recall rereading the splendid opening chapter to *The World's Religions* as part of my preparation for the week's filming in Cape Town. Late one night in our hotel, I underlined the following passage in which Smith likens the voices of the religions to a choir and asks, "Does one faith carry the lead, or do the parts share in counterpoint and antiphony where not in full-throated chorus? We cannot know. All we can do is try to listen carefully and with full attention to each voice in turn as it addresses the divine."

The gift not only of inspired oratory but also of listening well—these are the traits of the truly wise soul. I watched Huston enact both when we filmed him interviewing Native American spiritual leader, author, and political activist Winona LaDuke in Cape Town. In response to LaDuke's impassioned remarks about the continuing relevance of the old ways of her ancestors, Huston affirmed her point of view, then contrasted it with his own experience: "I am too often criticized for calling for a return to a nonexistent Golden Age," he said, "but that's totally wrong. I am interested in what was true in the past, what is true now, and what will be true in the future. In short, I am interested in what is timeless."

Finally, perhaps the simplest and yet most characteristic moment with Huston took place the morning of my most recent interview with him, at his home in Berkeley, California, in May 2002. Knowing that we planned to address the timely but combustible issue of how much—more or less—religion matters after the tragic events of September 11, 2001, Huston excused himself for a few minutes so he could sit on the sundeck of his house. He needed to "put his mind around it," as he is fond of describing his meditations on important issues. When he returned to the living room to commence the interview, he sat down in his favorite chair, and as my producer and cameraman, Gary Rhine, assembled the equipment, Huston turned to my six-year-old son, Jack, who had accompanied us for the morning. Jack was sitting quietly on the nearby couch, drawing in his notebook, and it seemed to me then that something about his quiet concentration amid the chaos of a film shoot touched Huston's heart.

With an impish smile, as if he were going to spring a surprise on him, Huston leaned over and, recalling Jack's middle name, addressed him as

"Blue." Then he asked in his inimitable sing-song manner, "Jack Blue, do you know the song 'Old Dog Blue'?"

Jack nodded sweetly at the play on words.

"Good!" Huston said, happily, and then began to sing in a raspy but tender voice:

> I raised a dog and his name was Blue,
> And I betch-a five dollars he's a good one, too.
> *Go on Blue, I'm comin' too. Go on, Blue, I'm comin', too . . .*
> There's only one thing that bothers my mind.
> Blue went to heaven, so first thing I'll do,
> Grab me a horn and blow for Old Blue.
> *Come here, Blue, I got here, too.*
> Then when I hear that Blue dog bark,
> Blue's treed a possum in Noah's Ark.
> *Come here, Blue, you good dog, you!*

As Huston sang his eyes locked with Jack's, as if there were no one else in the room. My son's shoulders rose and fell, like they do when he is almost giddy with happiness. By the time Huston came to the last few words of the song, Jack was in a rapture. But I am convinced his mood wasn't merely due to the extra attention he was getting. His response came from a flash of boyish pride that Huston had recalled his rather colorful middle name and that he had made a playful connection with an old (what else?) *blues* song just to please him.

Perhaps Huston only wished for him to feel as much at home as the adults in the room, and only had reached back into the archives of his ample memory to recall a little ditty with the word *blue* in it. But then and there it occurred to me that I had just witnessed a sterling example of why Huston Smith has become one of the most beloved teachers of our time. One of his sagely secrets is that he treats everyone alike—children and adults, struggling students and esteemed leaders—with respect for their being singular souls. It is his way to greet everyone he encounters on the road of life, in the hallowed tradition of the Old Testament and ancient Greek myths, as if they might be angels or gods in disguise.

As the song came to an end, and Huston smiled a smile as wide as the

Jordan River, I recalled his beaming face at the end of his lecture at U.C.L.A. Triumphantly, he repeated something he had recently heard from a rabbi, that it is an ancient belief that each of us have an angel marching in front of us in life, shouting exultantly, "Make way, make way for the image of God!"

Together, these moments have taught me that the way things are for Huston Smith is sacred not only under exalted circumstances, such as in an ashram in India or at an international conference of religious scholars in Chicago, but in everyday life with everyday people. This belief infuses his practice of what he calls his "karma yoga," which compels him to balance the scholastic first half of his life with work in the trenches of life, spreading his knowledge and enthusiasm in the public forum. With that vow in mind, he continues to speak to nearly every group that asks him, from third-grade classes in Oakland, California, to groups of neurologists at the University of Chicago looking for evidence of God in the brain to Unitarians in Amsterdam seeking the middle ground of spiritual practice. And always with equal grace and often puckish humor.

My experience with Huston has taught me that there is no time for small talk in this precious time we have together; instead, each encounter we experience with each other is an opportunity to participate in what medieval philosophers called "the long conversation." Every time we talk about the things that matter—life and death, love and hate, religion and philosophy, the way things are not, and the way things are—we are also speaking with our ancestors, and the pervading issue is invariably Eternity. It was in that spirit that Huston told Bill Moyers during the filming of "The Wisdom of Faith" that "religion is a living conversation between the human and the divine that goes on generation after generation."

These golden threads—wisdom and method, speaking and listening, witnessing and community—tie together the wide-ranging and free-spirited interviews of this book. I believe they reveal Huston's greatest gift to be the way he inspires others to cultivate their own kindness, compassion, and tolerance, qualities he feels are direly needed in our tempestuous world. In this way he has fulfilled the destiny he envisioned for himself as a callow young student, to become a philosopher of religion (from the Latin *religare*, "to bind"), literally "a lover of wisdom that binds people together." Perhaps that is why he often ends his lectures with the provocative thought, "Beware of the blindness to the unity that binds us." For Huston Smith, the wisdom of religion is a unifying force that holds the world together.

This book has been created in that spirit, along with the hope that Huston shared with the eminent Native American scholar Vine Deloria Jr. years ago, "We may be brothers yet."

A note to the reader: The interviews and essays collected in this volume have been edited slightly to eliminate repetition and for consistency.

A Theological Autobiography

Socrates told his tribunal that he didn't fear his sentence because if death was the end it would be like falling into untroubled sleep, while if his soul migrated to another realm he would meet the heroes of the past and a just tribunal, which would make it no wasted journey. When I found that passage from the *Apology* inscribed on a historical marker in Athens, the words *no wasted journey* jumped out at me, for I was on my first trip around the world, and they captured my mood perfectly. Not only was girdling the globe not a waste. Neither was life's journey, for I was learning so much!

I mention this because, though the prospect of writing my memoirs has never appealed to me (not even for grandchildren), I have toyed with the thought of what an appropriate title might be were I to do so, and in early manhood, "No Wasted Journey" was the obvious choice. In my forties, though, it gave way to "That Strong Mercy," for I underwent a midlife crisis which only mercy (it felt like) pulled me through. And in these later years, "Bubble Blown and Lived In" displaces both preceding candidates. For though I am not a constructionist, it does feel (now) as if I have spent my years sweeping out a horizon of beliefs, soap-bubble thin, that I could live in.

This essay by Huston Smith was first published in *Dialog* 33, no. 4 (Fall 1994), under the title "Bubble Blown and Lived In: A Theological Autobiography." Reprinted by permission of *Dialog*.

How that bubble took shape, together with the iridescent colors that swim on its surface, I have been invited to recount. Some things that I wrote in the introduction to the book I co-authored with David Griffin, *Primordial Truth and Postmodern Theology,* apply equally to the start of my story, so my first several paragraphs will follow that earlier statement closely.

SEARCH

I was born of missionary parents in China, and spent my formative years there. I don't suppose one ever gets over that. Because we were the only Americans in our small town, my parents were my only role models, so I grew up assuming that missionaries were what Western children grew up to be. As a consequence, I came to the United States for college, thinking that I would return to China as soon as I was theologically accredited, but I had not reckoned with the West's dynamism. Never mind that my landing pass was Central Methodist College, enrollment six hundred, located in Fayette, Missouri, population three thousand. Compared with Changshu (or even Shanghai of that day) it was the Big Apple. Within two weeks China had faded into a happy memory; I wasn't going to squander my life in its backwater. The vocational shift this entailed, however, was small. Instead of being a missionary I would be a minister.

My junior year in college brought a second surprise: ideas jumped to life and began to take over. To some extent they must have gained on me gradually, but there came a night when I watched them preempt my life with the force of conversion. Returning from a meeting of a small honor society that gathered monthly for dessert and discussion in the home of its faculty sponsor, several of us lingered in the corridor of our dormitory to continue the arguments the evening had provoked—as unlikely a knot of peripatetics as ever assembled. My excitement had been mounting all evening, and around midnight it exploded, shattering mental stockades. It was as if a fourth dimension of space had opened and my mind was catapulting into it. And I had my entire life to explore those endless, awesome, portentous corridors. I wonder if I slept at all that night.

In retrospect it seems predestined, but at the time I could only see it as providential that the faculty sponsor of our discussion group was a protégé of Henry Nelson Wieman, who had founded the school of naturalistic theism almost single-handedly. Wieman was at the University of Chicago, so it was inevitable that I proceed there for my graduate study. Having earlier shifted my vocational intent from missionary to minister, I now moved next door again by opting to teach rather than preach—although in moments of misgiving I suspect that I have friends who think I never accomplished that move. When Charles Kingsley asked Charles Lamb if he would like to hear him preach, Lamb replied, "I don't think I have ever heard you do anything else." That's too close to home for comfort.

Because those vocational adjustments were obvious and small, they occasioned no soul-searching; but as I think back, I am surprised that I didn't find the collapse of my youthful supernaturalism disturbing. I entered the Divinity School of the University of Chicago a committed Wiemanite. Despite World War II—I was headed for the chaplaincy, but the war ended before I made it—Chicago was an exciting time for me. Via naturalistic theism, my vocation was clear. It would be to align the two most powerful forces in history: science and religion. I was a very young man, and fresh to the world's confusions.

I can remember as if it were yesterday the night in which that entire prospect, including its underlying naturalistic worldview, collapsed like a house of cards. It was four years later, in Berkeley—but before I relate what happened, I need to explain how I got there. Chicago proceeded as planned, with one surprise. Although in my first year I would not have believed that such a thing was possible, in the second year I discovered something better than Wieman's theology, namely, his daughter. Two years later we were married. We celebrated our golden wedding anniversary last fall.

As I was now a member of Wieman's family, he couldn't direct my dissertation, but he did suggest its topic. Stephen Pepper at the University of California had written his *World Hypotheses,* one of which was pragmatism (or contextualism, as he called it), which was close to Wieman's metaphysics; so he sent me to Pepper to explore the fit. With a wife and an infant child, I spent 1944–1945 in Berkeley writing my doctoral dissertation, "The Metaphysical Foundations of Contextualistic Philosophy of Religion."

In the course of that year I chanced on a book, *Pain, Sex, and Time,* by Gerald Heard, who is credited for moving Aldous Huxley from his *Brave New World* cynicism to the mysticism of *The Perennial Philosophy,* and reading it brought the collapse of my naturalism that I mentioned above. The mystics hadn't figured much in my formal education, but when I encountered a sympathetic presentation of their position, I responded from the soles of my feet on upward, saying, Yes, yes! More than any other outlook I had encountered, it was their vision, I was convinced, that disclosed the way things are.

Mysticism pointed toward the "mystical East," so, Ph.D. in hand and teaching now, I cut back on philosophy to devote roughly half my time (as I have ever since) to immersing myself in the world's religions; *immersing* is the right word, for I have always been devotee as much as scholar. During my eleven years at Washington University (1947–1958) this involved weekly tutorials with a swami of the Ramakrishna Order who grounded me in the Vedanta and set me to meditating. When I responded to MIT's call to strengthen its humanities program by adding philosophy to it (my years there were 1958–1973), I shifted my focus to Buddhism and undertook Vipassana [a type of meditation] practice in Burma, Zen training in Kyoto, and fieldwork among the Tibetans in their refugee monasteries in North India. Angry at the hammerlock that analytic philosophers had on the field—in those days Harvard, Princeton, and Cornell constituted a "Bermuda Triangle" in which "planes" that entered from outlying territories disappeared professionally—I welcomed a bid from Syracuse University to move from philosophy to religious studies, and invested my last decade to full-time teaching (1973–1983), primarily in its graduate program. Asia-wise, that decade brought Islam into my lived world, through Sufi *sheikhs* [spiritual masters] that I encountered in pre-Khomeini Iran and North Africa—their five Arabic prayers continue to frame my day. On retiring from Syracuse we moved to Berkeley to be close to our children and their families. Until this year I continued to teach half-time: semesters here and there across the country, an occasional course at the Graduate Theological Union, and the last three years at the University of California. The new incursion on my religious front has been the primal religions. I helped edit a book with Reuben Snake (a leader of the Native American Church), *One Nation Under God: The Triumph of the Native American Church,* to help restore to that Church the rights the Supreme Court stripped it of in its 1990 Smith decision.

This all sounds flagrantly eclectic, and I can't argue that it wasn't, for the truth of the matter is that in culling from the world's religions what was of use to me, I was largely ignoring their differences. What they said about reality seemed sufficiently alike to carry me as I stepped from one to another like a hunter crossing ice floes, but I had no real idea what to do with their differences. I had been avoiding that question for some time when, in the course of a year-long around-the-world seminar that I co-directed in 1969–1970, I ran into Professor S. H. Nasr in Iran, who pointed me to a small group of thinkers who had the answer I was looking for. Referred to sometimes as Perennialists, sometimes as Traditionalists, their roots were in the *sophia perennis* and "Great Chain of Being." René Guénon and Frithjof Schuon have been their chief twentieth-century spokesmen, and I also recognized the names of Ananda Coomaraswamy, Titus Burckhart, Martin Lings, and Professor Nasr himself. Meeting those men changed everything. As their position has remained in place for me since I encountered it, autobiography will enter into the rest of what I have to say only to indicate why I found its key features plausible.

DISCOVERY

In the foreword to his collection of essays by Perennialist writers, titled *The Sword of Gnosis,* Jacob Needleman puts his finger on what struck me first about these thinkers.

> [They] were not interested in the hypothesizing and the marshaling of piece-meal evidence that characterizes the work of most academicians. On close reading, I felt an extraordinary intellectual force radiating through their intricate prose. These men were out for the kill. For them, the study of spiritual traditions was a sword with which to destroy the illusions of contemporary man.

I shall come back to those illusions, but let me begin with the contrast with academicians. None of the teachers I had actively sought out— Huxley and Heard, Swami Satprakashananda, Goto Roshi, the Dalai

Lama, and Sheikh Isa—had been academicians. They had served me as spiritual directors as much as informants; I know the ashrams, *viharas,* and monasteries of Asia better than I know its universities. When I found Schuon writing that "knowledge only saves us on condition that it engages all that we are: only when it constitutes a way which works and transforms, and which wounds our nature as the plough wounds the soil," I recognized him as standing in the line of my preceding mentors. With two additional resources. Schuon worked all the major traditions. And he was a theoretician, actively concerned with the way those traditions fit together.

The kingpin in constellating them, he insisted, is an absolute. Only poorly can life manage without one, for spiritual wholeness derives from a sense of certainty, and certainty is incompatible with relativism. Every absolute brings wholeness to some extent, but the wholeness increases as the absolute in question approximates the Absolute from which everything else derives and to which everything is accountable. For (as the opening lines of my *Forgotten Truth* state the point), "people have a profound need to believe that the truth they perceive is rooted in the unchanging depths of the universe; for were it not, could the truth be really important?" If a human life could be completely geared to the Absolute, its power would course through it unrestrictedly, and it would actually be a *jivanmukta,* a soul that is completely enlightened while still in its body.

So much (momentarily) for the Absolute, the One. What of the Many? As the succeeding sentence in *Forgotten Truth* puts the question, "How *can* we [hold our truth to be the Truth] when others see truth so differently?" As I think back on the matter, this is one of the two issues on which the Perennialists have helped me most. The other is the character of the modern world, which I shall take up in my closing section.

THE RELATION BETWEEN RELIGIONS

Having found Hindu, Buddhist, and Muslim (as well as Christian) teachers I had grown to revere, there was no way I was going to privilege one religion over the others. The question was where (within them) was there an absolute I could live by. (It needed to be an ontological absolute, not just a moral absolute, like tolerance or the golden rule, for only ontological realities wield objective power.) I knew that such an Absolute couldn't be slapped together from pieces gleaned here and there, for it was obvious that the power of the historical revelations derived from their respective patterns, or gestalts. To think that I could match such power by splicing *chi* [spiritual energy], say, to *pratiyasammutpada* [literally, "dependent arising"] and the logos made about as much sense as hoping to create a great work of art by pasting together pieces from my favorite paintings. Or creating a living organism from a heap of organ transplants.

The alternative seemed to be to find a single thread that runs through the various religions. This, though, ran into the problem of essentialism. Who is to say what the common essence of the world's religions is, and how could any account of it escape the signature of its proponent's language and perspective?

Caught as I was in this impasse, the Perennialists called my attention to a third possibility that resolved it: Don't search for a single essence that pervades the world's religions. Recognize them as multiple expressions of the Absolute, which is indescribable. One reason it is ineffable is that its essence is single, and knowing requires a knower and a known, which means that we are already in duality. The more understandable reason, though, is that descriptions proceed through forms, and the Absolute is formless.

This solution to the problem of the One and the Many has satisfied me since it first came to view, but I have had to recognize that it is not widely available because most people hear formlessness as lack. To them, if formless things exist at all, they are vague and abstract. Others, though, see matters differently. To distinguish the two types of people, Perennialists call the first type esoterics and the second exoterics.

The lives of exoterics are completely contained in the formal world. For them the formless is (as was just noted) abstract at best. It is incomplete. Lacking in important respects, it is not fully real. Esoterics, on the other hand, find reality overflowing its formal containers into formlessness, though this puts the cart before the horse. Because the formless is more real than the formed, the accurate assertion is that the formal world derives from the formless. The logical argument for the esoterics' position is that forms are finite and the Absolute is infinite, but for genuine esoterics the formless is more than a logical inference. It is an experienced reality. Through a distinctive mode of knowing (variously called *gnosis, noesis, intellectus, jnana,* and *prajna*) esoterics sense the formless to be more concrete, more real, than the world of forms. This is incomprehensible to exoterics because they conclude that an absolute that lacks formal divisions must lack the qualities those divisions fan out. But for esoterics, not only are those qualities in the Absolute; they are there in superessential, archetypal intensity and degree. Opposite of abstract, the Absolute is superconcrete.

I said that the Absolute is indefinable, but we need indications of its character, and these are what the great revelations provide. In doing so, they resemble telescopes that "triangulate" the Absolute like a distant star. What in varying degrees of explicitness they all proclaim is that the Absolute is richer in every positive attribute we know—power, beauty, intelligence, whatever—than we can possibly imagine. This all the major religions assert, and we can understand the logic of their claim. For the only satisfying reason that can be given for the way things are is that it is best that they be that way, so the mind instinctively attributes to what is ultimate the best that it can conceive. The alternative is to accept meaninglessness to some degree.

The consequence of this approach for the relation between religions runs something like this. As the superconcrete Absolute includes all forms, it can deploy them at will. In anthropomorphic (which isn't to say inaccurate) idiom, it chooses to do so in the great formal constellations we call revelations, crowding as much of itself into each as is possible under the formal limitations that finitude exacts. Because the esoteric takes the Absolute to be the formless source of these revelations, he or she can endorse their plurality as alternative voices in which the Absolute speaks to be understood by different audiences.

While this format gave me exactly what I was looking for—(a) an Absolute (b) that didn't require that I rank order the religions I work with—it carries a stubborn consequence. There is no way to satisfy both parts of this two-fold *desideratum* on the formal, exoteric plane. To which hard truth Perennialists add: If it is necessary to choose, it is better to adhere to the Absolute as truly and sufficiently disclosed in one's own revelation than to displace it with the "civil liberties" principle of religious parity, which is no more than a personally arrived at guide for conduct. Somewhere within these last two sentences I sense myself as parting company with my liberal friends in "the wider ecumenism," for they seem willing to reshape the forms of the great, originating revelations to two ends: politically, to reduce conflict by rounding off their sharp corners and rough edges, and theologically, to improve on their truths by learning from others. For my part, believing as I do that each of the enduring revelations already contains "truth sufficient unto salvation," I am not enthusiastic about tampering with them. The project smacks of precisely the sort of human fiddling with the revelations that Perennialists find themselves charged with when their position is mistaken for (a) the cafeteria approach, or (b) articulated essentialism.

Continuing with the last point, the chief objection to Perennialism that I hear is that its universalism rides roughshod over differences. I suspect that many such critics would shift their attack from Perennialism's (presumed) New Age all-is-oneism to its (actual) conservatism if they understood that everything that esoterics say about such things, universalism included, presupposes the formed/unformed distinction I have outlined. I was a universalist long before I encountered Perennialism. Where it changed my thinking was in persuading me to balance my universalism with an equal regard for the differences that distinguish revelations. Schuon's *Transcendent Unity of Religions* really is transcendent—radically so in being formless. In our "formal" life, forms are decisively important; so important that the forms of revelation should be respected. The cosmologies and social mores of their day (which they assume) are negotiable, but for spiritual insight we do better to plumb their pronouncements than tinker with them. For those forms are not incidental to the clarity of the message they convey, which clarity accounts for their historical power.

So much for religious pluralism. What of the modern world? Jacob Needleman warned us that for Perennialists "the study of spiritual traditions [is] a sword with which to destroy the illusions of contemporary man." What are those illusions?

CRITIQUE OF THE MODERN WORLD

As long as the issue was the relations between religions, Perennialists was the appropriate name for the thinkers I identify with. When we turn to their view of modernity, it is their other appellation—Traditionalists—that makes their point.

It does so because Traditionalists consider the ethos by which people lived before the rise of modern science to be on balance more accurate than the scientistic one that has replaced it. Not (to repeat the point just mentioned) its science, which has been superseded, or its social mores, but its ontological vision. I wrote *Forgotten Truth* to celebrate that vision; and I wrote its sequel, *Beyond the Post-Modern Mind,* to expose the Procrustean epistemology—again, scientistic—that has caused traditional truth to be largely forgotten. I say forgotten rather than refuted, for there has been no refutation, merely an exchange of traditional ontology for one that derives from an epistemology that (in the short run, at least) caters to our material wants and wish to control, "the Old Adam." There are, of course, oceans of historical and psychological reasons for the West's having made this exchange, but no logical reasons. We simply slid into assuming that the most reliable viewfinder available to our human lot is the scientistic one that edits out spiritual truths in the way X-ray films omit the beauty of faces.

I know that this assessment will be disputed; though actually it is a good day when one encounters dispute, for typically it is simply ignored. When rejoinders are heard, they point out that the preceding paragraph doesn't even mention science; only scientism, with which (by tacit association) science is sneakily tarred.

That reply is useful, for it forces me to drop innuendo, come into the open, and say right out loud that science is scientism. I didn't have the wit (or was it courage?) to arrive at that conclusion by myself; a scientist at the University of Minnesota who teaches science to nonscience majors pointed it out to me at the close of an all-day workshop that I had devoted to distinguishing science from scientism and exempting it from the latter's pernicious effects. "Everything you said about the dangers of scientism is true," he said; "but there's one thing, Huston, that you still don't see. Science is scientism."

His assertion startled me, but on the long walk it provoked I came to see his point. If we define science as the procedures that scientists follow and the demonstrable results that thereby accrue, and scientism as the assumption that the scientific method is the most reliable method for arriving at truth and that the things that science works with are the most real things, thus defined, the two are clearly different. But here's the point. Although in principle it is easy to distinguish them, in practice it is almost impossible to do so. So scientism gets overlooked in the way the power plays that are imbedded in institutions get overlooked until the extraordinary eye of a Michel Foucault spots them and points them out.

The cause of the blur is the one that Baruch Spinoza stated abstractly: things tend to enlarge their domains until checked by other things. This applies to institutions as much as to individuals. The vanguard of science's expansionism is scientism, and it advances automatically unless checked. Religiously, it is important that it be checked, for the two are incompatible. So where are the guardians to keep scientism from sweeping the field? The Traditionalists are the most vigilant and astute watchdogs I see. And scientism is one area where I claim expertise, for my longest tour of duty (as they say in the military; fifteen years) was at MIT.

The chief places I have tried to keep an eye on scientism are:

1. Higher education. Rooted as the universities are in the scientific method, as a recent president of the Johns Hopkins University pointed out, they are *killing the spirit.*

2. Mainline theology. Looking up to their more prestigious counterparts at the universities, seminary professors tend to accommodate to their styles of thought. As those styles do not allow for a robust, alternative, ontological reality, our understanding of God has slipped ontologically. (When was the last time I heard the word *supernatural* from a lectern or pulpit?) This slip is having disastrous effects on mainline churches whose members are moving to evangelical churches, Asian religions, or New Age cults and frivolity in search of the unconventional reality that *homo religiosus* requires.

3. The science/religion dialogue, with evolution as a major checkpoint. The only definition of Darwinism that has survived its multiple permutations is that it is the theory that claims that our arrival as human beings can be explained naturalistically. Scientism must make this claim, but the evidence for it is no stronger than that which supports its theistic alternative. Yawning lacunae in the naturalistic scenario are being papered over with stopgap "god of the gaps" stratagems—the god here is Darwin—that are as blatant as those that theology has ever resorted to.

4. Deconstruction and postmodernism. These thinkers see through scientism, but their constructive proposals make the wrong mistake (as Yogi Berra would say) for being brilliant answers to the wrong question. The question of our time is no longer how to take things apart, but how to work responsibly at reassembling them. For as the opening speaker at the 1992, U.C.B./Robert Bellah–sponsored Good Society Conference put the point: "We have no maps and we don't know how to make them."

If those four one-liners seem extreme and my obsession with scientism a complete tapestry woven from a few threads of fact, I suggest that a reading of Bryan Appleyard's *Understanding the Present* would alter those judgments. In it he asks us to imagine a missionary to an isolated tribe. Conversion is slow work until a child contracts a deadly disease and is saved by some penicillin the missionary has brought along. With that single stroke, Appleyard argues, it's all over for the world the tribe had known, and by extension for the traditional world generally. For the miracle its medicine men and priests couldn't accomplish, science delivers. And "science has shown itself unable to coexist with anything."

Speaking for myself, if the chiefs of the tribe could reason as follows: This white man knows things about our bodies and how to maintain them that we don't know, and we certainly thank him for sharing that knowledge with us. But it appears that knowledge of that sort tells us nothing about how we and the world got here, who we are in the fullness of our being, what happens to us after death, and whether there are beings of other kinds—immaterial beings, some of whom may be more intelligent, powerful, and virtuous than we are, the Great Spirit, for example. Nor does it tell us how we should live with one another. There seems to be no reason, therefore, why we can't accept the white man's medicine with gratitude while continuing to take seriously the wonderful explanatory myths that our ancestors entrusted to us.

If, as I say, the chiefs could reason this way and hold true to that reasoning, science would not be a problem. But they can't. We moderns and postmoderns can't. And I can't—not wholeheartedly, so scientized is the culture that encases me. But trying to change it is happiness enough.

PART ONE | **THE HEART OF RELIGION**

For Huston Smith, the longing for ultimate meaning and the promise of its fulfillment are at the heart of religion. There lies within us—in even the blithest, most lighthearted among us—a fundamental dis-ease. It acts like an unquenchable fire that renders the vast majority of us incapable ever of coming to full peace. All great literature, poetry, art, philosophy, psychology, and religion try to name and analyze this longing. We are seldom in direct touch with it, and indeed, the modern world seems set on preventing us from getting in touch with it. But the longing is there, built into us like a jack-in-the-box that presses for release. Religion claims that this longing can be fulfilled. That claim cannot be proven true, but when the full complement of human sensibilities are drawn on, they strongly suggest its truth in the way the wings of birds suggest the existence of air.

In the interviews that make up part 1, Smith reflects on what he has described as "the tidal waves of influence" from various world religions. Smith tells journalist Timothy Beneke that the great religions of the world unanimously affirm Transcendence as the goal of the human quest. It is a journey that begins in ordinary knowledge, but when it is seriously pursued it crests in "an intuitive awareness of things, a discernment of *the way things are.*" This belief orients him in his search, which is "the search for the Real." With editor John Loudon, he discusses the importance of returning to the primordial tradition, the conceptual spine that is the ground plan, the "font and spring" of all religious traditions. But the five interviews also reveal that Smith's essential concern is with metaphysics, the search for the essential nature of reality. This avid seeking compels him to ask which worldview comes closest to being real and true and brings him back to religion again and again because he feels it offers a vision of Transcendence.

While forthright about the social sins of religious institutions—intolerance and fanaticism—Smith remains convinced that we should focus on their worldview together with its anthropological corollary, that the human self is in essence divine. This comprehensive outlook—stretched like a skin over the two crossbeams of a Transcendence including reality at one end and an inspiring anthropology at the other—is, Smith maintains, the unvarying storyline that shapes all the great religions. And, he is convinced, in the long run it prompts us to behave better than we would without it. That saving outlook is inspired and renewed by mystical experiences that weave through history like beautiful variations on a single theme.

As if in response to the old adage "The purpose of life is a life of purpose," Huston Smith's avowed purpose is to spread the good news that ultimately "we are in good hands." What may surprise some readers is that he is exceptional among public intellectuals in our secular times in that he stands up not only for religious worldviews but also for religious organizations—churches, synagogues, and so on. Without blinking their sins, which he acknowledges have been egregious, he believes that on balance they do more good than harm—not only by keeping alive the pivotal concept of Transcendence, but in the encouragement they give parishioners to live up to the ideal of compassion they all espouse. Their idealism is unquenchable, as is their hope. In the end, he tells John Loudon, they assure us that eventually we will make it to *sat, chit,* and *ananda,* infinite being, infinite awareness, and infinite bliss.

Timothy Beneke: Tell us how you started your day.

Huston Smith: I began with the Islamic morning prayer to Allah. That was followed by India's hatha yoga, and after that a chapter from the Bible—this morning it was the Gospel of John—which I tried to read reflectively, opening myself to such insights that might enter. Then I was ready for coffee.

Beneke: What do those practices do for you?

Smith: Rabbis say that the first word you should think of when you wake up in the morning is the word *God*. Not even *thank-you* should precede it. I begin my day with the Islamic morning prayer as an extension of that point. I say it in Arabic. Not that I know Arabic, but I learned to pronounce the prayer phonetically because Islam is one of the three religions that require their canonical, prescribed prayers to be said in their original tongues; the other two

This interview was originally published as "The Way Things Are: A Conversation with World Religions Scholar Huston Smith," by Timothy Beneke, in the *East Bay Express*, March 8, 1996. Copyright © Timothy Beneke. Reprinted by permission of Timothy Beneke. Timothy Beneke is the author of *Men on Rape* (1982) and *Proving Manhood: Reflections on Men and Sexism* (University of California Press, 1997). He is writing a book with Kaiping Peng on the cultural assumptions of mainstream Americans.

are Hinduism and Judaism. And, of course, I know what the Arabic syllables of the prayer mean.

Beneke: What do they mean? What do they mean to you?

Smith: A great deal. That so much of what is important in life could be packed into just seven short phrases is almost proof in itself that Islam is a revealed religion.

The prayer opens with "Praise be to Allah, Creator of the worlds." Right off we are given to understand that life is no accident. It has derived from an Ultimate Source that is divine. But what is the character of divinity? The prayer addresses that immediately, in its second line, "the merciful, the compassionate." The Sufis from whom I learned the prayer give different nuances to those two words. Allah is merciful in having created us, and he is compassionate in that he will restore us to himself when our lives end, in keeping with the Koranic assertion "unto Him all things return." Some Sufis use that verse to argue that everyone reaches heaven eventually. Unlike other Muslims, they see hell as a place where sins are burned away; no souls stay there forever. But to continue with the prayer: the assurances of its second line are comforting, but they run the danger of inducing complacency. So the third line counters that danger immediately by adding "ruler of the day of judgment." Not everything goes. Actions have consequences, so we had better watch our step.

Then comes what (from the human standpoint) is the crucial fourth line: "Thee do we worship, and thee do we ask for aid." I was taught that when you come to that central line in the prayer, you should take stock of how your day is going. If it's going well, you should accent the first phrase, "Thee do we worship," and pour out your gratitude like Niagara Falls. If, on the other hand, it is one of those days when you wonder how you are going to get through it, you ask for help: "Thee do we ask for aid." Swallow your pride and admit that we all need help at times.

Truth to tell, by then the prayer has done it for me. Its remaining three assertions basically recapitulate what has gone before and round it off. "Guide us on the straight path, the path of those on whom thou hast poured forth thy grace; not the path of those who have incurred thy wrath and gone astray."

Beneke: How long have you been saying the Muslim prayers—the same prayer, five times a day?

Smith: About twenty-five years. Bodily movements accompany the words, but if circumstances don't permit them—say you are in a shopping line or on a freeway when the hour of prayer arrives—you may say the prayer silently to yourself. The prescribed times for prayer—on awakening, at noon, mid-afternoon, sunset, and on retiring—frame the day nicely. Five times a day, distractions are suspended, and one's attention is drawn to the infinite.

Beneke: After the prayer you turn to yoga.

Smith: Hatha yoga centers me; it gets me into my body somewhat. Ambu, my yoga teacher in South India, would occasionally hold a pose for two hours. I hold the poses for about twenty seconds, a fair measure of the distance between our attainments.

What does hatha yoga do for me? I don't want to claim too much. In the eight steps of Patanjali's "raja yoga"—the way to God through psychophysical exercises—hatha yoga, which works with body postures, is the third step in the program that integrates body, mind, spirit. If you undertake that program seriously, you don't do hatha yoga, the body movements, unless you are also working on the minimal moral precepts that the first two preceding steps prescribe. And the eighty-four postures of hatha yoga lead to the lotus position, where you sit, legs folded, with each foot upturned on its opposing thigh. In that position, you proceed to the remaining five steps, where you work with breathing and meditation. That's raja yoga in its full sweep. I've done it along the way, but it's not my primary path, and now I can't say that hatha yoga does more than counter somewhat the stiffness that comes with age.

Beneke: And why do you follow this by reading the Bible?

Smith: That's more complicated. For over fifty years I've read a passage from one of the world's sacred texts before breakfast. I'm not the first person in history to undertake the spiritual quest, and it's only sensible to draw on the experiences of those who have preceded me. The Bhagavad Gita, the Tao Te Ching, the Koran, the Bible, and the like are data banks of what they learned, so I apprentice myself to them. They are my guides on the path.

So much for the general practice. Now, to why I'm currently reading the Bible? To answer that I have to review my odyssey briefly. My parents were Methodist missionaries in China, so I had a Protestant upbringing, and I was fortunate: it proved to be positive. It "took," so to speak. I find that many of my students look to me like wounded Christians, or wounded Jews, in that what came through to them was dogmatism—we have the truth and everybody else is going to hell—and moralism—don't do this, that, and the other. What came through to me from my religious upbringing was quite different: we are in good hands, and in gratitude for that fact it would be good if we bore one another's burdens.

China was a part of my childhood and youth, and since then I have spent about a decade immersing myself sequentially in the thought and practice of Hinduism, Buddhism, Islam, and the Native American traditions. That pretty much covers the bases except for Judaism, which came to me through a daughter who married a Conservative Jew and converted to his faith. My ongoing involvement (with my wife) in their kosher family means a lot to me. We have a grandson named Isaiah.

During the middle decades of my life it would have been more accurate to consider me a Vedantist, a Zennist, or whatever I was then immersed in, than as a Christian, but I never severed my Christian connections. In the last year or two, though, I've developed an interest in reconnecting with my Christian roots; there's a saying, I believe, that "the child is father of the man." In any case it feels like coming full circle. I have been approaching Christianity this time as if it were a foreign religion like the others I encountered, which in many ways traditional Christianity is in our modern, secular age. This calls for bringing to it the same openness and empathy I tried to direct to the other religions I have studied. Approaching it this way strips away many stereotypes. I'm finding that in its depths, St. Augustine, Dionysius, Meister Eckhart—not the third-grade Christianity one hears from most pulpits—this new (to me) Christianity is more interesting than that of my childhood.

It poses a problem, though. In its emphasis on loving Christ, Christianity is the most *bhaktic* of the world's religions—*bhakti* being (in Hinduism's four yogas) the way to God through love—whereas I am primarily the *jnanic* type that gets mileage primarily through knowing God. Interestingly, that makes Christianity the most challenging of all the religions I've tried to work my way into. *Jnanic* Christians do exist, it's just that you have to hunt for them. The Church fathers were heavily *jnanic*. They are not read much anymore, but it was they who gave Christianity the theological sinews that have powered it. Anyway, I like challenges. Perhaps working with Christianity will round out a flat side in my personality.

If it does, that will be all to the good, but having touched on the four yogas—the way to God through knowledge, love, work, and meditation—I want to put in a word for my own primary yoga, the first of the four. The knowledge it works with is not rational knowledge. It has nothing to do with quantity of information or logical dexterity—the kind universities tend to prize. It is, rather, an intuitive awareness of things, a discernment of *the way things are*. What could be more important or interesting than that? In any case, that is the direction of my religious search. Religion for me is the search for the Real, and the effort to approximate one's life to it. Such approximation should be easy because the Real is so real, but in fact it is difficult, because we are so unreal. "So phony" is the slang way to put it.

Beneke: Have you been much involved with religious institutions over the years?

Smith: No, I haven't. For one thing they take time—G. B. Shaw said the worst thing about socialism was that it takes too many evenings. And beyond that, institutions are ambiguous. They bring out the bad in people along with the good; I don't know any institution, religious or otherwise, that is pretty through and through. But it has occurred to me of late that in remaining aloof from the institutional side of religion I've been something like a parasite. I live by the truth of the enduring religions, but I've done precious little to help the institutions that have kept those truths alive. I am working now on changing that—trying to repay some of my debt to these religions—and Christianity (as the faith I was born into and am currently focusing on) is the natural place to pitch in.

So I am going to church again. To resurrect a phrase from the 1960s, it feels like I'm "walking the talk" more. As for which church, a friend who knows me well says, "Huston, you are the only Confucian Methodist I know. The only reason you stay with the Methodist Church is filial piety and ancestor worship. It keeps you connected with your parents." There is something to that. As I say, my friend knows me well. But while I hold no special brief for the Methodist denomination or even Christianity vis-à-vis the other world religions, it's the tradition I was born into. And Christianity does house profundities; that's beyond question. So I am exploring them. That is a long answer to why I read the Bible this morning.

Beneke: One of the major themes of your work is the idea that behind the major religious traditions lies a deep truth that most educated secular people do not understand. It is a metaphysical truth about the universe and eternity, which involves seeing the eternal in the temporal, and seeing all the universe as a manifestation of eternity. This consciousness of the world puts one's own personality and all its accidental qualities, like gender and nationality, in a different perspective, and alters one's orientation to life. I sense that you want passionately to convey this to people.

Smith: Fair statement. As I suggested earlier, what is more important than the way things are? Sometimes when I give a talk I discover from questions that the audience is only really interested in social issues. I agree that these are important, and though we should all do more, I pay my dues on that front, I think. My wife and I were charter members of the Committee on Racial Equality (CORE) in St. Louis in the 1950s. I do everything I can for the Tibetans, and my book *One Nation Under God: The Triumph of the Native Ameri-*

can Church is on the injustice of the Supreme Court's infamous decision that stripped that Church of its constitutional rights.

Still, isn't it also important to find out the way things are? Religion has many facets, but if you skip the question of what finally exists, it looks pretty much like wheel-spinning to me, and it's hard for me to think of its practitioners as really serious about life's quest. Even practical dealings call for knowing the lay of the land, so to speak. Orientation. Life requires it if it is to be lived well, and orientation derives from knowing the nature of the universe.

Beyond all that, if what exists is in the end incredibly wonderful, to know that fact infuses one's life with energy, call it psychic or spiritual energy, as you wish. Joseph Campbell made that point when he wrote, "It would not be too much to say that myth is the secret opening through which the inexhaustible energies of the cosmos pour into human cultural manifestation." I agree with that assertion, while adding that, at that level, myth and religion are indistinguishable. So beyond the minimal payoff of knowing *where* you are—the payoff of orientation—if where you are turns out to be breathtakingly beautiful, how much greater the reward that comes from knowing—*seeing*—that.

Beneke: Okay, so where are we? What is the lay of our land?

Smith: It sounds glib when I put it into words—as bland as E = MC²— but the truth is that absolute perfection reigns. In addition to being glib, it sound dogmatic when I say it that categorically, but please understand that I see myself as basically a transmitter, reporting what the intellectual and spiritual giants of the past pretty much attest to in unison. Arthur Lovejoy in *The Great Chain of Being*— one of the classics of intellectual history—says that up to the late eighteenth century, when the scientific worldview began to take over, virtually every great sage and prophet the world over saw reality as a vast hierarchy ranging from the barest entities at the bottom, which barely escape nonbeing, all the way up to the *ens perfectissimum,* perfect being, at the top. My studies confirm this report.

I admit that it sounds outlandish to say that absolute perfection reigns, but I have two arguments in its defense. First, Einstein said that if quantum mechanics is true, the world is crazy. Well, experiments since his day have confirmed quantum mechanics, so the world is crazy—crazy from the standpoint of what our senses tell us the world is like. We accept that verdict because we have to; it comes from science. But when the mystics make the same point about the world in its reach for values, we back off because they can't prove their claims.

Look at Bosnia, we say, or the Holocaust; how are you going to square them with absolute perfection? Well, in something of the way a physicist would try to explain to an eight-year-old that the ratio of solid matter to space in the chair he is sitting on is of the order of a baseball to a ballpark, which is to say, not easily. But truth is not easy or obvious in religion any more than in physics. In both we need to get beyond the third grade.

My second rejoinder to people who dismiss absolute perfection out of hand is to point out that if you do that it leads to life being incoherent and not making sense. Either we settle for its not making sense, or we press to the hilt the possibility that it is the way it should be.

Beneke: Even a tumor in your lungs?

Smith: Yes, if we can see that tumor in its total context. We are back to the point that religion takes up where our routine reactions to life leave off. At the center of the religious life is a peculiar kind of joy, the prospect of a happy ending that blossoms from necessarily painful ordeals, the promise of human difficulties embraced and overcome. We don't see the complete picture.

Eighteen months ago our oldest daughter died of sarcoma, one of cancer's most vicious forms, though what cancer isn't vicious? The anguish our family experienced was like nothing any of us had remotely known before.

Beneke: Did you have doubts about the perfection of the universe? Were you angry at the universe?

Smith: Not angry. But of course I couldn't *feel* perfection then. Or more precisely, in a way I *did* feel it, but paradoxically, through my tears. It was as if shards of perfection pierced my sobs through the heroic way our daughter and her immediate family rose to her death. These experiences gave me the conviction that her death was not the last word.

This is quite apart from my own experience. The point is that the only person who has a right to say that things are exactly as they should be is someone who at the time he or she is speaking is feeling the heel of the oppressor's boot smashing down on their face. If you can say it then, it is real. Otherwise, it is Pollyanna escapism.

Beneke: The most famous example I know of is Aldous Huxley, dying of cancer, saying, "Yes this is painful, but look at the perfection of the universe." I can at times experience the universe as a manifestation of eternity, some great being behind the universe. I can to a degree transcend my own immediate pedestrian needs and involvement, but when this happens I experience extraordinary wonder and terror as well. Castaneda talks about balancing the wonder of being human with the terror of being human. Religion is about this sense of deep belonging in the universe, but I am not so sure that it is benign or friendly.

Smith: I distinguish between my thoughts and my emotions here. The Hindus speak of the *jivanmukta*, a person who, perfectly enlightened, is uninterruptedly aware of the perfection of things while still in his or her body. They cite Ramana Maharshi [a Hindu spiritual leader] as an instance. For my part, much as I revere Ramana, I'm not sure that even his bliss was unvarying. For several decades now I don't recall that my head has doubted the perfection of things, but experiencing it is a different matter. I doubt that within these mortal coils it is possible to quiet the emotional waves of ups and downs that are our human lot. But my head sees farther than my emotions, and when I'm depressed I can hear it saying, "Poor Huston. He's got the spiritual flu, but he'll get over it."

There is more to be said about the tumor in the lungs, however. One of the reasons I did not doubt God or the eternal during the seven and a half months of our daughter's dying—I touched on this earlier, but want to spell out—was the way she and her immediate family rose to the showdown. Her life had had its normal joys and defeats, but the spiritual work that she accomplished in those thirty or so weeks of dying was more than enough for a lifetime. Her sarcoma cancer began in the abdomen and spread rapidly, exerting pressure on her vital organs. But even when her condition had her at the breaking point, her farewells to us, her parents, in our last two visits were "I have no complaints" and "I am at peace." Her last words to her husband and children (Kendra and I arrived minutes too late) were, "I see the sea. I smell the sea. It is because it is so near." She always loved the sea. I think it symbolized life for her.

Beneke: A lot of us lapse readily into self-pity when we are sick or in anguish and think that the universe stinks.

Smith: I have told you what I believe, but I don't think there is proof as to who is right. Life comes to each of us like a huge Rorschach blot, and people fall into four classes in the way they interpret it. First, there is the atheist who says there is no God. Next comes the polytheist who says there are many gods, gods here meaning disembodied spirits of whatever sorts. Then there is the monotheist who says there is one God. And finally, the mystic for whom there is *only* God. None, many, one, and only. Using God as the measuring rod, these are the basic ways we can interpret the universe. There is no way to prove which way is right.

Beneke: I don't hear you using the word faith.

Smith: That is because the word is so free-floating. Everyone who has not given up has faith in something. If not in God, then in science, life, himself, the future, something. My favorite definition of faith is "the choice of the most meaningful hypothesis."

Beneke: That sounds a little like William James's pragmatism, which would have us believe things because of their positive effects on us.

Smith: That was James the psychologist, carrying over into James the philosopher. I'm not a pragmatist; I do not believe in believing in things because of their beneficial effects on us. I reject the argument that says, "Here is this mysterious Rorschach blot, *life.* Let's interpret it optimistically because that energizes us and makes us feel good." To hell with that line of thought! The question isn't what revs us up and makes us feel good, but what is true.

Beneke: And your intuitive discernment, your jnanic *faculty as you call it, tells you that the universe is perfect.*

Smith: Yes, but I don't rely solely or even primarily on my own intuition here. The chief reason I accept it is that it conforms to "the winnowed wisdom of the human race," as I like to think of the enduring religions in their convergent metaphysical claims. The word *wisdom* needs to be qualified, though. Not everything in the "wisdom traditions" is wise. Modern science has retired their cosmologies; and their social formulas—master/slave, gender relations, and the like—must constantly be reviewed in the light of historical changes and our continuing search for justice. It is their convergent vision of ultimate reality, the Big Picture that impresses me more than any of the alternatives that modernity has produced.

Beneke: Could you tell us precisely what you experience when you "intuitively discern" the perfection of things?

Smith: Something like Plato's experience when he said, "First a shudder runs through you, and then the old awe steals over you." I would not mind stopping with that, but other sensations can be added. Excitement. Exhilaration. Confidence. Selflessness and compassion. Peace.

Beneke: Underlying religion is the problem of death. Socrates defined philosophy as practice in the art of dying. You embody the traditional notion of the philosopher as a seeker of wisdom, someone who is concerned with the great questions of life. What do you think happens when we die?

Smith: I need to hesitate for a moment, for this is another place where it's easy to sound glib. The only honest answer is, *Who knows?* This is the ultimate mystery. Still, the mind keeps searching for answers, or at least for insights.

To pass into death is an adventure, for sure. Near the moment of his passing, Henry James said, "This is the distinguished moment." What the passage does is to raise again the question of final perfection. I believe in universal salvation, which is to say that everyone eventually comes to something like Dante's beatific vision, which phases out of time into the Eternal Now. That term isn't easy to understand. I have heard even theologians deride eternity as boring. That flagrantly misrepresents the concept. Boredom presupposes time that endures without changes, whereas eternity is outside of time.

Beneke: Boredom is when time is a weight burdening you, and you want to get rid of it.

Smith: Exactly, which is why it could not possibly characterize eternity. There are, however, two conjectures as to what the soul experiences in eternity. We must keep in mind that we are out of our depth here, and that these are what Plato would call no more than "likely tales," that is, human imagination's best stab at the mystery. One conjecture is dualistic. Here the soul retains its separateness and beholds, timelessly, the Glory, in keeping with Ramakrishna's dictum, "I want to taste sugar, not be sugar." In the nondualist version, what the soul beholds is so overwhelming that it commands the soul's complete attention, all 100 percent of it. With zero attention left for itself, that self drops from sight, leaving only what its attention is fixed on. As the Hindus say, "The dewdrop has slipped into the shining sea."

Beneke: This sounds like the German mystic Meister Eckhart saying that "the eye through which God sees us is the eye through which we see God."

Smith: You have it word perfect, though I am still not sure I understand what those words say. Something like what I was saying, I suppose. All the traditions make the point, though, that unless you are the rare case of a Hindu or Buddhist nonreturner, your spiritual work is not complete when you "drop the body," as Indians refer to death. Something remains to be done. Hindus and Buddhists say that *something* gets accomplished in this same world in the new bodies into which they reincarnate. The Abrahamic religions, on the other hand—Judaism, Christianity, and Islam—defer that further work on other planes: purgatory, hell, or other *bardos,* to borrow Tibetan vocabulary. The similarity that underlies these different imageries is quite apparent.

In the period immediately after death there may be a lot of confusion and bewilderment. Swedenborg thought that the first job old-timers in heaven had respecting newcomers was to convince them that they were dead. (I find the thought that heaven is that much like Stockholm rather charming, but also fanciful.) But there are also indications from psychical research—which I don't totally dismiss, though you have to step carefully. There are souls on the other side that are as confused as we are. Channelers and mediums beware! A lot of static gets mixed into the messages. Some souls may even decompose into fragmented residues. The intermediate realm between heaven and earth may be a real mess.

Beneke: Do you think channeling—spirits running through people— provides evidence of the spirit world, a realm beyond the physical?

Smith: There is no conclusive proof that convinces the Bay Area skeptics. Still, Plato took his to his *metaxy,* his "intermediate realm," which housed spirits like Eros, and Socrates's daimon, who never told him what to do but warned him what not to do. Plato took the spirit realm seriously, and I am inclined to do so also. I treat shamanism, for example, with respect. Roger Walsh's book *The Spirit of Shamanism* finesses the questions of whether the shamans' "allies" are a part of their own psyches or exist objectively apart from them. But whatever the geography of the case, in spiritual matters, space never functions as more than a metaphor for difference. Walsh too, as a professor of psychiatry, takes shamanism seriously. Wherever we choose to position them, shamanic "allies" are objectively other than the shamans' conscious minds, and they function accordingly. By the way, shamans appear in the oldest cave drawings we have, which date back about twenty thousand years, and suggest that shamanism may be humankind's oldest religion.

Beneke: The conventional way to dismiss all this is to say that consciousness is a product of the brain; you alter the brain in certain ways and you alter consciousness. When the brain stops functioning, consciousness stops.

Smith: That could be the case, but I consider it a prejudice of minds that I have come to believe that what we can get our hands on is most real. My reaction to it is like T. S. Eliot's on reading Bertrand Russell's *A Free Man's Worship.* He said it left him with no idea where the truth lay except that it had to be in the opposite direction from the book in hand.

I find it most interesting that the science that saddled us with reductionistic materialism in its early centuries is now going beyond that position. Quantum mechanics is telling us that the universe of space, time, and matter derives from something that exceeds those matrices. Whether or not that Primordial X is conscious, as religion holds, science cannot say. But at least materialism is now old hat.

Beneke: Noam Chomsky talks about how no one expects a cat to do algebra; similarly, there is every reason to suppose that there are fundamental laws of the universe that humans will never be able to know because of our cognitive limitations. Perhaps our ignorance is inexorable.

Smith: I was Chomsky's colleague at MIT for fifteen years, and I honor him greatly, but here *mystery* seems a more precise word than *ignorance.* In principle ignorance can be dispelled, whereas mystery cannot be, because in its case every advance that we make opens onto horizons we didn't even know existed. We are born in mystery, we live in mystery, and we die in mystery. That is not going to change.

Beneke: Let me ask an impolite question. Religion appears to some people— Freud, for example—as a form of wish fulfillment. Because people want the world to be a certain way, and because it is emotionally satisfying to believe the world is a certain way, people hold certain beliefs about God or life after death. There is evidence that where there are harsh child- rearing practices with a lot of corporeal punishment, people conceive of God as very harsh and punitive. What do you make of this?

Smith: I take heart in your child-rearing example. The fact that God has been seen predominately as a loving parent suggests that harsh, punitive, corporal punishment has been the exception rather than the rule. But your question itself I don't take as impolite at all. It introduces an important issue, the appropriateness of psychologiz- ing. Philosophers consider psychologizing a logical fallacy for being ad hominem; it diverts attention from the content of an issue to the persons who are discussing it. "Two plus two equals four" isn't untrue because the person who said it was drunk at the time. That's a crude example of psychologizing, but Freud's critique of religion, and those of Marx and Nietzsche as well, have the same form.

This is not to say that psychological considerations are irrelevant. We should be wary of what drunks say, and if Freud had proved that religious beliefs derive only, or even primarily, from wishful thinking and father images, I would accept his reasoning and could live with it. But he didn't come close to doing that, so I see his theories as half-truths. There are textbook cases (I won't venture how many) in which they come close to being the full truth about beliefs. But to generalize from these and turn a half-truth into the full truth is a blatant case of disciplinary imperialism. Psychology— or, in the case of Marx's "opiate of the people," sociology—colonizes religion and tailors it to fit its theories. You can see that I'm worked up on the point.

Furthermore, the psychologizing sword cuts both ways. If my beliefs simply reflect my character, yours reflect yours. If I believe because I am infantile, you disbelieve because you are counterdependent. You see why philosophers aren't fond of ad hominen arguments. They degenerate into trading insults. I come back to the idea of the world as a Rorschach blot. If you see it as consisting only of matter, then immaterial things that other people believe in will appear to you as projections. They, in turn, will see you as prey to tunnel vision and blind to half of what exists.

Beneke: Tell us about your experience with your Zen master in Kyoto.
Smith: I was drawn to Buddhism through D. T. Suzuki, whose writings held out the prospect of at least a taste of satori, the enlightenment experience, if one practiced Zen. I was in my mid-thirties, and at that stage I wanted that experience more than anything else in the world, so I entered Zen training, which led eventually to a monastery in Kyoto and koan training under a Zen master.

Rinzai Zen (the branch that I was in) uses koans [traditional Zen mental exercises] in its training. Koans are of different kinds, but the beginning ones are rather like shaggy-dog stories in that they involve questions—riddles, really—that make no rational sense. The one I was given was longer than most, so I won't repeat it in full, but it came down to this: How could one of the greatest Zen masters have said that dogs do not have Buddha-natures when the Buddha has said that even grass possesses it? For two months, I banged my head against that contradiction for eight hours a day. I was sitting in the cramped lotus position and reporting to my *roshi*, or Zen master, one-on-one at five o'clock each morning, what I had come up with. Precious little! It was the most frustrating assignment I had ever been given. I seemed to be getting absolutely nowhere, though I did discover as the weeks slipped by that the final word in the koan, *mu* (which translates into "no"), seemed to function more and more like the *om* mantra that I had worked with in Hinduism.

The climax came during the final eight days in the Myoshinji Monastery in the middle of a kind of final-exam period where everything else gets tabled so the monks can meditate almost around the clock. As a novice, I was permitted to sleep three and a half hours each night, but I found that grossly insufficient, and the sleep deprivation was the hardest ordeal I had ever faced. After the first night I was sleepy, after the second I was bushed, and it kept getting worse from there.

I still don't understand how Zen training works, but it seems clear that the initial koans force the rational mind to the end of its tether, and that sleep deprivation figures in somewhere along the line. If you can't get your mind into an altered state any other way, sleep deprivation will eventually do it for you, for deprived of dreams, the mind becomes psychotic.

Something like that happened to my mind two days before the monastic term ended. That afternoon I went storming into the *roshi* in a frenzy. Self-pity had long since become boring; that day I was in a rage. I was furious. What a way to treat human beings, I kept telling myself, and charged in to my *roshi* prepared, not just to throw in the towel, but to throw it straight at his face.

I entered the audience room with the required ritual, palms clasped together. Turning only straight corners because there are no diagonal shortcuts in Zen, I made my way to where he was sitting in his priestly robes. His short, heavy stick (for clobbering if need be) was lying in his lap. Sinking to my knees on the cushion before him, I touched my head to the floor and flexed my outstretched fingers upward, an Indian gesture that symbolizes lifting the dust from the Buddha's feet. Then I sat back on my heels, and our eyes met in a mutual glare. For some moments he said nothing, then, "How's it going?" He was one of the two *roshis* in the world then who could speak English. It sounded like a calculated taunt.

"Terrible!" I shouted.

"You think you are going to get sick, don't you?"

More taunting sarcasm, so I let him have it.

"Yes, I think I'm going to get sick!" I yelled. For several days my throat had been contracting to the point where I was having to labor to breathe.

Then something extraordinary happened. His face suddenly relaxed, its taunting, goading expression was gone, and with total matter-of-factness he said, "What is sickness? What is health? Both are distractions. Put both aside and go forward."

What I despair of conveying to you is the impact those fifteen words had on me. Without reflecting for a moment, I found myself saying to myself, "By God, he's right!" How was he able to spin me around, defuse my rage, and return me to lucidity in a twinkling? I will never comprehend. Never have I felt so instantly reborn and energized. It was as if there was a pipe connecting his *hara*—his abdomen, where the Japanese locate the self's center—to mine. I exited in the prescribed manner, not only determined to stick out the two remaining days, but knowing that I could do so.

It didn't occur to me at the time that in that climactic moment I might have passed my koan, and I returned to the States assuming that I had not. But when I related my story to a dharma brother [someone with whom I'd undergone spiritual training] who had trained for twelve years under my *roshi*, he said he wasn't at all sure that I had not passed it. He reminded me that the answer to the early koans is not a rational proposition but an experience. That, at the climactic moment in my training, I was able not just to acknowledge the identity of life's opposites theoretically, but to experience their identity. In my case the identity of sickness and health struck him as a strong foretaste of the enlightenment experience.

Beneke: Therapists talk about interventions, which require a certain timing and art where the therapist picks just the right moment to say just the right thing that leads to insight. Your roshi intervened in just the right way.

Smith: Apparently so. It still seems to me like genius. He knew exactly where I was, and administered exactly the light tap—ping—that changed everything.

Beneke: Your early work focused on the historical religions, ones that have written texts and cumulative histories. At a certain point you came to appreciate oral traditions as well.

Smith: I now see that in addition to the three great families of historical religions—East Asian, South Asian, and Abrahamic, or Western—there is a fourth: the primal, tribal, and exclusively oral family which is not inferior to the other three. What enabled me to honor tribal peoples as our equals is that while writing adds, it also subtracts. We tend to think that because unlettered peoples only talk and we both talk and write, we have everything they have, and something in addition. I no longer think that it's true. Writing exacts a price, which is loss of the sense of what is important.

Visualize a tribe gathered around its campfire at the close of the day. Everything its ancestors learned the hard way, through generations of trial and error, from medicinal plants to the myths that empower their lives and give them meaning, is stored in their skulls, and there only. Obviously they are going to keep reviewing what is important for them, and let what is trivial fade into oblivion.

Beneke: Tell us about your encounter with the Masai warriors in Africa.

Smith: I was in Tanzania for a conference in the late 1960s and didn't want to leave without a glimpse of big game in its natural habitat. There were no tours, so I found a fly-by-night rental joint and took off in a rickety jalopy for the Serengeti Plain. There was no road map, but that was logical because as far as I could make out there were no roads. I did encounter one road sign during the day, but I couldn't read it, besides which it had fallen over, so I couldn't tell which way its arms pointed.

A couple of hours into the desert, it suddenly dawned on me that I was completely lost. And out of gas. When we rent a car here we assume the tank to be full. Not there. They give you about enough to get out of the lot, but I didn't know that and hadn't checked. At a total standstill, I could not think of a thing to do. The car was too hot to sit in, and there were no trees to shade me from the blistering sun. Giraffes were friendly; one virtually looked over my shoulder when I had had to change a threadbare tire. There were other animals, but at that hour no lions. Dry bones were everywhere, though—portents of my impending fate. I ate my packed lunch, started rationing my last bottle of water, and tried to think of a plan of action.

None had suggested itself when two figures appeared dimly on the horizon. I started toward them, but with every step I took, they retreated. I quickened my pace, making frantic gestures of distress, and they gradually slowed their pace to allow me to catch up with them. They were disconcertingly large and wore nothing but spears taller than themselves, and flapping cloths over their shoulders to ward off the sun somewhat.

What then could I do? I was in human company but without words to communicate. *Something* had to be done, so I seized one of them by the wrist and marched him to my dysfunctional car, his companion in tow. This seemed to amuse them, and why not? What had our move to a pile of metal accomplished?

The two of them conversed and then started to leave, but I seized my hostage's wrist again. Human beings were my only lifeline, and I wasn't going to let it be severed. More laughter and conversation between them, and then one of them started off while leaving his companion with me. When he returned he had in tow a small boy who knew a few words of English, such as *hello, good-bye,* and the like. So, pointing in different directions, I said, "School, school!"

He gave no signs of comprehension, but after more conversation, he and the man who had fetched him went off, leaving my hostage with me. In about a hour, the man returned with ten adult cohorts, and the sun set that evening on as bizarre a scene (I feel sure) as the Serengeti Plain had ever staged: a white man, seated in state at the wheel of his car steering, while twelve Masai warriors pushed him across the sands. My propellers were taking the experience as a great lark. Laughing and all talking simultaneously, they sounded like a flock of happy birds. My first thought was,

Who listens? then immediately, Who cares? They were having such a great time.

Six miles across the plain they delivered me to the school I had asked for, which turned out to be Olduvai Gorge, where a decade or so earlier Louis and Mary Leakey [with their son Richard] discovered the tooth that "set the human race back a million years," as the press reported their discovery. That encounter left me with a profound sense of human connectedness. There we were, as different in every way—ethnically, linguistically, culturally—as any two groups on our planet. Yet without a single word in common, we connected. They understood my predicament and responded with a will and with style.

Beware of the differences that blind us to the unity that binds us.

John Loudon: The latest published writing of yours that I've seen is your enthusiastic introduction to the new edition of Frithjof Schuon's The Transcendent Unity of Religions. *There you speak of the primordial tradition. What do you mean by it?*

Huston Smith: If we look at human beings, the first thing that strikes us is how different they are—different heights, different shapes, different complexions—and yet we know that underlying this manifold diversity, the structure of the human spine that holds all these bodies erect is surprisingly similar. Now, it has come upon me that the collective outlooks of humankind are analogous to this situation concerning human physiques. That is to say, when we first come upon the Native American Indian outlook or the Hindu outlook or the Islamic outlook, what strikes us first is, again, how distinctive they are, how much they differ from one another. But the intriguing—more than intriguing, the important—thing that has become ever more evident the longer I work with these traditions is that at the heart of all of them is what we might call a

This interview with HarperSanFrancisco editor and religion writer John Loudon was first published as "The Meaning of Tradition: A Conversation with Huston Smith" in *Parabola, the Magazine of Myth and Tradition* 1, no. 1 (Winter 1976). Reprinted by permission of *Parabola*.

conceptual spine that is extraordinarily the same. It's as though, behind the scenes, a kind of invisible geometry was drawing them all toward a truth, which in the final instance is single. That I call the primordial tradition. It has a certain resemblance to what people familiar with philosophy know as the perennial philosophy. I don't object to that phrase; I even rather like it. But to avoid taking over all the baggage that's become associated with that phrase, I prefer to speak of the primordial tradition.

Loudon: You don't mean primordial in the sense of primary in a temporal sequence, do you—so that there was some primary beginning of religion that was then diffused into various historical streams?

Smith: Well, yes and no. The word *primordial,* if I look it up in the most recent dictionary of American usage, is defined in terms of temporal origin. But in the *Oxford English Dictionary,* which indicates the way in which the word has been used, it is defined as "pertaining to, or since, the origin of things." In other words, it really means "no matter where or when," and that's the sense in which I support and like the word—"under whatsoever sky." So it's not basically a temporal word but a timeless word.

Loudon: So it's not unlike the word primal, *in the sense of absolutely root, basic, universal. What a primal therapist, for instance, seems to want to get back to is the origins of an individual's emotional state, which isn't strictly a sequential affair. The origins are always there as the* prima materia *of behavior.*

Smith: That's good. That's exactly what I mean.

Loudon: How is the primordial tradition related to the great historical religious traditions? How does this primordial tradition take on the different flesh of the various traditions?

Smith: To begin with, it is the font and spring of them all. But it takes on, as it were, different coloring as it enters into, and in ways is also the source of, differing civilizations. To take an analogy from human life, the same individual might couch the same point in different ways, depending on the audience to which he is speaking. A father talking about the same general subject might speak in different language to his wife or to his five-year-old child or to a professional audience. Such diversity is appropriate, indeed essential, for communication. If the primordial truth had delivered itself in the same idiom to all humankind, it would have been understood by none. I've spoken in terms of analogy, and that's useful and inevitable to some extent. But to speak more directly, more literally—and if one uses anthropomorphic imagery—one could say that God, to connect with the different temperaments of the different civilizations, perforce must meet them on their own ground. Now, if we don't like to think in those terms, then we could say that the deepest truths welling up from the unconscious of the great spiritual geniuses—Muhammad, the seers of the Upanishads, the Prophets of Israel, Christ, Gautama Buddha, Confucius, Lao-tzu—naturally are filtered through the distinctive sensibilities of the various civilizations, which we know are different, or there would only be one civilization. So the unity is, in this sense, transcendent in all the traditions. They point toward it, converge toward it, and yet it eludes being fully deliverable or describable in any finite mode.

Loudon: Friedrich Heiler, in an article in The History of Religions, *a University of Chicago collection, listed seven elements common to the great world religions. Do you think that it is genuinely possible to articulate such elements and thereby give a skeleton outline of the primordial tradition itself?*

Smith: Well, I think you can. Indeed, some people—not everybody— should. At the same time there should be no mistaking the finger that is pointing at the moon for the moon itself, and there should be recognition that every articulation will itself be finite and relative. But it's a useful *upaya,* as the Buddhists would say, a useful means.

Loudon: My suspicion would be that Heiler's academic, Western intellectual way of putting it wouldn't be the same as the formulation of Daisetz Suzuki, for instance, or somebody from a very different background. In fact, if you were to ask scholars from the various traditions to come up with these common points, you might get the same diversity of formulation that you have in the traditions at large.

Smith: Yes. But I'm not sure that it would be equal in degree. And there is the fact too of different modes of expression. Archaic man would probably dance it out, and the Sung painters would paint it out, and we philosophers try to use words.

Loudon: You also seem to like very much Schuon's distinction between the esoteric and exoteric dimensions of the traditions and to find this a useful way of talking about unity amid diversity. Could you explain the basic distinction between the esoteric and the exoteric?

Smith: The key difference has to do with the notion of infinity. A true infinite is without limitation of any form and, by the same token, beyond any positive definition, because definition would demarcate and therefore limit. Some minds, faced with this notion of the infinite, are enticed, one might almost say entranced. Their response to it is affirmative, embracing. They are like a moth before the candle flame: they go for it. Other minds are rebuffed by such a notion. *Repelled* may be too strong a word, but they are certainly turned back by it. At best, they can't get their hands on it, their minds around it, and so it's meaningless. At worst, it's frightening, a little scary, or at least certainly unappealing. So the esoterics are those for whom the infinite is a positive notion; the exoterics are those for whom it is a negative notion. Actually, in the Western world, it's doubtful that one finds true philosophical esoterics before Plotinus, because even the Greeks, with all their passion for abstraction, saw the infinite as an inferior concept. They saw it merely as an indefinite, and that which is indefinite is without form, amorphous. And for the Greeks, the perfect is the formed rather than the unformed. Just as in French today, *ouvrage fini,* a finished work, is a good work, completed, articulated, defined. So in the West we have to wait till Plotinus for a positive infinite to emerge, and even he was probably influenced by India. For Indians, unlike the Greeks, viewed the infinite from very early times, certainly by the time of the Upanishads, in the positive or esoteric way.

Loudon: Then, just to round this off, Schuon finds a converging unity in the esoteric dimensions of the traditions and a growing diversity as the traditions become more fully exoteric?

Smith: Right.

Loudon: In the distinction in a specific tradition, between the esoterics, who I understand are always a minority, and the exoterics, who follow more closely and more literally the specifics which their tradition gives them, might the esoteric be regarded as a privileged or higher state and the exoteric following of the tradition somehow for the more ordinary people?

Smith: Either can be saints, so sanctity is no monopoly of one or the other.

Loudon: So is the distinction more one of personal calling or constitution?

Smith: Spiritual temperament, I think we might say. But to speak of temperaments generally, you can't say, for instance, that an extrovert is inferior to an introvert, or to use Jungian terms, intuitive types are preferable to sensate types. It's a matter of living one's type to the fullest that it allows. It's along that line that virtue and vice, or attainment and limitation, are to be viewed.

Now, if I were to be fully honest and expose myself, I should probably add that I may have hedged a little bit in that answer. Because if we talk about truth, it may be the case that the esoteric enters more fully into the divine nature. I'm not totally certain of that, but it may be more complicated than my initial answer suggests.

Loudon: You seem to indicate in the introduction to Schuon's book that at least the matter of discerning the transcendent unity of religions is more readily intelligible to the esoteric than to the exoteric.

Smith: That's true. For seeing the relationship between religions, I do think the esoteric has an edge. But that's a rather special problem. It doesn't put one ahead on the score of religious attainment.

Loudon: What do you think of the idea that occurs in Paul Tillich's work, and more fully in John Dunne's, that by "passing over" to other lives and other traditions one can come back to one's own expanded and enriched and discover there dimensions that had been closed to you or unnoticed before? Is this a fruitful way of experiencing the infinite potentiality of one's own tradition?

Smith: If it does indeed open you to resources in one's own tradition, it is to be lauded, and I can readily see that it could do that. In fact, I would say that my passings-over have done that. But if one were to make religion out of that method, which I don't think Dunne does, I would, of course, have misgivings. For one thing, though this is one way of discovering the resources of one's own tradition, I don't think it's the only way. There are ways of ferreting out our unexplored corners other than the method Dunne proposes. One way would be to dialogue with other seekers within one's own tradition, the expectation being that they will have seen things you have missed. Also, I think it would be a mistake to think that we, by virtue of our cosmopolitan perspectives, have more resources for sanctity than a Bedouin, say, who may never have heard of a religion other than Islam.

Loudon: So then perhaps it's a way for those for whom religious pluralism is a genuine question or challenge?

Smith: Yes, that's a good way of putting it. Because once that problem has broken over you, then to stay completely confined to your own tradition might have an element of rejection and dismissal which doesn't occur in the case of the Bedouin or an Australian aborigine. And that shutting it out might have an element of closure about it which would be spiritually detrimental.

Loudon: With the influx of Eastern tradition at all levels into the West, the related question arises of just how tradition-bound we are, simply by growing up in a culture. Can an ordinary, churchgoing, publicly educated person growing up in Syracuse, New York, really become, say, a Zen monk in a truly authentic sense? How transportable are the traditions?

Smith: I think it's possible. More than that, I think it is being done— Philip Kapleau at Rochester has done it; Richard Baker at the Zen Center in San Francisco has done it. By saying this, I am saying in the same breath that I think Carl Jung was mistaken in his claim that it splits a person apart. Albeit even with the pluralistic situation today, it is atypical, and the more natural route is to follow the tradition in which one is raised.

Loudon: Referring again to the diversity of your experience, how do you view your colleague David Miller's interest, shaped by the work of James Hillman, in polytheism as an authentic contemporary religious option and his sense that, for many today, there are many numinous centers, none of which can be said to be preeminent, and that for them monotheistic consciousness is inappropriate, even stultifying?

Smith: The issue that links the way I see things and the way David describes them in *The New Polytheism* is the issue of freedom and form. He picks up on the freedom end of that polarity. He sees modern humanity as restricted, or to put the matter another way, as having aspects of personality that are undeveloped and in need of being rounded out. I pick up on the form aspect of the polarity, seeing us as needing to find life's center and to discover its abiding priorities. David talks like Oscar Wilde, wanting to "taste all the fruit on the tree of life." I respond more to the prophetic injunction "Choose ye this day whom ye shall serve."

Loudon: Which way would you point a person who has become alienated from his or her tradition, or whose development has been arrested, or who has become acutely aware of the pluralism of religious traditions— back to his or her own tradition or outward to exploring another one?

Smith: The important point to be stressed is the parity and importance of the great traditions—both the ones I deal with in *The Religions of Man* [reissued as *The World's Religions*] and what Mircea Eliade calls the archaic ones, like those of the Native American. Parity: that in principal and practice the authentic traditions are equal. Importance (and this is likely to be the most controversial thing that I will say): that these traditions have a saving power which in all likelihood is greater than the saving power in any one of us as disconnected individuals. I know very well that Gautama Buddha says, "Be ye lamps unto yourselves." But in the traditions, statements like this assume a corporate base. One must also remember that "the spirit bloweth where it listeth." There will always be exceptions that prove any generalizations. Still, on average, as between a private *sadhana* [spiritual quest] that an individual Scotch-tapes together for him- or herself and one outlined by an enduring tradition, I place my confidence in the latter. That's somewhat out of tune with the temper of the times, and I may be less convinced about this than about the other things I've said, yet I more than suspect that it's true. It's a case of "I believe, help thou my unbelief." The moral is not necessarily that one return to his or her own tradition. There may be alienating factors at work there—a bad Sunday school experience or whatever—that would take a whole lifetime to undo. The moral is to find some tradition and to steep one's soul in it. To me it is immaterial which tradition; it is of maximum materiality that it be a tradition.

Loudon: Amid the myriad current religious options available, from Reverend Moon to Zen centers, how can a novice tell an authentic teaching from an inauthentic one? Is connection with a tradition essential?

Smith: I think it is. With due respect to the innumerable innovating gurus that are around today, I see their departures from tradition as, on the whole, aberrations. There are many personal-growth programs that can help to some extent, but in terms of life's final potentials I don't find innovative or eclectic systems to equal the tried and the true.

Loudon: There seem at least two types of entry into a tradition, besides birth, of course. One would be more along the line of "blind faith," that is, after an initial encounter, putting your hand in the hand of the guru and committing yourself to this way unconditionally. It has the advantage of being an absolute involvement without which true experience of a tradition seems impossible. The other is a more gradual entry by which the truth you experience and know personally is confirmed and enhanced by the tradition you are entering.

Smith: I think that puts it very well, and both are open options, and much depends on the circumstances—whom one finds oneself in the presence of—as well as, again, one's spiritual temperament. The Indians talk about the "monkey way" and the "cat way." In the monkey way, the baby monkey with its own arms will embrace the mother's neck, but in the cat way, the mother picks up the kitten by the nape of the neck. Perhaps the experience of [twelfth-century Muslim theologian] al-Ghazzali is relevant here. He went through three stages: one very orthodox, becoming versed in the law, but finding that rather dry; then coming upon the Sufis, whose way was entirely esoteric, ecstatic, and mystical; and then finally—this is the important thing—he came to realize the dangers of excess if ecstasy is not curbed by orthodox guidelines. Thus he came in the end to a definitive blend of form and substance that has remained normative for Sufism. I respect that model.

Loudon: For many your book The Religions of Man *was a first introduction to the study of comparative religions. What do you see as the importance of this study?*

Smith: Everything turns on how it is done. For me, the opportunity to work with this gold in its various historical veins has been a continuing joy. I am ever grateful for the opportunity to attend to such vivifying, salvific—it is nothing less than that—material. At the same time, I can remember the courses that I took in world religions in my collegiate days. They were without doubt the dullest, least profitable courses in my curriculum. I went through them without encountering a single item that would tempt me to pursue them on my own. Looking back, I sometimes feel that those teachers must have been geniuses of a kind—geniuses in reverse, if you will—to have been able to conceal the material from us to the extent they did. There's nothing very special about learning certain facts and dates: it could easily turn people off.

Loudon: So you would regard as unprofitable, even counterproductive, an approach that treats traditions as assemblages of historical information, propositional truths, and ancient curiosities?

Smith: The main thing was that those teachers did not themselves value what they were teaching. At most, they were cultural historians, curious as to how the old boys felt way back in the old benighted days.

Loudon: I wonder if the contemporary increased awareness of the variety of religious traditions, through courses and books, encourages individuals to develop their own personal syntheses.

Smith: It probably does. The question is whether such individual syntheses are likely to change people as much as involvement in a living tradition can. As you know, I side with the latter. Even so, by the mere fact of living in our polycultural times, there is likely to be some borrowing. Look at the art around my office here—from India, Japan, China. To a degree, that's eclectic, and it can be welcomed, I think. What we have to realize, though, is that a religious outlook, and a religious way, is in the end more like an organism than like a mechanism. That means it is not basically constructed of random or interchangeable parts. We are learning from the difficulty with heart transplants that organisms tolerate intrusions from the outside to some extent, but not beyond given limits. We can learn from this analogy that each of us needs a religion that is not just a collage but an organic whole. And for me that means a tradition whose various ingredients have over the centuries (if we put the matter in human and historical terms) settled into relations with one another that are organic and whole. We need to ground our lives in a center that is holistic in this way. Fixed in that center we can, with appreciation, borrow some trimmings from one another, so to speak.

Loudon: *Do you think that people are inescapably religious, that even without a great tradition patterning their lives they constellate their existence about an ultimate and a series of hierarchically related values?*
Smith: I think in a meaningful sense that's true, though the degrees may vary.

Loudon: *There then would be two senses to religious conversion: one, converting to one of the traditions, not excluding the one in which one was born, and learning from it how to articulate, symbolize, actualize one's religious concerns; the other, shifting from one lifestyle to another.*
Smith: That's true, but I wonder if the alternatives are equally promising. You see, I don't see serious involvement with a tradition as merely the adoption of a set values—look at Martin Lings's *What Is Sufism?* and you will see my point. There is a dynamic, substantive power to traditions. Assuming that a tradition is alive, it is like an artery, and to be incorporated in it is like receiving a spiritual transfusion. To change the image, it's like a wave which can carry

one forward. It follows that an important question about any ad hoc eclecticism is, Does it possess that kind of *barakah*, as the Muslims would say, that kind of substantive grace? You can see here that I am passing beyond a purely humanistic point of view to posit a flow of spiritual force which the traditions channel. Granted that to some degree this force seems spent today, I think it continues to some extent and is the world's best hope.

Loudon: Backtracking a bit, would it be correct simply to identify the esoteric dimension of the traditions with what is more popularly called the mystical dimension?

Smith: I think they certainly lie in the same direction. The problem is the many senses in which the word *mysticism* is used. Sometimes it means nothing more than a direct experiential encounter with the transcendent, whatever its form. From there it can go on to specify a dramatically different kind of experience. And the word is also used to emphasize the experience of unity, of the oneness of things. All of those would be involved in an esoteric encounter, but in addition, that encounter, since to some degree it is of the Infinite, would be ineffable; it could not with any degree of adequacy be put into words. But esoterism doesn't turn wholly on direct experience; it can take its stand on the conviction that the esoteric perspective is true without claiming a great deal in the way of experience of its truth.

Loudon: So that a philosopher, for instance, who had a certain position about the nature of reality without having a so-called mystical experience could be in the esoteric camp?

Smith: Correct. The Sufis have a nice way of putting the point. They speak of the lore of certainty, the eye of certainty, and the truth of certainty. The lore of certainty they liken to hearing about fire, the eye of certainty to seeing fire, and the truth of certainty to being burned by fire. Now, an esoteric can be one to any of these three degrees. With respect to what strikes me as true, I see myself as an esoteric, but I would not lay any great claims to having experienced the truth I feel confident of. I think the moment when I first realized I was an esoteric, though of course I didn't use the word, was when I first opened the Upanishads and found the truth of those writings pouring through to me. My wonder was that truth of this depth could be articulated to this extent in words. There was a rush of conviction regarding the truth of that perspective, but it wasn't *samadhi* [the highest state of self-realization].

Loudon: My assumption, in listening to you, has been that some traditions have a larger dimension of the esoteric, and others have a larger dimension of the exoteric. I would assume, for instance, that in Zen the esoteric dimension would totally predominate.

Smith: Yes, but I wouldn't, of course, consider Zen a distinct tradition apart from Buddhism. You might think of it as an esoteric dimension within Buddhism, though not the only one. But I do think that by and large the Asian traditions tend to accommodate the esoteric perspective more routinely than do Judaism and Christianity, with Islam a border case in which Sufism is explicitly esoteric and much of Islam is not.

Loudon: Well, could there be a sense in which Sufism itself has both an esoteric and an exoteric dimension? Isn't there an external, formal tradition of teaching which functions almost as an exoteric dimension?

Smith: Yes, there is. There are degrees of Sufism, as elsewhere. The esoteric presents itself as circles within circles, its teachings becoming more and more esoteric as one approaches the center. That means, as you say, certain doctrines will be readily available to everyone, but there will be certain teachings and methods that are initiatic, just as early Christianity was initiatic, with stages of entry and the Eucharist reserved to those who were in the inner coterie. Another point on Sufism: it almost seems that the more refined the esoteric core, the more it tends to draw a rabble, one might almost say, to its outer fringe. So in Sufism one finds the loftiest spirituality ringed about with jugglers and magicians—spiritual riffraff, almost. In places Sufism has acquired a bad name, precisely through such hangers-on. But though one might not be totally pleased with that picture, there is a kind of naturalness about it too, because the bizarre element on the fringes at least senses that something important is present at the center of the circle that attracts them.

Loudon: What would be the standard term for what you mean by the exoteric?

Smith: One of the reasons a term doesn't immediately come to mind is that in the West it is generally what we think of as mainline, institutional Christianity, or whatever the religion is, where the doctrines are articulated, the observances specified, and the laws laid out.

Loudon: How would you characterize the freedom the mystically inclined person has in regard to his or her tradition?

Smith: It is difficult to generalize on that, because the answer differs at different stages. In early stages when the individual life really needs to be made over—cast in a different mold, one might say—too much individual discretion could compromise needed rubrics. I am assuming, of course, that one begins the quest because one wishes to be born again, or changed into something different from what one already is. But then later on, as one's feet are more firmly planted on the way, overdependence on external authority could be, in certain cases, debilitating. There's a wonderful *mondo* [a question-and-answer teaching system] in the Zen tradition on that. When one of the students went to his *roshi* to report a great satori, the *roshi* heard him out but said, "Well, that wasn't such a great satori; it was just a little satori." Whereupon the student replied, "I don't care what kind of satori you think it was; it was a great satori!" To which the *roshi* responded, "Well, in that case, it was a great satori." So there comes a time when the independence and appropriateness of private judgment comes back into the picture.

Loudon: I would think that Thomas Merton's experience might bear out the legitimacy of this gradual independence within an ongoing dialectic between freedom and form.

Smith: It is a dialectic. The Zen tradition, as we know, has many stipulations like "When you see the Buddha, kill the Buddha!" or "Tear up the Sutras!" Such teachings have their place, but we tend to overgeneralize them, divorcing them from the contexts for which they were intended. Too early in the game, we appropriate to ourselves the right to take the liberties they counsel.

Loudon: Might there be a special temptation for Westerners, with the emphasis on freedom and individuality, to avoid the early stages of initiation into a teaching?

Smith: Yes. And there is a sizeable streak of counterdependence in our culture. "Don't tell me what to do!" The Fritz Perls attitude toward life.

Loudon: And if you say that at the start, you may never get off the ground.
Smith: Exactly.

Loudon: Does following a religious way, a path of faith, necessarily involve spiritual disciplines of some sort?

Smith: Yes. Again, we must recognize that "the spirit bloweth where it listeth," so there may be one in a million who may be the exception. But overwhelmingly the need is for wisdom and method both; all the traditions so teach. As the saying goes, we need to walk on both feet: right views and right practice.

Loudon: How can a person understand a religious tradition that he or she does not practice?

Smith: Very imperfectly. There are those who see the promised land, get some intimation of what lies there, but for some quirk within them just do not take the steps to cross over into it. But the rule in religious matters is that understanding proceeds through living what one is trying to understand.

Loudon: So it is only by living a tradition that one comes to understand it and gains thereby the resources to understand other traditions?

Smith: That's true. Noam Chomsky once said that there is a very real sense in which to understand fully how one language functions is to understand how they all function. The situation with religious traditions is comparable.

Loudon: Is the advanced, scholarly study of the particular traditions a necessary or vital part of the interplay between knowledge and practice?

Smith: One has to ask, "Necessary for what?" You see, I believe that
Black Elk [Lakota Sioux medicine man] or an Australian aborigine
living the Dreamtime that Eliade talks about had everything
"necessary unto salvation," as the saying goes. Scholarly equipment
would be irrelevant to the depth and quality of their awareness.
When it comes to religious living, the kind of information that
appears in scholarly journals is quite expendable. Even so, the mind
is a part of the human complement, and one can become interested
in comparative religions as one can in other things. Lunching with a
colleague, Bertrand Russell listened attentively to his report of a
discovery in brain functions that he had made, and then commented quietly, "It's nice to know things." That holds for religions
too. I am constantly grateful for such historians of religion. As you
may know, I chanced myself to stumble on one remarkable fact in
this area: the capacity of certain specially trained lamas to sing
multiple tones simultaneously. Was that discovery important?
Probably not. It was a grace, you might say; a grace, moreover, from
which one can learn something beneficial.

Loudon: So it's not necessary, but such study can be enriching.

Smith: It can also be distracting, because if one isn't careful one's
attention can get sidetracked into merely collecting information. In
which case living, organic wholes get pulverized and become like
dry sand.

Loudon: Regarding the interrelationship of religious traditions, what about
the individual traditions' claims of exclusivity and preeminence?

Smith: It's totally understandable, because that to which one gives one's
life one must think is ultimate. Otherwise, it doesn't deserve
ultimate allegiance. If one gives one's life to Christ, exoterically
conceived, then it's almost as though one wouldn't be wholly
committed to Christ unless that Christ were absolute above all
other exoterically nameable deities.

Loudon: Otherwise you'd always be on the threshold of commitment and
never committing yourself actually.

Smith: That's why Schuon says that for the exoteric the preeminent, privileged status of one tradition is not only inevitable, but appropriate. Now, such people are going to have problems, because we live in a world where people are aware of other traditions. And how God's mercy is to be reconciled with his apparent favoritism for one tradition will probably be a lifelong koan for those people. But whatever one says, this is no problem for the esoteric, because the esoteric core is common to them all.

Loudon: The Jesuit William Johnston, in his comparative work with Zen and Christianity, has found a very close correlation in the stages of mystical ascent, but he raises the question of whether they really reach the same goal. Might it be that there are many mansions in inner space that are reached, and perhaps different ones by different traditions?

Smith: Oh, it's logically possible. The only question is whether, at the end of the road, it is in any decisive sense true. Johnston, I assume, thinks it is true that there are many mansions and that maybe Zen gets only into the antechamber. Is there evidence for that?

Loudon: You would see the difference more in terms of language about, or the interpretation of, what is essentially a common experience in the two traditions.

Smith: In the end, yes. Whether in addition to being common the experience is identical is another question. Probably it's a matter of theme and variations. In those moments when you are romantically in love, is your romantic love exactly like your roommate's, or does it have idiosyncratic shades and nuances? But I would say that substantially, just as one instance of romantic love is like another, so it is with the theophanies.

Loudon: Referring back, for a moment, to your earlier statements about your personal odyssey, would I be right in assuming that the next wave after the strong influence of Zen in your forties was Sufism?

Smith: Yes, you would be. It does happen that around the turn of this decade [1969–1970], abroad in Iran and later in North Africa, I found myself swept in contact with some Sufis in a sequence of experiences that were eye-opening. If I fantasized this, its almost though some man in the sky was saying, "Well, Professor Smith, you've ranged broadly, but there's one tradition that you really don't understand, and that is Islam." And that would have been true, because when I wrote *The Religions of Man,* all the chapters were easy except the one on Islam. I really had to work at that chapter, and even with all my labors I felt I didn't succeed very well. The Koran itself had seemed to me the least accessible scripture in the world. So it took me totally by surprise that in the present sector of my journey there surfaced persons in the Islamic tradition who seemed spiritual paragons. Moreover, standing as they did in the tradition of al-Ghazzali and [twelfth-century mystic and theologian] Ibn Arabi, they were able to meet me on my own mental ground—philosophy—with an emphatically esoteric bent. So I find myself currently most occupied with sounding that tradition.

Loudon: Do you think the stages in your odyssey involve not only changes in teachers and in language and symbolism but also new dimensions of your personality that were opened up?

Smith: That's possible, but I don't really resonate to this sort of Jungian idea that there are flat sides of myself that need to be rounded out, and that different traditions develop different sectors of these. If that were the case, it might counsel that everyone should do something like what I've done, but I want to stress that on balance I see my own trajectory as aberrant rather than as normative. Though who knows what is appropriate for an individual life? In one sense, our trajectory is our destiny. I have to affirm mine as apparently curiously fitting for my odd circumstances, but it is nothing to emulate. As I have said, I think the Thomas Merton way gets farther.

Loudon: It seems ironic that you who have taken the tour, so to speak, feel that it's an abnormal course, and not necessarily the most fruitful way, whereas many of those who advocate an odyssey through the traditions, some claiming to follow Jung, have really kept pretty much within their Western perspective, or outside of a tradition altogether.

Smith: I can't say. But what would Jung himself have said? He says that such experience splits a person apart. How can a Jungian hold that this pattern is somehow normative, when the master gives that opinion?

Loudon: I suppose Jung would say that you should find these different dimensions within your own culture and make the odyssey within it.

Smith: That strikes me as a reasonable generalization. And it accords with my premise that each religion suffices and that there are many mansions within each. Hinduism is simply more explicit than some of the others in noting that there are different yogas for different spiritual types.

Loudon: You tell me you are planning a major new book, entitled Under Every Sky: A Primordial Philosophy of Religion. *[Editor's note: The book was never written, but its concept remains relevant here.] What is its basic argument?*

Smith: It is that human outlooks, taken individually, are too numerous to submit to any pattern—they range all the way from village atheist to agnostic to pious believer. But if one takes collective outlooks, that is, the outlooks of tribes, civilizations, religions, outlooks in the aggregate you might say, they admit to an overview. When one looks at the pattern as a whole, at first the collective outlooks appear very different—Asian from Western, Occidental from Oriental—but as one studies them one becomes progressively aware of a common conceptual spine behind them, as I mentioned at the outset. This common conceptual spine I call the primordial tradition, and I argue that it is universal. It represents, one might almost say, the human unanimity. The only exception is ourselves— the contemporary West over the last two hundred years. Why are we different from the rest of humanity? I think the obvious reason is because of modern science. It has maneuvered us into a distinctive position. Now, if it were actual scientific findings that dictated our unique outlook we could regard it as a breakthrough: a new departure for humankind. In point of fact, however, it's not science that dictates our modern outlook, but a misreading of science, one that deserves the name scientism. Scientism may be defined as the view that the scientific approach to truth is the only reliable one, the only one that gives "news of the universe," one might say, and that the realities that science turns up are the only true realities. But that is a mistake. Science doesn't show that its own outlook is the only valid one. It's we who assume, because of the marvels it has wrought in its own sphere, that its epistemology is privileged.

Loudon: An essential element of scientism seems to be a reductionistic mentality that measures things on just one level and eliminates any sense of a hierarchy of being.

Smith: That's right. Scientism reduces what in the West has been called the "Great Chain of Being" to its ground floor alone.

To continue with the thrust of the book: our modern atypical outlook is grounded in a mistaken reading of science, but aberrations can be corrected. If we come to see through our mistake, we might rejoin the human race. We could get back on course by returning to the primordial outlook, which I take to be the one that most naturally emerges when the full complement of human sensibilities is pondered seriously.

Loudon: Regarding the parity and importance of the various traditions, what role, if any, do you see for missionary work?

Smith: I think it has a place. I can speak autobiographically both ways on this. First, I think my parents did useful things in their years in China. For one thing, starting the only school for girls that had ever existed in the city where they were, vaccinating against smallpox— these are merely secular spin-offs. But I also think that their level of spirituality had an invigorating effect on the religious environment they were in. By the same token, I am enduringly grateful to Swami Satprakashananda in St. Louis, who for a decade was a cornucopia funneling into my consciousness insights and perspectives that have left me forever indebted. If he had not come to America, I don't know where I would be today.

Loudon: So the value of missionary work lies in people representing their own traditions authentically in other cultures?

Smith: Perhaps invariably there will always be some for whom, for whatever reasons, beginning with plain alienation, a voice from afar speaks more authentically than do the voices at hand.

Loudon: Should there be religious secrets?

Smith: Yes, I think that an authentic tradition must always harbor an element of the esoteric. The text is "Cast not pearls before swine." There is a sense in which the kingdom is not of this world, and to expose it totally to this world is a bit like letting the human heart loose in the world without a protective casement of bone and tissue. This may go a little against our notions of openness, democracy, and egalitarianism, but if we balk at the esoteric rights and necessities in religions, it is evidence that we do not understand the actualities involved. This is not foreign to our own tradition: Christianity emerged in its early, eminently vital period as a highly esoteric religion. It was an initiatic faith, with echelons of entry; more and more of the truth unfolded according to the preparation of the novice and catechumen to respond to such information appropriately.

Loudon: And there would be a sense in which even if the secrets are divulged they're not really revealed if one's not in a position to hear them. One hears something other than what is really being said.

Smith: Exactly. When truths are revealed beyond the capacity of assimilation, either the hearer is harmed or the dharma is harmed, in the sense of being trivialized, demeaned, debased. I brushed with one such case, when I came upon the special mode of chanting among the Tibetan lamas I referred to earlier, because it turned out to belong to the esoteric dimension of Tantra. Normally that sound would be uttered only under protected, ritualized conditions, and here I have put it on a commercially available phonograph record. The episode confronted me with a problem of conscience, but in the end I referred it to the lamas themselves, and the album contains a covering phrase from the performing abbot to the effect that under the peculiar circumstances of today a few limited stanzas may be released "for the benefit of all sentient beings."

Loudon: The discussion of the unity of religions seems to be growing now, and there is an increasing awareness of the pluralism of religions as a central issue. Does this augur some change within the great religious traditions themselves?

Smith: Growing awareness of other faiths is an undoubted fact, but we should not assume that our degree of awareness here is typical. Would an average villager in India be more aware of Taoists, say, than his great-grandfather was? But in the West, at least, increasing consciousness of other religions is raising in a rather acute way the question of the relation of one's own tradition to other traditions. Beyond those obvious facts, the matter grows more subtle. There has been an emphasis lately on ecumenism, with spotty results. In trying to combat prejudice and divisiveness, it is well motivated, but it has not brought a clear gain, because much of the empathy toward other faiths has been at the cost of a diminished confidence in one's own tradition. It has been said that a Muslim in the Middle Ages respected a crusader who sought to kill him out of conviction more than he respected a man who preached tolerance toward him but believed nothing.

Loudon: Do you think, then in terms of an extended "Axial Age" in which the great religious traditions were founded, ending with the emergence of Islam, with the result that the great traditions are already with us? Or is there the possibility of the emergence of another great religious tradition or of a tradition that is somehow synthetic?

Smith: I'm not waiting for it. There is a clear assertion in one of the traditions, namely Islam, that it will in fact be the last major revelation of this cycle. And it happens that for thirteen hundred years, that has proved true. My personal feeling on this question is one of equanimity and ease. I don't see the need for a new religion. What is lacking in the vehicles, the rafts, the *yanas* we how have? They are distinct, and there is a certain awkwardness in that. But I'm inclined to view the prospect of a tensionless world as utopian and unrealistic. If it were to be realized, it would be indistinguishable from paradise and would thereby lose its separate existence. I don't think that this attitude is pessimistic, because it is balanced by the fact that ours is a transitional stage and not the total picture.

Loudon: What would the ordinary, virtuous, nonreligious American miss out on by not aligning him- or herself to a religious tradition?

Smith: *Satchitananda:* "infinite being, infinite awareness, infinite bliss." Does the ordinary, decent, secular American aspire to that? Does he or she see it as within his or her register? There is a special circle in Dante's hell that is populated by souls whose only fault was that their aspirations were too low.

Mark Kenaston: Did theological differences with Christianity play any role in fostering your interest in other spiritual traditions?
Huston Smith: Not really; I was a late bloomer, or a slow learner.

Kenaston: I find that very difficult to believe.
Smith: I had none of those questions regarding the theology of Christianity. These questions were not major for me—what I became aware of was a belongingness to the universe, or reality. In our community the focus was Jesus, but I wasn't considering the particulars of religion.

Theological issues that are so alive for many people just passed me by. Christianity always seemed an affirmative message as to how one should live and what one's basic connection with the ultimate should be. Maybe I have a too-easy conscience, but in moving from my parents' narrow Protestantism into a "universalism" of my later years, there were never any severe conflicts. Why that should be maybe you can tell me!

This interview with journalist Mark Kenaston appeared in the *Bodhi Tree Bookstore (Los Angeles) Newsletter,* no. 3 (Summer 1992). Reprinted by permission of the Bodhi Tree Bookstore.

Kenaston: I have a suspicion. A discontentedness with Christianity has led me to explore other spiritual traditions. On the other hand, you appear to have embraced these traditions out of an appreciation of the universal qualities they share, an inclusion based on attraction to truth in many forms. An embracing rather than a rejection.

What was the religious climate at that time in China? Did most people practice a form of Confucianism or Taoism?

Smith: Remember that I was a boy at the time. I was interested in flying kites and fishing. But what one noticed was folk religion, which tends to be the same the world over. A lot of concern with spirits—mostly evil—and how to ward them off. One would see all kinds of evidence of that, ghost money and paper houses at funerals so the deceased would have a home in the afterlife.

There was a fine Buddhist monastery about three miles from town in the country, and we would take lovely walks out there for picnics. But to us that was a nice picnic place, and that's about all it was. So that's what the local religion looked like. Of course, later on, I found that the Shanghai area was very rich in its history for Chan, or Zen, Buddhism. I'm sure that Confucianism and Taoism were being buffeted by modernity and yet were still alive and to an appreciable extent continued.

Kenaston: Your description of the paper houses for the dead in China reminds me of the ghost houses I saw in Thailand—miniature houses placed on stilts on a family's property to give shelter to spirits. Have the Eastern traditions woven old folk beliefs into contemporary religion to a greater extent than have their Western counterparts?

Smith: There is some difference between religions on this score. As a generalization, I think the Semitically originated ones—Judaism, Christianity, Islam—tend to draw lines more sharply than the others. On the other hand, this accommodation and "folding in" of folk belief happens everywhere. Take Christianity in Latin America. Two weeks ago I was down in Mexico to attend two all-night vigils. One was with the Huichol—the peyote people—and another was with a Native American church. The contrast was very striking because the Huichol's ceremony was entirely their own. On the other hand, at the Native American church I was amazed at the interweaving of Native American belief, language, and terminology—and Christianity was all the way through.

Kenaston: Was it Catholicism?

Smith: Not necessarily. I think the leader was a Winnebago and was Protestant.

If you take Christianity in southern Italy, I hear that it's practically the patron saints that are worshiped—in effect, local deities. Jehovah is probably in there somewhere but is off the chart as far as the dynamics of the religion are concerned. What I'm saying is, I think there is probably a difference in spiritual personality here and probably analogous to the Jungian type. But the similarities are universal and cut across all the traditions. Some people are what you might call polytheistic in the sense that a more finite God rivets their attention as opposed to an abstract, universal deity.

Kenaston: An individual who needs a "personal" God?

Smith: That's right. This notion of spiritual "personality type" feels original to me because I haven't picked it up anywhere else. You can study all the major religions—Christianity, Islam, Judaism, Buddhism, and Hinduism—and slice them as traditions. Additionally, cutting the other way and across all of them are these reoccurring four spiritual personality types.

The first is the atheist for whom the obvious, the mundane, is all there is. And you find those people everywhere. You even find the atheist in tribal/oral cultures; and as you know, there are some who are just "meat-and-potatoes" people.

And then you get the type we were just talking about, the polytheists. These are people who really come to life religiously in the broadest sense in terms of concrete spirits. For example, each shaman in the tribe has their own personal "guide," a spirit that helps, guides, and empowers them. But there's no thought that this guide is the only spirit or that this personal spirit created the world.

So we've got the atheists and the polytheists. Then come the monotheists, where it all comes together in a single universal being, but it's a personal God. You mentioned this personal God earlier. Beyond these three spiritual types you get the mystics, where again it's a "world spirit," but the personal imagery of the monotheist becomes too anthropomorphic to really seem real. So I'll give you a little test. On one hand you have the atheist who believes in no God. Next there's the polytheist who has many Gods, and after this person is the monotheist who has one personal God. Now the test: What does the mystic say?

Kenaston: Can I answer with an analogy in a few words?
Smith: By all means.

Kenaston: For me, a rough analogy is that the universe is composed of spirit that is analogous to an amorphous block of "clay." The clay can be used to make a beautiful figure or pot but can also used to create something hideous or disgusting. Everything is created from this material: nice people, bad people, beautiful sunsets, and natural disasters. The mystic sees the clay as the creative stuff of the universe, inert in the sense of not having intrinsically dualistic qualities of good or bad—what [ninth-century Zen master] Huang Po might call the "One Mind," or the pregnant void from which all things are possible. In short, the spirit or stuff that permeates the entire matrix of our universe, both manifest and unmanifest.
Smith: I'll mount the ladder again. Atheists have no God. The polytheists have many Gods, and the monotheists have one personal God. The mystic—only God.

Kenaston: I used one hundred words trying to say something that you said much more coherently in two.
Smith: You got to it when you said "entire matrix."

Kenaston: Can we move on and talk a little bit about what you call the "wisdom traditions?"
Smith: First of all, not everything in these traditions is wise. So we begin by "red-penciling." We red-pencil their science because that's been superseded by modern science—we have proof of various things by way of controlled experiments. We should see their science as antiquated and shouldn't take it literally.

Second, we red-pencil their social patterns because these traditions picked up the social mores of the time. We've learned some things about social relationships in the course of time. So, you see, I'm not totally down on modernity. I think one of the great learnings is that we have come to realize that social structures vary from culture to culture, and they're not ingrained in the nature of things as if they were natural laws—as they tended to be viewed in the past. They are human constructs, and therefore we're all implicated and have responsibility for them. So we red-pencil these in the sense that we scrutinize and winnow very carefully gender relations, for example. We don't look to them for wisdom in these two areas.

What's left? What's left is how an individual spirit works out his or her destiny in the face of the way things finally are—ultimate reality. Now, on that score, I keep being set back in respect for these traditions, and they have seemed to me, with continued study, to be infinite reservoirs of wisdom on that particular point. When the Hindus speak of the "Eternal Dharma" and other traditions speak of revelations, I think they are revelations whether we imagine this as coming down from "on high" or welling up from the unconscious of the spiritual geniuses of the human race. In any case, they do come from beyond, wherever we envision that is, and I see nothing elsewhere that rivals them in their wisdom.

What would you suggest? A generation ago we might have said Karl Marx or maybe Freud or so on, but they have all been shown to be paper gods.

Kenaston: Do we have a problem in the West because we've divorced the spirit from so-called scientific inquiry? You find very few scientists who freely admit to a spiritual/mystical orientation because it's not seen as good empirical science. Ironically, the Buddha was an empiricist and a mystic. He said time and time again, "Don't believe something merely because I tell you it's true—find out if it's true for yourself." Consequently I've wondered if Western science and psychology are severely limited because, by and large, they ignore the spirit.

Smith: I think that they do, and I think this is really what's behind the movement of humanistic psychology and transpersonal psychology. These are practicing psychologists who sense this Procrustean bed of the reductionistic, mechanistic view of the human self. Both movements are alive and vigorous, but it is an indictment of the university because they have made virtually no inroads into these areas in twenty years. There are, to my knowledge, only two major academic institutions where you can get a higher degree in psychology with a humanistic or transpersonal orientation, and both of those only in the master's degree—one at Sonoma State and the other in Georgia.

Kenaston: Can we talk a little about how some of the wisdom traditions of the East are being transplanted to the West? An example that comes to mind is the group that formed around the Tibetan Buddhist Lama Trungpa Rinpoche in Boulder during the seventies.

The press picked up on several rather sensational issues, such as Trungpa's alcoholism and the recent revelations that Trungpa's successor, Osel Tensin, may have knowingly passed the AIDS virus to others before his own infection became public knowledge. Many in the American Buddhist community are deeply divided over these troubling events, and some question whether a vital and dynamic Western Buddhism will survive.

Smith: I think that the invariant guidelines are that when a tradition, which began in one civilization or culture, moves to another it always changes and yet retains a certain identity, which remains distinct from the culture in which it came. Now, you've been using the example of Buddhism, and that's a particularly good example because it is one of the three great missionary religions in the sense of seeing itself as universalistic in its relevance to humankind. And we have a very clear sequence; about six hundred years in India and then it moves to China, and then six hundred years later it moves to Japan and now a little more than six hundred years later it come to the West.

And our history is clear enough to see certain discernible modifications as it moves into these cultures. Now the question is, What about coming to the West? Some of the modifications are clearly apparent. In Western practice, men and women are together, whereas they were segregated in traditional practice. That is just one example. In spite of modifications, it hasn't become indistinguishable from the culture in which it came.

Now let us talk about the mistakes in making a move, and there frequently can be and are mistakes. Trungpa is a very good example, although *mistake* may not be the right word when talking about Trungpa Rinpoche. I think what happened in Trungpa's case was a genuinely grounded and gifted teacher who, in coming to the States, loosened his grounding in the Kagyupa [one of the four main schools of Tibetan Buddhism] tradition so he became independent. He no longer had the controls that he was used to in terms of his religious mentors.

Kenaston: He was young when he came to the West, wasn't he?

Smith: He was very young, and I just have to write it off to human frailty. The blandishments, the inducements were so powerful, and the ties to the Kagyupa relaxed to the point that they no longer had any discipline over him to keep him in line, and it was just too much. You bring in alcohol and other things, and he just succumbed. Maybe it would have been expecting too much under the circumstances not to.

Kenaston: He found himself in a culture in which the structure for his monastic training was nonexistent.

Smith: And that happens time and time again.

Kenaston: It seems another factor in the equation relates to the lack, to a large extent, of a guru-pupil tradition in the West. We are taught that it's important to be self-reliant, and we harbor an abiding suspicion of authority. I've heard the Dalai Lama remind people of the Buddha's admonishment to verify truth empirically yourself. He has related that it was typical in Tibet for people to scrutinize a potential teacher for as much as seven years before making a commitment to the guru-student relationship.

Smith: Absolutely. We seem to be so hungry spiritually as a people that we tend to latch on—uncritically—to something that has an aura of authenticity.

Kenaston: In the past few years we have seen many people explore perfectly legitimate traditions under the auspices of a charismatic teacher—jump in with both feet and be 100 percent for a period of time and then bail out when this teacher turns out to have human foibles. How can an individual remain enthusiastic and positive about religion or practice and at the same time have his or her feet on the ground and remain discriminating?

Smith: I like [nineteenth-century Hindu mystic] Ramakrishna's formulation regarding religion. In his usual folksy way he says, "Religion is like a cow. It kicks, but it gives milk too." I don't know that we could, if we spent all day, winnow it out any more precisely than that. In other words, there are two sides.

It comes down to a view of human nature. I think that people want and need a sense of orientation—a sense of where they are in the world. Without orientation you have no direction, and you need a sense of direction to give you your bearings because life fires at us point-blank. It doesn't wait. We can't say, "I'm sorry I don't have it figured out yet. Just hold back and don't require a decision from me today." It doesn't do that. We have to decide. And with no sense of direction or orientation, how do we make our decisions?

Now, this orientation knows no cutoff point short of the whole. And then we come down to, "Do we belong or do we not?"

Kenaston: Are some people asking, "What do I belong to?" In other words, many people are so unsure of how life fits together, or what their role is in the world, that they aren't even sure where to apply for membership. People are just drifting.

Smith: I hear that as a different wording of the same question. My wording was, "Do we belong or do we not?" The nineteenth-century zoologist Ernest Haeckel said that if he could have one question answered it would be, "Is the universe friendly?" If we don't belong, that is another way of saying that it is not friendly.

Now, the universe is ambiguous; it comes to us in both moods. So therefore, there is no objective stance from which you can decide this question: Is it friendly or do we belong? From that point it comes down to William James—the choice of the most creative hypothesis. Now, if I defend religion, it's a close call between the kicks and the milk it gives!

Kenaston: Sometimes the kick is the milk isn't it?

Smith: Well, that's true. When we come down on the side of religion, we have faith that ultimately it makes sense. So when it comes right down to it, I'm not finally a pragmatist—although you can go a long way, almost to the end, pragmatically.

Okay, if it's ambiguous and it's not going to tell us unambiguously whether it's friendly or not, then it's up to us which is the most creative hypothesis. It seems we shouldn't throw in the towel too soon but press the more creative hypothesis. This I think the traditions do, and I think that is why religion has persisted over two and a quarter million years, or however long human beings have been around.

I know a sociobiologist named E. O. Wilson who hates religion, but as a biologist he had to concede that there seems to be a religious gene in the human makeup, and he doesn't know how to get rid of it! The functionalists would say that the reason that anthropologists have found no society that doesn't have a religion is because it has a function. It serves a purpose and would have disappeared long ago if it didn't. I believe this to be the creative hypothesis on this particular question.

Now, let me see if I'm still on course in terms of your question. It is on those general and maybe minimal lines that I find myself standing up for these traditions. I think there is a danger they will just go down the drain. If they do, what will take their place when people need to have some sort of orientation?

Kenaston: We have seen people, as I mentioned earlier, that appear to be searching for anything that is seen as an alternative and giving it validity in their own minds simply because it's an alternative. People take bits of this tradition and bits of that tradition because it seems interesting or exotic. If they see something they don't like, they throw it out! If things get a bit difficult or the practice takes too much time, it goes into the garbage. They seem to be attempting to create narcissistic, "feel-good" spirituality without enduring the discipline needed to bring the mind under control. Any thoughts on this?

Smith: That is true. On this subject Trungpa Rinpoche was very good. In his book *Cutting Through Spiritual Materialism* he coined the term "Saint Ego." These people are really worshipers of Saint Ego, and if they happen to like something then they decree that it's true. If they don't like it, they declare it not true.

First of all, one has to be compassionate and generous. Who really knows what works for different people? So I wouldn't start going around saying no, no, no, don't do that. But if you ask me, I don't have a great degree of confidence in a kind of pastiche or cafeteria religion where you pick up this, that, and the other— where you weave your own religious cocoon around yourself. We're not the first to face the problems of life, and that's where I find an endless wisdom in people who have endured—the Jews, for example. I also find that when I study the Tibetan teachings, to use another example, I find this wisdom that puts Freudian psychology to shame.

I did want to wedge something in here, if I might. I have tremendous gratitude for older people who, when I was young, opened their doors to me. Aldous Huxley, one of our great perennial philosophers, would invite me in to talk for hours, because the topic was of mutual concern.

Kenaston: *Now you, in turn, have become known as a person who is very generous with your time. Without taking up much more of it, I did want to ask you about two spiritual personages and your thoughts about them. I discovered modern Christian mysticism when I found the writings of Thomas Merton. Do you have anything to say about Merton?*

Smith: Oh, yes. It's a moving story. We were both invited to what was pretentiously called a "Spiritual Summit Conference" in Calcutta. I went at some considerable inconvenience because I was teaching at MIT, but when I saw that Thomas Merton would be there I knew that I would move heaven and earth to go.

It was a glorious week. Well, conferences aren't glorious— anything but glorious. But because of his presence it was so colorful.

I arrived at the hotel and in the evening went down for hors d'oeuvres before dinner, and I entered the dining room and there was Merton all by himself. He was alone at a table with his fruit punch, and so I went over and right off I had about half an hour with him before anyone else arrived.

I can still remember my first real question I asked him after a couple of preliminaries. I said that I had recognized a very sizable monastic pull in me, but it was also clear that it wasn't for this incarnation. The man-woman thing, family, householder clearly outweighed that other. Nevertheless, it was really there, and I was drawn to it and so to come to the point right away, I asked him, "What's it like to be a monk?" And his answer really just swept me away. He said, "You know, it's very nice." And my thought was, "Very nice? It's about as difficult a way as I can imagine."

Later on, I came across what he said about his three vows. Poverty, he said was a snap—a cinch. Chastity is more difficult but manageable. But obedience is a bugger! And we know from his life how that weighed upon him. I really liked the guy; he was just wonderful. We ended the week by flying together from Calcutta to Delhi. I was going up to the Tibetans in northern India at Dharamsala, and he was going down to Thailand to his death. [Thomas Merton died in Bangkok, on December 10, 1968, of electrocution after emerging from a shower and touching a faulty floor fan.] Of course we didn't know that.

I still remember that ride to Delhi. He said he always wanted to do this trek from Kathmandu to Pokhara. He said, "Come on, let's do it!" We were fantasizing that I would wire my dean and say, "Fire me if you must, but I won't be home for another ten days!" And he would cancel his schedule—it was all fantasy, but it was fun.

Kenaston: Did you ever make that trip to Nepal?
Smith: Oh, yes, but I've never done the trek to Pokhara. I hear it's a seventeen-day trip.

Kenaston: I was in Nepal a year ago and really enjoyed myself. The people are very nice, and the landscape is breathtaking, although I have to admit that I was troubled seeing the extreme poverty. It reminded me of my own relative affluence as a North American.

Smith: I'll throw Mother Theresa's comment into the picture: "Desperate material poverty in India, desperate spiritual poverty in the West." It's just one take on the situation, but I think there's a lot of truth to it. Look at the disparity between our potential and what we're doing.

Kenaston: I know that you've met the Dalai Lama. Do you have any thoughts you would like to share about him?

Smith: [Taking out a picture of himself with his arm around the Dalai Lama] I was on a panel last year at U.C.L.A. They put me on for a half an hour with His Holiness solo—which was wonderful, because I've known him for twenty-eight years. The amount of time we've spent together isn't that much, but each time has been so meaningful. There have probably been eight meetings over the years.

On the U.C.L.A. panel was a psychiatrist who really pressed the Dalai Lama about anger; psychiatrists tend to have a particular "take" on the subject of anger. When the day was ending in the afternoon, the Dalai Lama had to leave to go to Santa Barbara, and we had a half-hour wrap-up, and the chair went around the room to ask our reflections on the day. And I was very interested in the psychiatrist. He said, in effect, "Incarnations are not my beat; I have a Jewish background, and I tend to be very skeptical. But I have to say that after today, if there is such a thing as a human incarnation, I have come closer to it today than I ever thought I would."

I can't get over the fact that here is someone who was raised like a king, surrounded by people who are convinced that he is the divine incarnation for Tibet, and he has escaped the slightest trace of an ego. He's so human, and the combination of the keen intellect and the compassionate heart—you so rarely see these come together.

I would be happy to tell you about my first meeting with him. The first time that I went among the Tibetans I didn't have a visit to His Holiness on my shopping list. I thought that he was too busy, and what right do I have asking him for any of his valuable time? The lamas I met when I was there said, "You're certainly not going home without seeing His Holiness." And because they said it in such a matter-of-fact way, that idea grew on me very quickly. I very much wanted to.

So I made the trip to Dharamsala. Before I went in to see him, because he's so generous with his time to give me an audience, I resolved to stay no longer than ten minutes. No more. So I spent the ten minutes expressing concern for the Tibetan people and proposed the idea of his coming to North America—he told me later that I was the first one to propose a trip. Because of problems with our State Department, the trip wouldn't come about for some time.

At the end of the self-allotted ten minutes I stood to take my leave. Even though he was speaking through an interpreter, his English was already partly functional and I overheard him say softly to himself in English, "I must think what is important." Then he turned to me and said, "Please sit down." And when I next stood up an hour and a quarter had passed—it was the most wonderful morning of my life.

And what had caused that change (staying longer than ten minutes) was a deception. The calling card that I used when I was traveling in Asia has Massachusetts Institute of Technology under my name, and he thought he had a live scientist in his living room! We all know about his scientific interest; he wasn't going to miss the opportunity to ask, "What is important" in terms of the questions he had about science.

There were two things in which he was particularly interested. He wanted me to fill him in on the "Steady State" and the "Big Bang" cosmogonies. Coincidentally, I had just heard a lecture on the "Bang, bang, bang theory," which holds that the world expands like an accordion, collapses, and expands again, ad infinitum. When he heard about that, the Dalai Lama said, "Well, that's the right one." As a matter of fact, the "Steady State" theory was dropped, and the issue is now between the other two.

The other subject was DNA. He was sorting out in his own mind the interface between reincarnation and DNA. It was interesting listening to the interpreter trying to get the equivalents of sperm, semen, and genes. He finally concluded that it has no bearing on reincarnation; in other words, it didn't undermine reincarnation.

Kenaston: He is always making the point that when science conflicts with religion, one must adapt to the scientific position. I think that is a very courageous attitude.

Smith: It is a very courageous attitude. Again this brings us back to the point on the wisdom traditions. When it comes to the cosmology—the science of it—we don't venerate the tradition on that point, because that's not where its genius lay.

Kenaston: To shift gears a bit, by the time this appears in print, the State of California will have most certainly executed a human being for the first time in twenty-five years. Despite a crackdown on crime that has our prisons overflowing with criminals, our society seems to be coming apart at the seams. [This interview occurred before the Los Angeles riots.] Any thought on where we are and where we're headed?

Smith: The surface signs seem very dismal, often overwhelmingly so. This leads to the question, "Is that the whole picture?" and to my mind it is not. One can bring out some countervailing thoughts, but I must acknowledge the fact that in voicing them, I speak from a position of privilege and immense good fortune. To shout from the safe shore to a drowning person, "Chin up!" is an insult. And so one has to be mindful of that and take courage from the fact that anything that I say is not just mine, but has been also said by people who were in the valley of the shadow of death when they spoke these things.

First, *When was it ever different?* Sometimes it's seemingly a little better, sometimes worse. The fourteenth century had the Black Plague, and there were witch-hunts where towns put the entire female population to death for being witches. Now, we have many terrible problems such as in our ghettoes where we have poverty beyond belief. But at least we're not sweeping it under the rug *to the extent* that we have in the past. We're beginning to look at it, and our affirmations indict us on terms of what we say we believe. Okay, there's that. Then you can bring in the Indian perspective of samsara [cycles of misery caused by karma] always being infinitely removed from nirvana. And it's only those who can find nirvana in samsara that the salvation comes—the society as a whole will never be remade to rival paradise.

If one becomes more abstract, life is like a tapestry that we view from the wrong side. *We* see all the strands and knots, and it makes no sense from the back. But there is a different view of the whole thing to which we are assured some day we will be privy. In the meanwhile, there are all these knots we have to deal with existentially; the path has been charted—compassion and justice—imbued by vision. And it's up to each individual.

Kenaston: I've wondered if detachment is less important now and action may be more necessary. The leadership in this country has been assumed by people who, in my mind, appear to be anything but spiritually minded—despite what they say about promoting the family, values, and morals. And believe me, I'm not just talking about Republicans!

Smith: Is the present time really any different? I'm reminded of *A Tale of Two Cities* when Dickens begins with that great line "It was the best of times, it was the worst of times." I confess that tends to ring true. Each time has its challenges and its demands. But when you say for this moment that democracy needs to be spiritually infused— absolutely. There's no qualification in my mind on that.

How is that to be done? And if we take it in terms of contemplation and action, it's absolutely clear to me that the two must be fused. But not simple-mindedly, because there are different modes of action. Who knows how much effect it might have on society to realize that there are people for whom the spiritual is so important, that they will forego everything else. A little bit like the *sannyasin* [homeless renunciates] who don't do anything in an overt way but exercise a magnetic pull on the general population through their dedication and unswerving single-mindedness to the human spirit.

I think we have to be very generous in terms of the various forms that action can take. And political action is a very important one, and by and large we should all be involved and doing more than we are. On the other hand, I would be very uneasy about some people I can think of being involved in making policy decisions—I would be very nervous!

You cannot solve the crucial economic problems in simply economic ways. It is clear that we need to do more, and don't forget simple acts of kindness.

Kenaston: Thank you for being so kind and generous with your time.
Smith: Thank you.

Richard Marranca: What do you think of the guru tradition?

Huston Smith: In principle, it is important. Basically, it's only a special case of having a role model—someone you look up to and try to imitate. Children couldn't develop if they weren't surrounded by people who have mastered life's basics and can show them the way. Language is a particularly obvious case. When it comes to how life should be lived, we are children to the end.

The shadow side, of course, is that like every good it can be perverted. And, as the Latin warns us, *corruptio optimi pessima*—the corruption of the best produces the worst. We've had evidence to spare us of that in the last thirty years: shoddy gurus who let their power delude them into thinking that they were above the moral law. But abuses don't annul the principle, which remains valid. Christ was a guru, the Buddha, and Muhammad were gurus.

Only once did I enter into a formal master-disciple relationship, but I have had role models—informal gurus—all along. One of the

This interview with creative writing teacher and fiction writer Richard Marranca appeared originally under the title "Mosaic of the Spirit: An Interview with Huston Smith" in *Yoga International,* no. 37 (September 1997). Reprinted by permission of *Yoga International,* RR1, Box 1130, Honesdale, PA 18431–9718; 570–253–4929; www.yimag.org.

most memorable was a college professor. The college itself was small and modest—Central Methodist College of Fayette, Missouri—but it has several good teachers and one great one, and that's all it takes. I was born and lived in China until I came here for college. I knew nothing, really. I was fresh to a new world, and by comparison this teacher seemed omniscient. My life was unformed, and I needed a pattern, a mold to pour my life into, and at the time he provided it. Eventually I discovered that he wasn't omniscient, but by that time I was in graduate school and another professor had replaced him. Still, my gratitude for his being there when I needed him has never waned.

There's a humorous side to the graduate professor I cathected to. For two years under his aura I wouldn't have believed that anything on earth could have topped his philosophy, but then I discovered his daughter and realized that I had been mistaken. So I married her and eventually abandoned her father's philosophy. I outgrew the naturalistic worldviews of both of my academic mentors, but I stand as a living witness to their importance as role models. They showed me the excitement ideas can infuse into life, and that steered me into teaching. I cannot imagine a vocation that would have brought me more satisfaction.

The best discussion of the guru role that I know of is by Joachim Wach, who was Mircea Eliade's predecessor in world religions at the University of Chicago. In his essay "Master and Disciple," he brings out the tragic element in that relationship. For when it's authentic, the master works from the start for his own death as master. His object is to bring the disciple to the point where he can stand on his own feet spiritually and no longer needs him. When Stephen Mitchell concluded his formal training under his Korean Zen master Soen Sunim, he told Stephen, "Now you must kill your parents. Then the Buddha. And then you must kill me."

My own *roshi,* Goto Zunigan, gave me an inside view of how the process works. In my next-to-last meeting with him (before I went to say my final farewell on returning to the States) he took me backstage on a guided tour of the small pavilion in the Ryoanji temple complex to which he had retired. Introducing me to a tiny old lady with a delightful twinkle, he said, "This is Oksan. She attends to my physical needs." And in the next room: "Here is my television set. Do you watch sumo wrestling? No? Too bad. It's wonderful!" As we stepped outside the back door, he gestured toward a crate of empty bottles, noting, "Here's the residue of the beer I drink while I watch wrestling." The whole point of the tour was to make sure I wouldn't be leaving with the thought that he was all austerity and piety—the illusion that spirituality was all there was to him.

Marranca: What have you learned from your study and practice of a variety of religions and spirituality traditions?

Smith: *The World's Religions* is my detailed answer to that question, but to select a few points, Hinduism's doctrine of the four yogas throws a lot of light on the religious quest. Before encountering it I had not realized how differences in temperaments affect people's religious quests. Those who are reflectively inclined advance by knowing God. Those whose emotions are strong do better to concentrate on loving God. The actively inclined make time by serving God, while experimenters become good meditators.

Vedanta taught me the difference between *Saguna* and *Nirguna Brahman*—between God's describable aspects and God's infinity, which exceeds description. I later learned that every religion recognizes that distinction. Taoism has its Tao that can be spoken and its Tao that cannot be spoken. Christianity has its God and its Godhead. I could continue with the list. But it was Hinduism that first brought the distinction to my attention. When people came to Ramakrishna, he would often begin by asking, "Do you like to talk about God with form or without form?" That simple question cuts through libraries of theological polemics. The two styles needn't be pitted against each other. Each has its place.

Marranca: Why do all traditions have esoteric and exoteric elements?

Smith: Because the notion of formlessness—something that can't be put into words—doesn't connect with most people. Things without nameable properties are simply nothing as far as exoterics are concerned. That's not the case with esoterics, who see forms as boundaries and therefore limiting. However, though esoterics regard the formless as more real than finite things, which by definition are bounded, they recognize that forms have their place, which is why Ramakrishna was quite happy to talk about God as possessing form if people wished to do so. The Infinite, esoterics see, must exceed forms because forms would constrict it, but they accept forms as pointing in its direction. The finger pointing to the moon isn't the moon, but it directs us toward it. As for Buddhism, its bodhisattva vow is endlessly inspiring: the image of the person who, posed on the brink of nirvana, turns back to help others enter it before she or he does.

Marranca: Do you think the bodhisattva shows up in Plato's Allegory of the Cave—the idea that those who have escaped from the cave should go back to help others escape?

Smith: Certainly. One of the chapters in my *Essays on World Religion* is titled "Western Philosophy as a Great Religion." It traces the line in Western philosophy that runs from Pythagoras, through Plato and Aristotle, to Plotinus and the Middle Ages, and argues that Judaism, Christianity, and Islam all adopted that lineage and made it their esoteric strands.

Continuing with what I have learned, in Islam Sufism has been decisive for me. To have times explicitly prescribed for calling one's mind back to transcendence is so valuable that once I started the practice, I have found myself unwilling to leave it. It pours each day into a sacred framework. In Judaism, the prophets' demand for justice echoes through history right down to Martin Luther King Jr.

A fascinating feature of East Asia is the way it configures its religions as partners rather than rivals. It regards them as strands of a single rope, so to speak. Traditionally, all Chinese were Confucian in their ethics. Taoist priests would be summoned when people fell ill, and Buddhist priests presided over funerals. If we untwist this rope to examine its strands, Confucius's strength was in his social emphasis, his insistence that character is forged in the crucible of human relationships. He would have thought it crazy to suppose that you could perfect yourself by hying off to a cave in the Himalayas to meditate for forty years in isolation. Philosophical

Taoism's greatest input was its concept of *wu wei,* nonaction that succeeds because it generates minimum friction.

As for the tribal religions, of which the Native Americans are our closest neighbors, their reliance on speech rather than writing teaches us that writing can subtract from understanding as well as add to it. Unlettered peoples are ignorant of many things, but they are seldom stupid because, having to rely on their memories, they are more likely to remember what is important. Literate peoples, by contrast, are apt to get lost in their vast libraries of recorded information. Indigenous peoples don't have that problem.

That is my Cook's Tour of something I have picked up from each of the religions I have worked with.

Marranca: You visited Auroville in Pondicherry a couple of times. What was your impression?

Smith: My first visit was brief. It was my first time in India, and I was trying to touch all the holy bases. Fifteen years later I returned and stayed for six weeks. It was impressive to see how much had been accomplished. A small city had sprung up with a truly international population. There were residents from Europe, Australia, the United States, all over. People were contributing their respective talents in return for simple maintenance.

There was a remarkable philosopher at Aurobindo's ashram, Professor Basu, who had resigned from an important Indian university to follow Aurobindo. I am a *jnana yogi,* one whose primary approach to God is through knowledge, and I had daily tutorials with Basu to deepen my understanding of Vedanta. Aurobindo had "dropped the body," as Indians say, but I did have *darshan* [time spent with a spiritual teacher] with his spiritual consort, the Mother, who survived him. I also took up hatha yoga under the resident instructor, Ambu, and though I never got very far, I do continue my kindergarten practice each morning. In some ways the ashram was a strange scene, because along with classical yoga the residents did Western calisthenics in sport shorts and white middies. The Mother played tennis into her late eighties.

Much as I learned from Professor Basu, he did not convert me to

Aurobindo's reconstruction of Vedanta. I felt that his Oxford education (which he acquired at the time when evolutionism, even social evolutionism, was in the saddle) colored his reading of the Vedas.

Even so, Aurobindo's impact has been enormous. To cite but one example, Professor Friedrich Spiegelberg, who taught philosophy at Stanford, used to tell his students that the forty-five seconds in which he gazed silently into Aurobindo's eyes during his annual *darshan* were the most important in his life. That led one of his students to go to India and spend two years at the Aurobindo ashram. His name was Michael Murphy, the founder of Esalen Institute, in Big Sur, California. We overlapped briefly at the ashram, and he told me that he had inherited some coast property in Big Sur, and along with meditating at the ashrams he was using his stay to try to figure out what a Western ashram might look like. I think he would have been startled if he had foreseen some of the bizarre turns Esalen was to take, but it weathered its craziness to become the mecca of the human potential movement.

Marranca: You and Aldous Huxley were friends. Could you tell us a bit about his connection with your interest in Vedanta?

Smith: Huxley was very important to me for about a decade because he converted me from my academically produced worldview, which is sometimes called naturalistic. That is the outlook I had after four years of undergraduate education and five years of graduate school at the University of Chicago. But in that view there is not much of a place for mysticism, so I paid no attention to it. It was Aldous Huxley's book *The Perennial Philosophy* which converted me from naturalism to a mystical view of the nature of reality. That has stayed in place ever since I came upon it in my late twenties.

You may never have heard that name of Gerald Heard; he figures in this picture. Actually I came to Huxley through Heard. They were fast friends, both English, both pacifists. There was a lot of feeling against them for their pacifism at the time, so they came here, to the United States. Huxley was the better writer of the two, but Heard was the one whom Huxley credited for shifting him from the cynicism of his early writing—*Brave New World* and the like—

to the perennial philosophy. Before encountering *The Perennial Philosophy*, I came upon a book by Heard. I came to this book thinking that it would assist me with my dissertation, but by page two I found out that it had nothing to do with it. It's the only time I've read the whole night through, because he was the first mystic I ever read.

That seems incredible now. I was in arm's reach of my Ph.D. and hadn't even read any mystics. In those days, Protestantism was in control of the mind-set of the universities in religious studies, and the Protestants have not been strong on the mystics. It was really Heard who changed my mind. My naturalistic worldview collapsed overnight like a house of cards when I saw this mystic's vision.

And so Heard was the one who converted me that night. I made two vows before the sun rose, and I finally closed the book. The first was that I would not read another line this man wrote until I had my degree firmly in hand; I was obviously afraid that I would just peel off academia. My second vow once I had my meal ticket in hand was to read everything this man had written. I kept that vow—about twenty-five books. Then I decided I wanted to meet him. I wrote to his publisher, and I got a note back saying he would be happy to see me but that he was in seclusion in Tribuco Canyon, near Los Angeles. I was in Denver, poor as I could be after graduate school and with a wife and child, and I had agreed to go to St. Louis to teach.

A week before we were to go there, I hitchhiked from Denver to L.A. to see Heard. He was living a hermit's life, not in any formal sense, but he lived that way and gave a lot of time to meditating. After I had hitchhiked all that distance, when we were face-to-face, I found I didn't have any questions, which is fine. I didn't go because I had burning questions. I just wanted *darshan*. After supper, we sat on the brown hills and looked out, sitting in silence. The next morning as I was saying good-bye, he asked if I wanted to meet Aldous Huxley, who was interested in the same things. Well, I was twenty-eight years old, and of course I did.

Heard gave me the address of Huxley's L.A. apartment, but he wasn't there. He and Maria were in his cabin in the Mojave Desert. His maid put me on the phone to him. When Huxley found Heard recommended me, he invited me out. I went out and had a wonderful walk through the Mojave Desert with them, making beds, and sweeping sand out of their cabin. It was a wonderful visit. When I was saying good-bye, Huxley said, "Oh, you're going to St. Louis; there's a very great swami there."

I'm not sure I knew what the word *swami* meant at that time, but of course I held Huxley in such high regard that the first week I was there I looked up the Swami Satprakashananda and visited. I returned home with a copy of the Katha Upanishad under my arm, and before I went to bed I opened it. By the second page I was glued to it and said, "This is it!"

Philip and Bridgett Novak: The Religions of Man *has been the most successful world religion text of our times. Its insight and clarity have been widely praised. Yet you wrote it at age thirty-seven. How did you do it?*

Huston Smith: One wishes that one knew. It's the kind of question that teases out autobiography. If I was not born with a religious impulse, at least it got built in early in a Christian missionary family, in China. I have always had a positive attitude toward the subject matter and a sense of its importance. In the beginning, that was entirely in the Christian mold. But as a young man, I met Gerald Heard, and through him Aldous Huxley. I absorbed their espousal of mystical traditions, which neither my undergraduate major in religion nor my graduate education in the philosophy of religion had paid the slightest attention to. Because the mystics tend to speak a universal language, I moved from Christianity (when I say moved, I don't mean abandoned, but extended, across religious

This interview with Philip and Bridgett Novak was published in *The Quest* (Winter 1991). Reprinted by permission of *The Quest* magazine, a publication of the Theosophical Society in America, www.theosophical.org.

lines) to find in each new domain the same basic essential and existentially meaningful truths.

This process really began to snowball when I moved to my position at Washington University in Saint Louis. I was then about twenty-eight. I had been teaching for two years entirely in Western and philosophical material. In the late forties and early fifties, the big move in education was to globalize our universities: a directive came down from the dean that every subject outside the sciences should try to offer something of a non-Western nature. I was the young man on the totem pole, and so the assignment came to me. Having met Heard and read Huxley's *The Perennial Philosophy,* I was eager for it. But I was also ignorant and needed help. Just before going to St. Louis, I visited Heard, who talked to me about Swami Satprakashananda of the Vedanta Society. Meeting him was a revelation. I instantly sensed, like a kind of ontological jolt, profundities that drew me in. After that it unfolded sequentially, and I was able to move into comparable existential encounters with each of the major traditions.

Novaks: But those encounters came after the original writing of The Religions of Man.

Smith: That's true. Buddhism had come in just at the end. I went to Japan for Zen training in 1957, and *The Religions of Man* came out in 1958, so my account of Zen is informed by that. China, of course, was not wholly unknown to me. My first seventeen years were spent there, I knew a vernacular dialect, and I felt a congeniality with aspects of the Chinese religious complex.

Novaks: You seem to be saying that you wrote The Religions of Man *with a "beginner's mind." Fair enough. Its early success, too, might be attributable in part to a relatively virgin market. But thirty years later, amid a host of competitors,* The Religions of Man *is still going strong. I'm still fishing for the secret.*

Smith: Something else does come to mind. The book emerged out of a television program. A few years ago before I wrote the book, what is now PBS [then National Education Television] was born. Educational television seemed like a good idea, but nobody knew what to do with it. And TV is ravenous, you know. You have to keep feeding it. So they were looking for food. A couple of NET producers wanted to televise university courses. Washington University was one of the schools they approached. They conducted an informal popularity poll, and my course surfaced. The dean let me off that semester, and I taught via television. Out of a number of courses (from various universities) that were taught this way, two took off. One of them was mine; the other was a Shakespeare course at the University of Southern California. *The Religions of Man* attracted a very large audience in Saint Louis, and, like the Shakespeare course, verged on competing with commercial stations.

I was blessed beyond words because my young producer was splendid. We were both University of Chicago graduates and were interested in ideas. Later he became a playwright, but at the time was working in television to make ends meet. He saw what was needed. He was very hard on me, which, of course, was why he was so good. Every evening, before we went on the air, he would come to our house or I would go to his apartment, and he would stand me up and have me do a dry run. I can still remember his withering comments along the lines of, "It doesn't sound too red-hot to me," which meant: back to the drawing board. He would also just keep bearing in on me, saying, "With this medium, if you lose them for twenty seconds, they switch the knob, and you don't get them back." He was pounding on me to sprinkle my talks with concrete examples, and they found their way into the book. So one answer to why other texts might not have taken off the way mind did is: they didn't have Mayo Simon put them through that regimen! Of course, one has to be interested and involved and studious, but a lot of people have those virtues. However, nobody else had Mayo Simon. That's at least part of the answer.

Novaks: So why have you decided to offer a revised edition, now called The World's Religions, *after some thirty-three years?*

Smith: Several factors contributed. Within the discipline of world religions, new information had been coming to light every year, and it was adding up. And some glaring holes in the original began to appear. The first of these was Tibetan Buddhism. I have since been chagrined that the term doesn't even appear in the index of the first edition. A total blank. I had once approached John Blofeld to pick his brain on Zen (I thought his translation of *The Zen Teachings of Huang Po* and *Hui Hai* were brilliant), only to find that his personal teachers were Tibetan. I resolved on the spot to learn more about that tradition, and that led to a considerable association with the Tibetans. Later, on a trip around the world, I came upon the Sufis. Again, Sufism is a word that's not even in the original index. Then, when I moved to Syracuse University in 1973, I found myself five miles from the Onondaga Reservation and Native American traditions. There, too, I discovered something that just wasn't in my horizons when *The Religions of Man* was written. So there were three holes that needed to be plugged.

But it was actually the gender issue, ticking away like a time bomb that finally transformed intention into action. The gender issue had gotten more and more painful every year until at American Academy of Religion meetings I would almost start hiding from certain faces. It was actually in late 1989, at the meeting in Anaheim, when I realized I could wait no longer. So I searched out John Loudon (my HarperCollins editor) and said, "Okay, let's go."

Novaks: Can you give us a glimpse of the other substantive changes that occur in this new edition?

Smith: First, I want to say that thirty years of working with these ideas have caused them to be handled at a deeper level this time; the new edition is a more reflective book. I can best tick off the other substantive changes by doing a brief sequential rundown.

Hinduism is the chapter that is least changed; indeed, it contains no substantive changes at all. Buddhism has the aforementioned Tibetan addition. After probing devoted, living Confucianists about their way of life, I have added a section to Confucianism that describes how one would live one's life if one were trying to steer it by Confucian principles. The Taoism chapter is the most changed. Certain of my thoughtful Taoist friends have never been happy with the way I handled popular and mystical Taoism. Reimmersing myself in the whole issue, I was quite thrilled to bring forth from the bewildering mass of phenomena that crowd under the Taoist umbrella an original typology. Using *chi* [spiritual energy] to designate the Tao as it courses through human beings, I propose that philosophical Taoism aims at efficient, effective deployment of our *chi* primarily by spending in the mode of *wu wei* [nonaction]. Energizing Taoism, a term covering the Taoisms that work with nutrition, yogic exercises, and meditation, seeks for its part to increase the supply of *chi*, while popular/religious Taoism aspires to vicarious *chi*, a *chi* whose power can be made available to others. I'm happy with this typology; it feels as if it cuts where the joints are. Besides the obvious change with the addition of Sufism, the Islam chapter as a whole is the one in which the deepening, seasoning process that the entire book has undergone is most evident. The reason is that Islam is the religion about which I have learned most during the interval. The Judaism chapter now has a section on Messianism, which I had inexplicably overlooked in the first edition. The Christianity chapter has an added section on the historical Jesus. Finally, the chapter "The Primal Religions" is completely new. It is short and does not attempt to do those many traditions full justice, but it does acknowledge their existence and salutes them. In addition, it does something that nothing else in the literature that I was able to find attempts. It tries in short compass to indicate how religion, as expressed in an oral, tribal mode, differs from religion in its historical text-oriented genres.

Novaks: What of the traditions not addressed? I mean such traditions as Zoroastrianism, Sikhism, Jainism, Shinto, the Latter-Day Saints, and so on. What is your rationale for exclusion?

Smith: I do have an appendix (to the Hinduism chapter) on Sikhism now. As for the others, it comes down to my decision not to introduce a religion unless I could stay with it long enough to convey its flavor, and beyond that, the meaning that it has for its adherents. That takes space, and I didn't want to turn the book into a tome. It's a focused book, specific in terms of its aim and its audience. No volume of whatever length could present them all; I didn't want to make the book a catalog. One does have to select. Two criteria that I use are first, the numbers of human beings a religion has included over the centuries and second, its prominence in the world today. Thus, the

Tibetan tradition, though small in numbers, has jumped to world importance. People know about it and are interested in finding out about it. One could say the same thing about Judaism. It is small in numbers, yet in terms of world impact, its influence on the other traditions and on world politics today, it is important. I do feel apologetic, personally and emotionally, most to the Shinto tradition because that's the Japanese miracle, and aspects of it, its affinity with nature and its simplicity, are very compelling. In regard to this and other worthy traditions, in the end, one just had to apologize.

Novaks: I've heard you say that thirty years ago you sensed the unity of religions but didn't have a fully satisfying theory of their unity-in-diversity. Since then, you've been deeply impressed by the writings of the Swiss seer Frithjof Schuon and his various articulations of the transcendent unity of religions. Has this clearer philosophical grasp of religions' unity-in-diversity played a role in the revised edition?

Smith: Not explicitly. Even back then, Huxley's *The Perennial Philosophy* had given me a kind of loose working definition of the unity: there is an absolute; the relative world is conditioned by it; human life should be vectored toward it. These near-truisms define the position, and they have proved sufficient for the revised edition. I have reworked the last chapter to articulate some of the commonalities in a way I don't do in the first book. Indeed, this is a new note. The book's new epigraphs are also telling. One of them is from E. F. Schumacher, who says, "We need the courage as well as the inclination to consult, and profit from, the 'wisdom traditions of [hu]mankind.'"

I have come to love that phrase: "the wisdom traditions." It has certain advantages over the word *religion*, which designates the institutional aspects, which are always a mixed bag. That phrase was operative in my mind in the revision, and I present the religions more explicitly as wisdom traditions than I did previously. That rather than Schuon's more technical and abstruse schema has been the noticeable influence.

Novaks: In a book called The Fragile Universe, *philosopher of religion Patrick Burke observes that "the great traditions are everywhere in decline." Though there are pockets where this generalization does not hold, for example, in certain fundamentalist Islamic and Christian sectors, do you feel it is generally true that the great traditions are evaporating? If so, where are we headed? If not, why not?*

Smith: When it comes to taking the pulse of our time, let alone trying to divine the future, my mind gets no traction. I don't trust myself, but I will say something. I personally believe that we are *homo religiosus,* religious creatures, meaning that the spirit is an ineradicable part of our makeup, and, like a jack-in-the-box, it will always seek expression. But what form will it take? What channels will it flow in? I vacillate in my sense of the future of the great traditions. They have certainly been severely wounded by three centuries of triumphant modernity. But modernity itself is now facing serious problems, and that at least puts us into a different ball game. If modernity is called into question, then what truly speaks for the human race? Personally, I do not see an outlook, an ethos, that is more profound than the wisdom component of these traditions. One could ride the momentum of that thought and say that there might well be a resurgence of interest, even confidence, in that component. A science writer in the *New York Review of Books,* not a pious journal, recently reported his sense of a revival of the "ism" among intellectuals. But even if such a resurgence of religion were to occur, it might occur outside traditional institutional channels. Certainly the difficulties facing the traditions are enormous. I guess that's about where I'm left with the matter.

Novaks: I have a couple of other questions about that tractionless realm of the future. The great religions may be in decline, but Walt Anderson tells us in Reality Isn't What It Used to Be *that "we seem to be in a world with more religion than there has ever been before. Beneath the rational surface of our more or less secular realism lurks a seething cauldron of faiths of all descriptions." How do you see the New Age proliferation of spiritualities? Are they distortions of the great traditions which alone are the privileged disclosers of the sacred, or are they hopeful signs of what Willis Harman calls "distributive revelation," a kind of religious democratization in which a thousand spiritual flowers bloom to our betterment?*

Smith: Walt Anderson has a fine eye for this kind of thing. Part of my conviction that we are *homo religiosus* is that if the formative power of traditions has been played out, the spirit will seek outlet elsewhere, which it manifestly is doing. Personally, I find depth in these New Age movements only to the degree that they tap into or flow from the great historical traditions. That's just the way it looks to me. When the traditions erupted and entered into history, they did so with a certain congruence with the minds of the public that these new movements, with all their sometimes dazzling effects, do not seem to have. They do not strike the hearts of multitudes in the way that the great traditions in their formative periods did. Let me add, too, that I am a *jnana yogi,* and, therefore, the Gnostic depth of long-developed traditions makes a great difference to me. I see it as very important. Many of these new movements seem to me to be riding *experience,* a magic word these days. For me, experiences come and go. One day my experience of the world is rose colored, the next dismal gray. It's like ice packs floating on the sea. The mind is capable of more stability than that. It can remember and remain constant through the ups and downs of experiences. And the limitlessly deep cognitive contours of the great traditions give the mind what it needs. They have included towering intellects, spoken to multitudes over millennia, and in the process a winnowing and seasoning has occurred.

Novaks: So, on the one hand, the spirit will blow where it wants, but on the other, if we lose these traditional structures or if they peter out into "distributive revelation," some very important structural shapings of the spirit will be lost?

Smith: That puts it very well, yes. Another of my four epigraphs on the flyleaf of this book *[The World's Religions]* is by Robert Bellah. Recently Bellah said, "In 1976, I was writing about a post-traditional world. Now, I believe that if we lose our traditions we will have no world at all." I confess I agree. From all our available spiritual resources, the great traditions continue to impress me as the most promising. Not that we have to perpetuate them blindly, but fathoming their wisdom still strikes me as our best hope.

Novaks: In a similar vein, Huston, what of the oft-dreamed dream of a new world religion, one that gets rid of all the premodern cultural baggage of the existing traditions and makes the sacred newly available to earth beings of the postmodern global order? Could there ever be such a universal religion, if not in the near future, even in the distant one?

Smith: Well, one can never issue prohibitions when speaking of the spirit. It is bigger than we are. So, logically, it can happen. But there are reasons to think that it won't. To begin with a banal yet important one, we have to realize that when we're talking about religions, we're talking about very human institutions, despite their divine infusions. Now, there are some people who just want to be at the head of whatever group they're in. They would rather be first in a storefront church than second in command to the pope. This fact of human nature just has to be reckoned with. This means that if we got a single world religion today, we would, very likely, have two tomorrow. That's one problem. And then there is the question, Is bigger necessarily better? When I look to my own background, I see Protestantism in shambles and splinters, and yet maybe these differences have providently given a little play for different facets of the human spirit. One must also be aware of the degree to which our age, an age of gigantism in education, the "megaversity" and so on, feeds this single-religion fantasy. To my way of thinking, religious unity dwells in the Absolute in God Itself, and will not be found among the multiple and relative, that is, where we live. It may be a mistake to look for more unity than human existence allows on either the individual or communal level. And yet, of course, the longing is natural and appropriate too.

Novaks: The theologian Thomas Berry, a sensitive student of the religious traditions, has nevertheless argued that all of them—even the so-called historical traditions of the West—were born out of a predominately spatial conception of reality in which time was mistakenly seen as an ultimately unreal reflection of the eternal. Now that evolutionary thought has revealed a universe that is time-developmental down to its roots, the argument goes, none of the old traditions is fully adequate to describe the Real in its Creative Advance. Nor do they have sufficient resources to respond to our ecological/spiritual predicament. So comes the call, once again, for new wisdom traditions, since the old ones were hatched within an outmoded form of consciousness. Your response?

Smith: I don't resonate. The world is in a mess, but perhaps it always was. It's a bit like the craving for unity we were speaking of. We can say we want something different. But until we specify what we want different, it's just a vacuous gesture. What is the claim? Do we want time-consciousness? Even the Australian aborigines knew that there was time, but they also had an urge for the timeless. Do we want to absolutize time? All right, then we have to assess the plausibility and possible advantages of doing this. My own feeling is that we live between the poles of time and eternity. Both must figure in the picture. If the move is to eliminate eternity, again, I'm not sure it can be done, and I don't see what's gained by the move. I understand the feeling that things are terrible and that we've got to do something different. But, again, until we say exactly what it is that will be better than what we've got, we're merely riding a human frustration, and that's thin ice.

Novaks: Some have glimpsed a silver lining in the ecological cloud, suggesting that newly awakened concern for the earth and identification with an earth community might provide an "immanent unity" of religions or at least help erode intercultural and inter-religious antagonisms. How do you see it?

Smith: The way I have said it to myself is to go back to William James's essay "The Moral Equivalent of War." James argues that war can bring out the goods of patriotism and idealism and that war can inspire the individual to heroism and putting the group's concerns above his or her own. But it's so destructive. So we need a moral equivalent of war. Our environmental predicament could be that equivalent. That predicament is new in human history. I guess I am just affirming the tenor of your question here, namely that our environmental crisis may be the catalyst that could draw peoples together.

Novaks: Do you harbor any hope that the linkage between religion and violence can be broken?

Smith: First of all, my persuasion is that what really breeds violence is political differences. But because religion serves as the soul of community, it gets drawn into the fracas and turns up the heat. I remember being asked to speak to a political science class during the Iran hostage crisis. I never have gone to a lecture with such dragging feet, because I knew they wanted me to describe the religious differences and to say that if they were resolved the political problems would be resolved too. But that's not the way it works. That's a confusion of cause and effect. Still, politics and the spirit are too intimately linked to be placed in watertight compartments.

Novaks: In your considerable writings on the religious traditions, spanning some forty years, you seem to shy away from one aspect of religion where differences are most apparent, and that is what happens after death. All religions seem to speak to the issue, but you seem reluctant to do so. Why?

Smith: Because it's a mystery; respecting human beings, the ultimate mystery. I do have some opinion on the subject, though. The differences among the religions that you refer to are real, but they all pretty much agree that something in the human self survives bodily death. I don't mean material components like atoms or minerals, but something that is continuous with our awareness. I accept that surmise. Where the religions differ is on what that "something" is, and where (in their respective symbolic cosmologies) they locate it. The Hindu/Tibetan doctrine of reincarnation has the human spirit returning to this world to continue its odyssey in another body, usually a human one. Other religions have the soul (or its counterpart) passing through purgatories or intermediate realms of other sorts. Given the immensity of our ignorance on this subject, I find the variety in these subsidiary depictions neither surprising nor disconcerting. Underlying virtually all of them is the thought that with rare exceptions the human enterprise isn't completed in this life span; further work with its attendant ordeals is required before we reach our final destination. If any religion unequivocally held that some souls are destined for eternal damnation, that would be a position one couldn't equivocate on. But even Christianity (which comes closest to the view) includes alternative interpretations that have the fires of hell exhausting themselves eventually. Siding with that reading of the matter, I find a commonality in the world's religions, even in their teaching on the afterlife, as long as we stick to the essential.

I must confess that the prospect of sharing what it's like to have a day-to-day, moment-to-moment personal relationship with God made me apprehensive. Why? Was it presumption that I have a moment-to-moment relationship with God—one that I am consciously aware of? Or was my reluctance one of good taste, the issue of whether it's appropriate to parade intimacies in public? Underlying these doubts was the question of whether I know what my relationship to God is. The arrangement feels more like a mystery that is open to my conscious awareness and direct inspection.

In the end, though, the premise that prompted this book *[For the Love of God]*—that we can learn from one another on this matter—prevailed.

When, on the National Broadcasting Company's *Wisdom* series I asked Daisetz Suzuki if he was born with a religious impulse, he answered, "Not born, but it awakened."

"When did it awaken in you?" I wanted to know.

"Well, I do not know exactly. But the starting point was marked, per-

This essay by Huston Smith, based on a conversation with Dr. Benjamin Shield, was published under the title "Encountering God" and excerpted from the book *For the Love of God,* edited by Richard Carlson and Dr. Benjamin Shield. Copyright © 1992. Reprinted by permission of Huston Smith and New World Library, Novato, CA 94949, www.newworldlibrary.com.

haps, when I was sixteen or seventeen. I wanted to get my religious yearnings somehow settled."

I could have answered the same: the deepest yearnings of which I am consciously aware have always been religious. I consider the religious impulse to be a part of the human makeup; the search for cosmic understanding is as much a part of the religious impulse as the search for cosmic belonging. In my case, though, early conditioning doubtless contributed to the strength of the drive.

My relationship with God through my mid-twenties was cast in a Protestant, pietistic mold wherein God was approached through a personal, love-and-service relationship with Christ. I continue to honor that mode and to work on it in part. But, in addition, the Hindu doctrine of the four yogas—the notion that people are of different spiritual temperaments and therefore will approach God in different ways: *jnanis* through knowledge, *bhaktis* through love, *karmic* types through service, and *rajic* types through meditation—freed me to see that there were other channels through which spiritual energies may flow. My personal relationship with Christ, though real, was not very intense, whereas *thoughts* of God could hold me spellbound for an entire night.

Such *jnanic* knowledge is apt to be misunderstood by those who have not experienced it—by those whose yogic strengths lie elsewhere. It has nothing to do with quantity of information or logical dexterity. It is rather that thoughts, for the *jnanic,* possess a body of sorts, a three-dimensional substantiality that makes thoughts real in ways they are not for other people. Plato's ideas, for example—the Good, the True, and the Beautiful—for the *jnanic* (or Gnostics, as they might be called in the West if that word is distinguished from gnosticism) are not the empty abstractions that others take them for. They are almost palpably real. And their reality excites; they all but dance and sing. This distinguishes the *theoria* that discusses them from theories as these typically function in science. The Greek word *theoria* derived from theater, which makes *jnanic* knowledge closer to vision than to thought as we usually use the word. It is seeing, albeit with the eye of the soul. And the vision attracts. Aristotle compounded Goodness, Truth, and Beauty into this Unmoved Mover, which moves the entire universe by force of attraction. But my point is that ideas attract *jnanis,* who are drawn to ideas because they love them—and we are drawn to and become like that which we love.

Socrates said that to know the good is to do it. St. Paul disagreed, but he was a different temperamental type—so knowing was not the same for the two men.

This all relates to God, for though I have not used the word, I have been speaking of nothing else. God is the Good, the True, the Beautiful—and Power and Mystery, we should add—fused so completely that the five are not five but one. In my best moments I am drawn to that God as moth to flame, and at such times I do not know whether my happiness is the rarest or the commonest thing on earth, for all earthly things seem to reflect it. But I cannot hold onto it. When those grace-filled moments arrive, it does not seem strange to be so happy, but in retrospect I wonder how such gold of Eden could have been mine.

It is easy to make too much of direct mystical disclosures. Desert stretches provide opportunities for growth that are as important as mountaintop experiences, and theologians assure us that souls can be established in an abiding relationship with God without being sensibly aware of God's presence. The goal is not altered states but altered traits. Aldous Huxley's observation that the task of life is to overcome the fundamental human disability of egoism comes in here, for every step we take in overcoming that is in God's direction.

If the heart of religion is faith in the reality of another world, then the heart of science is evidence of the deep structure of this world. For Huston Smith, the problem with modernity's worldview is that it accepts the second half of that sentence but not the first, producing a truncated worldview. In limiting us to what science and common sense tell us exist, it discounts what our highest intuitions register as the noblest part of the objective world.

In this second part, Huston Smith tells Steve Reuys of MIT, "Between religion and science proper I see no conflict whatever." The problem arises from modernity carelessly slipping from science into what Smith calls scientism. This term, he explains to radio interviewer Michael Toms, denotes the illicit conversion of two philosophical assumptions—philosophical assumptions are always debatable—into proven scientific fact. The first of these assumptions is that science is the most reliable road to knowledge that we have; the second is that matter is the fundamental stuff of the universe from which everything else derives. Neither of these assumptions is proven by scientific findings, but they are the working principles for science. We mistakenly assume that the staggering success of modern science—in the material realm, we should not forget—elevates the guidelines by which it rightly proceeds to the level of philosophical truths. This logical mistake demotes the noble project of science to its bastard counterfeit, scientism, Smith explains to Jeffrey Mishlove. As that counterfeit leaves little room for the human spirit, there can be no compromise between religion and scientism, but between science and religion there are only resolvable misunderstandings.

Smith points out that materialists themselves emphasize how much the human mind is conditioned, and thereby limited, but in doing this they concern themselves with the mind only in its ordinary mode. That mode can be compared to the narrow border where the sea breaks on the shore. In this limited region, the coastline certainly exerts an influence. Farther out at sea, however, this influence disappears faster and faster and soon completely. The lower, worldly experience and the exact investigations of science play their parts exclusively on the shoreline of the boundless sea of

Mind-at-Large. Such half-awakened consciousness must rest in the delusion that we are nothing but this body, and that our mind is this body's consciousness.

In all this Smith's concern is not engaged in academic debate. He is motivated by an existential fear that the modern, reductionist worldview has harmed our cultural soul, leading us to lose our grip on Transcendence. He tells Michael Toms that he believes science has become for many *the* "sacral mode of knowing," which it is for the material world, but not the immaterial one. It is a mistake, he says to Richard Smoley, to "think we can prove spiritual truths by science, because science can't speak to the things that concern religion." The beauty of religion, for Smith, is the way it provides human beings with the means of relating to an invisible realm that is both powerful and good. His call for a reconciliation between the two modes of knowing is reminiscent of author Karen Armstrong's description of our natural capacity for "binocular vision," the ability to see and know both logically *and* intuitively.

Toward this end, he remains guardedly optimistic. Smith's recommendation for getting beyond the current impasse, which he reveals to freelance writer Marsha Newman, is a return to a worldview that validates both scientific fact and spiritual realities. For Smith, that is the primordial tradition, the transcendental philosophy to which all traditional civilizations were drawn. It credits a divine origin for everything in the universe and is the philosophy that gives life meaning, purpose, and worth. When asked by journalist Richard Gazdayka what a lifetime of studying and practicing the world's great religions has given him, Smith's response sounds like the perfect note for reconciliation: "The world—and I mean that quite literally."

Steve Reuys: You'll be leaving MIT, at the end of this term, is it?
Huston Smith: Yes.

Reuys: Are there any particular reasons you decided to leave? Is it the kind of thing you are willing to discuss, or are the reasons private?
Smith: I wasn't job-hunting, and when Syracuse University first approached me, I told them they could try but I didn't think they would succeed. But in the end they did succeed for two reasons. Here my interests are peripheral to the main thrust of the philosophy department and I am, as it were, token representation for other kinds of philosophy. There I expect to be part of a continuing dialogue, an ongoing colloquium. Second, I'll be actively involved there in graduate teaching, whereas here my work is almost entirely with undergraduates. I haven't felt restive here; students are first-rate, and my position has provided unparalleled freedom and stimulation, which are no small virtues. The move to Syracuse is going to involve a trade-off at every point: in graduate teaching I'll

This is the earliest interview included in this book; it took place in April 1972, with Steve Reuys, staff writer at *Free Parking,* the MIT newsletter. Copyright © Steve Reuys. Reprinted by permission of Steve Reuys.

be able to push my interests deeper but at the price of the scope of my survey courses here, which I've liked too; at Syracuse I'll have more influence but at the price of greater involvement and responsibility, which will end my loner's independence.

In the end it came down to something like this: I found myself saying, "I know what this is like, and it's been good, but I really don't know what that other life is like. Before it's all over I think I'd like to find out."

Reuys: You speak of token representation and a loner's role. What distinguishes your interests from those of the rest of the philosophy department?

Smith: There isn't a complete divide. A lot of what my colleagues do interests me very much. It's what they leave out—the part of the marrow that's missing.

How to characterize what's omitted isn't easy; in fact, it's one of the deepest issues in philosophy today. A sign that an issue runs deep is that the two sides can't agree on where it lies. If my colleagues agreed that there is a cavity I'm sure they'd take steps to fill it, which is a way of saying that one feels sure in advance that they won't agree. In the interests of "equal time" it might be useful to ask them sometime how they see the difference—if they answer "quality" I'll flip—but here you're asking me, so I'll say where I see the divide.

At root is the question of the adequacy of scientific canons of knowing. No one doubts their adequacy for science; the question is how well they work in other inquiries, in this case philosophy. Logical positivism said they are the only valid cognitive canons anywhere. Analytic philosophy, the name for the dominant philosophy in England, America, and at MIT today, stands in positivism's line of descent. Descendents aren't necessarily clones of their forebears, but they tend to carry resemblances. Analytic philosophy isn't crudely scientific, but (I would argue) it is subtly so.

First, the knowledge it allows must, like that of science, be objective in the sense of being compelling to all who are capable of following its arguments.

Second, these arguments must be consistent. So esteemed is this requirement that analytic philosophy departments are sometimes caricatured—it isn't fair, but like all caricatures it has a toehold in fact—as departments of applied logic.

Third, the terms that appear in the arguments should be unambiguous. As words notoriously lack this virtue, being multilayered in meaning and open to alternative readings—to the delight of poets, and all humanists, to some extent—I would say, but to the despair of scientists who instinctively reach for numbers which are unequivocal—analytic philosophy is increasingly couched in terms of symbolic logic.

That these rubrics of analytic philosophy are likewise those of science is, I think, evident. But what's the alternative? Am I going to argue for a truth that is subjective, contradictory, and ambiguous?

To put it this way is to see why analytic philosophy has difficulty seeing that there are alternative ways of philosophizing that deserve respect, for the three alternative ways that have tried to secure a respected beachhead here—I am thinking of existentialism, phenomenology, and Asian philosophy, none of which enjoys a place in our graduate program—argue, each in its own way, that truth does indeed have subjective, contradictory (or better, paradoxical) and ambiguous aspects—not perhaps from God's standpoint (this is my way of putting it) but from man's.

The deepest concern of existentialism is to critique the belief that objective truth is truth's only or most important kind.

The deepest concern of phenomenology is to undercut, through careful description, the reductionism that results when everyday experience is accepted uncritically instead of seen as in part a fabrication from our everyday concerns; from other concerns—art, science, religion, dreams—other worlds derive, each of which enjoys a logical and epistemological status equal to the others.

The deepest concern of Asian philosophy in the face of analytic philosophy's reduction of mysticism to feeling, à la Bertrand Russell's *Mysticism and Logic,* is to hold onto the fact that knowing admits of degrees, with satori [intuitive illumination] or *samadhi* [total fulfillment] at the top. In the past the West knew this too— medieval philosophy distinguished between *ratio* and *intellectus* and Baruch Spinoza between rational knowing and intuitive vision— but analytic philosophy brooks no comparable distinctions.

Reuys: And you see underlying all this—what analytic philosophy accepts and what it rejects—an espousal of scientific canons of knowing?

Smith: Not completely, of course, but to an unwarranted degree. Ludwig Wittgenstein perceived the danger as clearly as anyone, having himself succumbed to it in his early career: "Philosophers constantly see the method of science before their eyes, and are irresistibly tempted to ask and answer questions in the way science does." He also said in his Blue and Brown Books of the 1930s that circulated as typed manuscripts among his students, "This tendency . . . leads the philosopher into complete darkness." That he saw clearly is shown by the fact that the most influential American philosopher for the past twenty years, namely Willard Quine, is one who holds that "there is fundamentally only one kind of entity in the world . . . the kind studied by natural scientists . . . and . . . only one kind of knowledge . . . the kind that natural scientists have."

Reuys: Is the analytic bent of MIT philosophy disproportionate for the nation as a whole?

Smith: For colleges, yes, but for universities with ranking graduate programs, not much.

Reuys: Is the trend increasingly toward analytic philosophy?

Smith: I don't know. I'm not aware of any clear trend in the last decade. The situation appears to be fairly stable.

Reuys: Do you see it as detrimental to students?

Smith: I do see students as in certain respects the losers, not in what they get but in what they don't get. To put the point I was making earlier in another way, everyone who philosophizes does so in accord with certain sensibilities—can you imagine a Pythagorean who was tone deaf? These sensibilities guide him as he fashions epistemological probes that help illumine the regions of his concern. Analytic philosophy appears to serve logical sensibilities admirably, but onto transcendence, the sacred, the meaning of life and humanity's potentials it opens no vistas. Who, here at MIT, will be working with students whose sensibilities and concerns lie in these directions? Are we to say that these concerns are unimportant? Spawned by neuroses? Tangential to the life of the mind? Or to philosophy?

Reuys: You mentioned Asian philosophy at one point, and that seems to be what your name is linked with most in the minds of undergraduates here. What is there that we have to learn from Asia?

Smith: Before answering your question directly I want to say that I've moved toward Asia partly as a fugitive. It's true, as you may know, that I was born and grew up there, so when I get to Zen and the Tao, the tea and the chopsticks and the calligraphy connect with the "wonder world" of my childhood, and a part of me feels like it's home. But the comfortable feeling derives from a source that lies deeper than personal biography. Despite the inroads from the West, the outlooks of Asia remain profoundly premodern, which in my vocabulary is to say places where the human spirit can roam and breathe. In so saying I betray the fact that it's not just analytic philosophy I experience as a bed of Procrustes. There's something about the whole modern outlook that's gone awry—analytic philosophy is merely the philosophical derivative of this fact. Basically the mistake has to do with a misreading of science, which is why these years here have been invaluable for me and why I shall miss MIT enormously, for one lives here in daily contact with something—science—which in ways that no one fully understands is fatefully at the heart of where humanity is and where it's going. Whether we pull through or go under depends in part on whether we can come to see the place of science in the human venture.

Reuys: I'm not through with Asia, but to stay with the present point for the moment, what is the place of science in our life?

Smith: To be life's yang without eclipsing its yin. Science isn't any one thing—it's more like a village than a single individual—but one makes one's way toward the heart of the village through objectivity, then prediction, and then control, with quantification increasing at every step, numbers being (as earlier noted) the key to precision. It's a marvelous venture, the most important for us since our discovery of language. And by my lights it's full speed ahead, provided only that the ship not capsize. But for it to remain upright the ballasts of science need to be balanced by equal attention to their complements: objectivity balanced by subjectivity, prediction balanced by wonder, control balanced by commitment and self-giving, and quantity balanced by quality. It goes without saying that the humanities are (or should be) the special though not exclusive custodians of the yin side of this equation. Education, like humanity itself, needs to walk upright on both legs, not hobble or hop indefinitely.

Reuys: One often hears that science and religion conflict. Have you found it difficult to teach religion in MIT's predominately scientific environment?

Smith: Not at all. I get agitated, as you notice, when I suspect humanists or social scientists of modeling their knowledge after the scientists', but that's another matter. That's not science, it's scientism. Between religion and science proper I see no conflict whatever. On the contrary, I find in science all kinds of suggestive analogies as to what religion is up to and what it tries to say.

For example, science and religion both say that reality is infinitely beyond our normal capacity to perceive; science says this about being's quantitative aspects—light years, angstroms, and the like— religion about its qualitative aspects. Or again, religion agrees with science that the way things really are is anti-intuitive, which is to say, beyond humankind's capacity to visualize or describe in ordinary language. Science's recourse in the face of this difficulty is mathematics; religion's, the mystic vision. Both are at one in saying that the imagery deriving from our normal space-time perception won't fit.

Reuys: Perhaps your yin-yang image of a moment ago can take us back to Asia from which we got diverted.

Smith: Good. Asia, said Jung, is the West's unconscious, and it does look as if Asian values and virtues are ones that the post-Enlightenment West has to a large extent repressed. Bent on *control,* the West has lost sight of the virtues of *surrender.* Bent on changing the world, it has seen comparatively less to be gained by changing oneself. In Paul Tillich's contrast, its "prophetic faith" (aliveness to the holiness of the *ought*) has partially eclipsed its "ontological faith" (sense of holiness of the *is:* Buddha's insight under the Bo Tree that all things are intrinsically Buddha-nature already, precisely as they now are). Again, as with the science-humanities dichotomy, it's a matter of redressing an imbalance. I see Asia as providing cues for helping us to see disproportions that have crept into our value system, most of which we aren't even aware of.

Reuys: One of your articles that appears in Earth Might Be Fair, *a collection of ecological essays, suggests that the oriental concept of Tao might be useful in our ecological crisis.*

Smith: That's true. I play there with the fact that "Dow," which is the way Tao is pronounced, denotes in the orient the most ecological concept humankind has conceived, while in the West it denotes Dow Chemical and by extension napalm, deforestation, and the most antiecological acts humankind has perpetrated. Within this tiny phoneme the opposites have met.

Reuys: Are there other specific ways Asian perspectives can be useful to us?

Smith: In a day when *interdisciplinary* has become a necessary word in science and a wistful one in the humanities it might be helpful to see how Asia has managed to keep philosophy, theology, and psychology together. I'm sure we've gained things by letting them divide into compartmentalized specializations, but we've lost something in the way of wholeness of outlook.

China appears to have evolved a rather viable social philosophy that I find worth studying. A book by Herbert Fingarette, professor of philosophy at Santa Barbara, *Confucius: The Secular as Sacred,* begins by saying that he used to read Confucius for historical reasons. Now he reads him for contemporary reasons, as a major teacher saying things that need to be said and are not being said elsewhere.

India's delineation of personality types strikes me as more perceptive than that of the Greeks, Jung, William Sheldon, or any other I have found in the West. And the clarity with which Vedanta distinguishes between personal and transpersonal aspects of God is theologically invaluable.

Having cited several specifics, however, which is what I heard you asking for, let me say that the greatest value in studying another culture lies beyond any such list of particulars. Cultures resemble organisms more than mechanisms, which means few if any items can be picked from one and stuck down into another to good effect. What cross-cultural study can provide is a perspective on one's self, one's own condition. A single eye can give us up and down, but it takes two eyes converging on an object from different angles to provide the dimension of depth.

Reuys: The two dichotomies that you have spoken of—science and humanities, and Asia and the West—do you think they can, or better, will, be integrated to effect a balanced life?

Smith: Now, that's interesting, for of all the questions you have asked, this is the first on which I don't even have an opinion. I guess I'm nothing of a futurist. Many of my associates are. Some see us stepping cleanly into the Aquarian Age, others say disaster must come first, that at least California must fall into the sea. I feel like the British, that one way or another we'll probably muddle through, but I don't expect unambiguous social progress.

And now that I warm up to the subject, I think I know why it is that I feel this way. People differ, and I'm more inward-private than outward-public orientated. I know that collectivities are important—politics, social structures, and all that. A police state, unemployment, or a war on home soil could bring me to my knees in an instant. So I don't advocate privatism or books on how to live on a farm in Vermont and love it. I even hold a tiny political office in my own township.

But I can't say that my heart is in it. Perhaps it is the fact that I've been socially privileged—not poor, not persecuted, not discriminated against, and not victimized by war—that makes me realize that social or collective well-being doesn't solve the human problem. As Marianne Moore puts it in her poems, "There never was a war that wasn't inward."

Jeffrey Mishlove: It's a pleasure to have you here. One of the points that you make in your book Beyond the Post-Modern Mind *is that we tend to think in the West, in our contemporary culture, that our worldview has expanded from earlier generations, and that we are progressing. We think of our time as a time of great progress. You point out that this may not necessarily be totally the case.*

Huston Smith: Well, let's begin with the first of those. Progress is one thing, and the question of whether we are enlarging our view of reality is a specific aspect of that. Let's start with the latter. It's unquestionably true, I think, that our knowledge of nature, of the physical universe, has just ballooned incredibly. Who could have believed, when we were back working with the naked eye, a universe that's 18 billion light years across, and still expanding—stretches of that mind-boggling vastness? And also, comparably, the smallness and the intricacy and even the mystery—we shouldn't forget that—the mystery of nature, the paradoxes of matter being both a wave and a particle. So our knowledge of nature has indeed, unquestionably, expanded beyond belief.

This interview with Dr. Jeffrey Mishlove is a transcript from the television series *Thinking Allowed: Conversations on the Leading Edge of Knowledge and Discovery.* Copyright © 1998. Reprint of this transcript by permission of Thinking Allowed Productions.

Mishlove: I would imagine that at this point there are hundreds of thousands of scientific papers published each year.

Smith: Each year. It's just impossible to keep up with it—a deluge, an avalanche. But what I think we don't realize is that with that enormous expansion there has occurred—well, I might as well come out and say it—what I think is a comparable contraction. And the way we might put it is that horizontally, if we take that image, the world of nature, our view of reality, has expanded incredibly. But vertically, if we take that to symbolize the regions of value and worth, it's almost as though we have pulled the shade down on the realms of being that our forebears believed in implicitly, but we have shut them out simply because our honored way of knowing in the modern world—namely, the scientific method—has no way of getting at those realms of worth.

Mishlove: Realms of being, realms of value.

Smith: Right. There's one quite simple way, I think, to get a fix on this truly important point. What has introduced and changed our world and our worldview, is, of course, modern science. And the crux of modern science, of the scientific method, is the controlled experiment. Now, everybody agrees to that. But I think what we don't go on to add and to think about is that we can control only what is inferior to us. Now, what that comes to is that our scientific worldview, which is what we really, implicitly believe in, in the modern world, consists of nothing except us and things that are inferior to us.

Mishlove: In terms of their level of consciousness, or their level of power.

Smith: Yes. By inferior, I mean by every standard of worth that we know. If we turn it around, we can say that the scientific worldview shows us nothing in reality, nothing in the whole of existence that is greater than we are by every criterion of worth that we know.

Mishlove: You seem to be suggesting that we somehow set ourselves as superior to, say, the 18 billion light years of the physical universe that we look at.

Smith: The point is that apart from life on this planet, science shows nothing in that enormous but quantifiable matter, because the expanse of space is what the instruments of science can pick up.

Mishlove: Cold, inert.

Smith: That's right. And there's no comparable extent of value infusing them. Value in the scientific worldview is confined to sentient organisms. We can speculate on whether there are others in the universe, but all we actually know is our own planet, as far as life is concerned.

Mishlove: And there seems to be a strong tendency in the scientific community, and those moved by the scientific community, to deny that there is intelligent life out there anyway.

Smith: There is a mixed report on that. There are many scientists who speculate that the probability is large, but the point is that we have no verified proof of that. There's a nice little example that puts this point vividly in a capsule, and that is Carl Sagan's *Cosmos,* the television series several years back, which was a striking and just beautiful and remarkable series, in a certain respect—namely, the scientific respect. But if you saw it—did you see it?

Mishlove: I saw part of it.

Smith: My memory is that it began with Sagan coming on the screen and saying, "The cosmos is everything that ever has been, or will be." Now, that's a great opening line. That's a marvelous hook. But then, what follows? Fifteen or seventeen programs which are just incredible in their awesome beauty, as far as the matter of space and size, and power, but did anything appear in Sagan's *Cosmos* that is greater than we are by every criterion of worth we know, which includes intelligence, awareness, compassion, perhaps? No. And so, "everything that ever was and will be" leaves out the possibility of there being realities that are indeed greater than we are.

Mishlove: In other words, by virtue of our culture's desire to control, to manipulate, through science, we exclude from our worldview that which we cannot manipulate.

Smith: We do, and the fault is in part that we have seized upon a method that increases our control. But I don't think we ought to limit it to that, because the scientific method is indeed also, of course, an avenue of getting toward knowledge. There is pure science as well as applied science, and that's all to the good. Yet even there, even in pure science, because the way of getting at it through science is through the controlled experiment, we are forced into dealing only with those aspects of reality that we are able to control. And to go back to what we were saying before, those turn out to be those regions of reality that are inferior to us.

Mishlove: The whole realm of knowledge that's included in the humanities consists of, I suppose, our image of ourselves—our realm of values. Are you suggesting that basically the humanities in our culture have in a sense become smothered by this dominant scientific worldview?

Smith: Well, I'm afraid that they have been thrown on the defensive. Historically, the role of the humanities is to be the custodians of the human spirit. This is their commission. But because the humanities ply their trade in the university, and because, as the president of Johns Hopkins University put it in an interview in *Newsweek* not too long ago, the university is dominated by the scientific method, then the humanities are willy-nilly—not intentionally—pushed into using canons of objectivity and verifiability. But the truth of the matter is that the more sublime regions of the human self are deeply inward and deeply subjective and do not lend themselves to objective purview by the methods of the university.

Mishlove: I believe that your argument is basically that experience is primary. It comes before observation of the so-called external world that science looks at—that the realm, for example, of religious experience, which you have studied extensively, is perhaps more real than the observable, so-called objective realm of science.

Smith: People can legitimately differ on the question of whether it is more real, but I think we ought to hold out for its being no less real than other aspects of reality which can submit themselves, expose themselves, to objective and verificational techniques.

Mishlove: Of course the positivist philosophers, who have had such an influence in our century, would imply that anything that's metaphysical, that's not testable by scientific methods, is by definition unreal.

Smith: It is certainly true that within philosophy, which is one aspect of the humanities, metaphysics and ontology have suffered a humiliating demotion, as Willard Quine has put it recently.

Mishlove: Let's just for our viewers define ontology. That's a term many people probably wouldn't know.

Smith: Right. Maybe I shouldn't have thrown it in. It comes from the Greek word *on*, which means "being." And so it is the science of being, or to simply put it in simple terms, it's reflection on what ultimately exists.

Mishlove: What is real.

Smith: Yes. R. D. Laing, in one of his books, *The Politics of Experience*, I think, says, "Everybody is a naive ontologist." I think that is true, meaning that we each have our views as to what is real.

Mishlove: One of the points that you make is that, for example, there is the realm of the psyche, the realm of the mind, which includes our thoughts, our thought forms, and perhaps even the realm of spirits and mythological figures, the realm of deities. In the modern materialistic framework these things are thought of at best as kind of an epiphenomenal by-product of matter, a by-product of neural activity in the brain. But you think it might be viewed differently.

Smith: It certainly is the case that all the peoples of the world, with the exception of us, we of the modern West, have believed that human beings stood sort of midway on the Great Chain of Being. Many things—animals, plants, and minerals—are below them. But by the same light they're not at the top of the heap. Marshall Salins, the anthropologist at the University of Chicago, said we're the only ones who believe that we have ascended from slime, or the apes. Everybody else assumes that they were descended from the gods. And it is true that we have a very isolated position. Now, if we look at the testament of what people believed in the past, they believed that the entire world was sentient, that it was filled with life and spirit.

Mishlove: This is a viewpoint that we sort of denigrate today and call primitive animism, or something of that sort.

Smith: We certainly do—and yet the belief that the entire world is alive can't be totally squashed. But certainly, as far as our official philosophy is concerned, we do not have a place, in the scientific cosmology at least, for angels, demons, or even what traditionally has exceeded them, namely, the Great Spirit, the World of Soul, or God.

Mishlove: Or some kind of a vital principle has even been excluded at this point.

Smith: Right. I think the point that at least comes through to me inescapably is, Why the change? Is it that we know now for sure that beings greater than we are do not exist? No, we have discovered nothing that indicates or proves that they do not. It is simply that we have turned a method of getting at truth, namely the scientific method, into a metaphysics—taking to be really real only what turns up through that probe as the privileged and reliable way of getting at truth. It *is* immensely powerful, but we don't see that its power derives precisely in trade-off for its limitation.

Mishlove: In other words, you seem to be saying that if we look at the modern Western mind-set, what it is is a kind of an imperialism, dominated by a materialistic metaphysics.

Smith: I think that is a fair statement, frankly, because just think of what it leaves out. Again, all credit to what it has done in the regions where it is effective. In fact, it is a near-perfect way of getting at truth in the material world. For example, science rides on values, but it cannot itself deal with value. It can deal with descriptive values, like market research. It can tell us what people do value, but it cannot tell us what they ought to value. A second thing is purpose. Is there any purpose in existence, in life, in reality? Jacques Monod, the Nobel Prize winner, says that the systematic denial of purpose is the cornerstone of the scientific method. And we can see why it has to be, because if you go back to explain things because God intended it so—namely, a purpose—why, of course that short-circuits the scientific investigation for secondary causes, which produces them. So we rule out purpose. And then—meanings. Now, the scientific endeavor is meaningful all the way through, but a certain kind of meaning it cannot get at, namely the meaning of the whole: What is the meaning of life?

Mishlove: Sort of like a gestalt.

Smith: Right. Existential meanings, they're sometimes called—the meanings by which we live. Science can't deal with them. Steven Weinberg puts it that the more comprehensible reality becomes—and he's a scientist—the more meaningless it becomes, because it comes down to equations and numbers, and those are not themselves existential meaning.

Mishlove: So the fact that our dominant worldview is scientific—one without value, without purpose, without meaning, without a sense of quality—

Smith: Yes, quality I haven't mentioned. I think if we're going to be careful here, we have to say that the scientific enterprise, and worldview too, itself rides on many of these things we've already mentioned—that there are values, like values of truth. But the point is, those values are not themselves turned up and revealed by science. They're assumed for science, and science itself cannot come to grips—let's just name them again—with values, purposes, meanings, and qualities. It deals with quantities rather than qualities. But look what we've left out if we leave out those four things.

Mishlove: Well, those things are the nourishment of life itself, I would think. And I would imagine that without that kind of nourishment being sustained by our mainstream cultural institutions, our mainstream cultural mind-set, that what we experience is what has been called alienation, discontent, social problems.

Smith: I think this is a direct result of moving our beliefs into the confinement of a scientific view of reality. But there's another thing

I'd like to say, if I may, and that is in all of these it sounds like we're bad-mouthing science. But there's nothing wrong with science itself. In fact, that's an understatement; it has given us incredible good. The problem is not science, but scientism—namely, to assume that what science turns up and can turn up is the sum of all there is. In a way it's a simple thing, but that's one of those things that we know but never learn, you might say.

Mishlove: It almost sounds as if what you're suggesting is what we need to have, rather than scientism, or a dominant science, is science at the service of other higher values.

Smith: At the service, and in place—a place for everything and everything in its place. And it has a very important place, but that place is not to presume to be the whole. And also I think it's very important to say that what we've stumbled into in these constricting aspects of our contemporary view is not the fault of scientists. It would be a vast mistake and an injustice to point fingers at them. This is something that has happened for which all of us, we denizens of the modern world—we're all responsible for it.

Mishlove: It's something that has taken place over centuries as well.

Smith: That's right. And we ask science to give us the view of reality. It's not that the scientists come out and sell it to us hard; because, of course they do have this wonderful treasure, and it comes to the controlled experiment—namely, that in science you can prove your hypotheses. And in the humanities, we cannot.

Mishlove: You know, in T. S. Eliot's great poem "The Waste Land" he seems to describe the whole modern worldview—

Smith: A very prophetic poem.

Mishlove: —as being like a waste land. And he suggests at the end of that poem that the antidote is the rose window of the cathedral.

Smith: Lovely image.

Mishlove: Do you feel that there's some way we can reintegrate religious values?

Smith: Well, logically there's no reason why we cannot at all. It simply means coming to understand what science is and what it can do, and what it cannot do. What happened was that the Western world stumbled upon this phenomenon. Modern science, as Victor Butterfield puts it, outshines everything since the dawn of Christianity—others would say since the discovery of language. We stumbled upon it without preparation and became absolutely ravished by its potential—which, we have to keep on saying, is immense in a certain region but is limited to that region. We became ravished by it. But if we come to understand it, as I think we really are doing—I think we really are coming now finally to see this—that the scientific method is not omnipotent, omnicompetent—then we can place it in its place, value it for what it can do, but not let it distract us from using other faculties to explore other regions of being which are there but which cannot be approached by that method.

Mishlove: The realm of the infinite.

Smith: Infinite, and infinite not just in space, but in worth. When we think about infinite now, that's been pretty much co-opted by science too. We think about infinite space or infinite numbers. Well, those are scientific terms. But what about infinite value? Frankly, I believe that reality holds as much in the way of worth beyond what we are able to see with our ordinary experience as it holds in quantity and size beyond what our naked senses can fathom.

Mishlove: You describe in one essay, "Flakes of Fire," that experiencing this sense of value is like a gift of grace, or something that is given to us by the gods.

Smith: There do come these telltale rifts in the clouds of ignorance that encompass us, when there are moments of discernment, when we see. And we see into being and existence in its qualitative dimension, beyond what we normally do. And those are saving insights that bring courage to the human soul.

Mishlove: Professor Huston Smith, it's been a pleasure having you with me. It is really a delight to get at the level beneath the normal mind-set that we live in. Thank you very much.

Smith: You're most welcome.

CHAPTER 9 | SCIENCE AS THE ORACLE OF OUR AGE

Michael Toms: Huston, why have religious structures seemingly lost the Vision, so that people have to seek it elsewhere?

Huston Smith: I think that they, like perhaps all the other institutions in the modern world, were taken in by a development that goes back about three or four hundred years and set the modern world on its course. That development was, of course, the emergence of modern science.

Science in the generic sense had been around as long as art and religion. But what was discovered then in the sixteenth, seventeenth centuries was the controlled experiment, which escalated science to a new order of power and exactitude. That power proved to be enough to create both a new world, this world that we now live in, and a new worldview. In the process it brought many, many benefits. But in terms of worldview, it inflicted a great blow on the human psyche by making it appear that life's material side is its most important side. Now, this is a logical mistake. Science didn't

---

This interview was conducted with one of the most popular and adept radio interviewers in the country, Michael Toms, of New Dimensions Radio. It was later transcribed and included, under the title "The Ground of Being," in Toms's book, *At the Leading Edge: New Visions of Science, Spirituality, and Society* (Burdett, N.Y.: Larson Publications, 1991). Copyright © 1991 Michael Toms. Reprinted by permission of Michael Toms.

really say this, but because its power derived from attending to the material aspects of nature, and because that power is great and effective and gave us many benefits, the outlook of modernity is unprecedentedly materialistic.

Now, you asked about religious institutions, the mainline churches. Unfortunately, they too succumbed to some extent to that slip. Not intentionally. But transcendence, as that which is not just larger than we are but also better than we are, got pushed into the background and lost our attention. All modern institutions, churches included, have suffered that loss.

Churches are doing many good things, social service causes, taking in the street people, and so on. They're doing very good work. But the reason that they've failed to inspire as they once did is that their grasp on transcendence has slipped. That also accounts for why Asian spirituality has begun to appeal to people in the West. Not having suffered the modern reduction of reality, they have maintained a firmer hold on transcendence.

Toms: Asian spirituality puts more emphasis on the experience. I think of my grandmother, for example. She was deeply saddened when the Catholic Church decided to change the ritual and go to an English Mass. The mystery of the Latin, the mystique, was changed, was transformed, in that simple act.

Smith: That's right. And the so-called liturgical reform that you're referring to is an ambiguous move. Certain re-emphases were perhaps called for, but there have also been losses. You mentioned one; I will mention another. I recently was at a gathering with Robert Bellah, the noted sociologist and author of *Habits of the Heart.* He's a wise and right-thinking man. But he claimed that when the priest stopped facing the altar and turned to face the congregation, the Catholic Church gained, for the congregation felt included. Well, I have to confess that my take is just the opposite. Togetherness is nice. But it can't match the symbolism of the priest and the people—everybody, the priest included—facing the Cross, as something that is beyond them all. That's what people need, more than they need the sense of togetherness or creating your own theology—the whole anthropological turn.

Once more I'll say that the situation is ambiguous. It's not totally black and white. Because the gains are tooted more than the losses, it's important to balance the picture. I'm glad you brought up the issue.

Toms: The aspect of community also comes up for me as we're talking about the shift. In the previous form—with the priest and the congregation facing the Cross, as you put it—there's a recognition, I think, of each individual on his or her own journey in community.
Smith: Right.

Toms: Whereas, shifting it around it's like, well, we're all in this together.
Smith: That's right.

Toms: But it's not quite that way, it seems. It's different. As you say, "ambiguous" is a good way to put it.
   Another thing that keeps coming up for me as we're talking about this has to do with the educational system, of which you've been a part for so many years. With the increasing emphasis on business, career, and opportunity—at the sacrifice of what's called the humanities, the bedrock of establishing values and ethics in ourselves—courses on those subjects are going by the by. What about that?
Smith: I think it is a serious matter. You may have seen, just in this last week, a poll of students, freshmen, throughout the nation. One of the questions in the poll was, "Why have you come to college?" Seventy-five percent said, straight out, that their top priority was to make money, make more money. Few checked the option "to develop a meaningful philosophy of life."

Toms: That's almost a direct reversal of the way it was twenty years ago, in the 1960s.
Smith: Exactly. I see the shift as ominous. The universities and colleges might say, "Well, that's just a problem of our time. We face the yuppies, and that's what they're coming for." But I personally think that we in academia have to take some responsibility for the shift. Again, there's been no wrong intent. We have simply not seen

clearly what has happened. And what has happened in academia is that, as President Steven Muller of Johns Hopkins said in an interview, "the university is rooted in the scientific method, and the scientific method cannot provide a sense of values. As a result, we're turning out skilled barbarians."

Now, I think that's basically true. But what academics do not see clearly enough is the way that their own disciplines, including their criteria for knowing, gravitate toward scientific ways of knowing which emphasize objective knowledge—public knowledge that can be verified.

Toms: All the proper footnotes and bibliographies.

Smith: That's part of it. There is also the jargon and the academese, much of which is unreadable. There is the added problem that because such a large proportion of our population is going to college, professors can get their books published just by requiring their students to read them. There is an ingrown character to academic writing. Professors speak to their colleagues and their own students. A gap emerges between the university mind and our public consciousness.

Toms: Huston, you're mentioning how a specific paradigm has crept into academic circles, how the scientific model has actually become part of the research into the humanities, and how it can stifle creativity and originality. But in your writings you've also referred to David Bohm's theory of wholeness and the implicate order. David Bohm is certainly one of the foremost theoretical physicists alive today and has pioneered, I think, a theory of physics that almost sounds like a spiritual philosophy.

Smith: It does indeed.

Toms: One very similar to some of the Oriental philosophies you're so familiar with. What is your view of the possible coming-together, the linking, with science coming back around to its roots in natural philosophy?

Smith: It is an immensely exciting time. The outcome hasn't been determined; we'll find out how things go, but the incursions are fruitful. On the one hand, the developments in science have undercut a kind of crass Newtonian view of reality as consisting of ultimate little atoms that are unrelated to other things—our century has undercut that. The interrelation between the parts of being—which David Bohm emphasizes with his concept of implicate wholeness—clearly is a move back toward the unity which traditional philosophies, those of Asia included, emphasized.

At the same time, I think we have to be careful here. Modern science has become a powerful symbol for transcendence—again I use *transcendence* to refer to that which is greater than we are by every criterion of worth we know, including intelligence and compassion. Modern science suggests such a realm, but I do not think that it proves it. Nor do I think that it can, for this reason: the crux of modern science is the controlled experiment; that is what distinguishes modern science from generic science and what gives it its power by virtue of its power to prove. It can winnow hypotheses and discard those that are inadequate. What we do *not* see is the corollary of all this, which is that we can control only what is inferior to us. Things that are greater than we are, including more intelligent, dance circles around us, not we they. So there is no way that we are going to get angels, or God, or whatever other beings there may be that are greater than we are, into our controlled experiments. So I think modern science will never prove anything in the area of the human spirit. But it can suggest, and I find it suggesting powerfully. For me, modern science has come to rival, even outstrip at times, sacred art and virgin nature as a symbol of the divine.

Now, if I can continue one more step, I think there's a trap if those who share our kinds of interests—let's just say here "New Dimensions" interests—rush on to say, "Well, that's true of science up to this point. But that only shows that we need a new science that is larger in scope and can prove these transcendent realities." When I hear that, and I hear it very often, my impulse is to say, "In proposing that move, you show me where your loyalties lie, namely, in science! You're for transcendence, but you won't really believe it exists until science proves that it does. So your move shows that you continue to accept science as the ultimate oracle as to what exists." That acceptance is the heart of modernity's problem, so the call for a science that proves transcendence only perpetuates the problem.

In probing the physical, material world, science is brilliant; it is a near-perfect way of telling us about that. And to know about nature is a great good, for nature is awesome in its own right. But science doesn't have to do everything. And if we try to make it do everything, with every step of its expansion we will decrease its power and will end up with a kind of mushy science. Of course, we can define *science* in any way we please. I prefer keeping it hard-nosed, powerful, and precise, while insisting that it can only disclose a *part* of reality.

Toms: It occurs to me as I hear you present your case here—which I think is very compelling—that it may explain why it's so difficult to get psychic and paranormal experiences to happen in the scientific laboratory.

Smith: Exactly. I believe that paranormal powers are real. But to get anything into a laboratory, we have to reduce the variables to a single alternative so we can discover which side of it is true. Where the object in question exceeds us in complexity, we can't do that.

Toms: This may explain why it has been so easy to change the agenda of colleges and universities, through the federal budget and the like. We've made science into some kind of god.

Smith: Oh, clearly.

Toms: And science has become our religion.

Smith: Alex Comfort has a nice line on that. He says, "Science is our sacral mode of knowing." Sacral is a coined word—it comes from *sacred*. I think he's right. Science has almost exactly replaced the role that revelation played in the Middle Ages. Then, if you wanted the final verdict on what is true, you would go to the scriptures and the traditions of the Church. Now we go to science. One intellectual historian has pointed out that as far back as a hundred years ago, more people believed, really believed, in the truth of the periodic table of chemical elements than they believed anything in the Bible.

In the century since then, we've moved further in that direction. Science *has* become the revelation of our time.

And to return to our previous point, it *should* be with regard to the material world. The slip is that we have turned science into scientism—scientism being defined as the assumption that science is the only reliable way of getting at truth, and that only the kinds of things it tells us about really exist.

Toms: It may require some sense of humility to admit that we have confused science with scientism.

Smith: It will. In a way, we know what we need to know. It is one of these things that we know but never learn.

Toms: Or that we know but haven't integrated.

Smith: That's right. It has to be assimilated. But everything in our culture—almost everything—works against that assimilation. The visible bombards us from dawn to night. The tangible is so much with us that it's hard to put it in perspective. That's all we need to do, just put it in perspective. But that saving grace is difficult to allow.

Toms: Having just a little bit of time to step back, being able to use that observing mind and that observing quality that all of us have to get that perspective, is really important.

Smith: Important and, in our time, difficult.

Toms: Huston, Joseph Campbell, in his work on the mythic quest and its symbols of myth, went a long way toward showing us why we're not able to get that perspective.

Smith: That is very true. Many times he referred to that "shape-shifting yet wonderfully constant story" that all the myths relate. I think "shape-shifting" is a beautiful phrase. In their specifics, their particulars, myths differ; yet the underlying theme is constant. Joseph was a master at going straight for the pay dirt—for what the underlying, constant story is—and then making it available to us.

Toms: I wonder where we can find that story in the midst of the scientific revolution, because it's obviously present. But how do you bring the symbology out, and how do you make it understandable and obvious to all concerned? Certainly it's there.

Smith: Part of it is there. Are you asking how science itself may be exemplifying this underlying story?

Toms: Well, in a sense, yes. In a sense, you can see the scientist seeking the ultimate invention or the ultimate product or whatever it is—trying to find the ultimate solution to this disease or whatever—as on the hero's quest, the mythic journey.

Smith: We need to distinguish here between science and the scientists. There is no question but that scientists are on a "hero's journey" second unto none. Their dedication, their devotion to truth, their ordeals, and then the exultation of homecoming when new truth is discovered—all of that, the whole symbology of the hero's journey is powerfully exemplified by them.

I'd like to illustrate this with an anecdote from MIT, where I taught longer than anywhere else. Ed Land, who later invented the Polaroid camera, came to MIT as a freshman and took a course in optics. Before the semester was over—I tell you the story as it came down to me—the teacher of that course had resigned a tenured position to go with this freshman student and start a company that later become Polaroid. My favorite moment in the story concerns the time when they were right on the cusp of their decisive discovery of how color film could be developed in the small space of a camera. They were working so hard that they were actually living in the lab. When they got exhausted, they would just put their heads on their desks. Finally, the ex-professor said to his ex-freshman, "Ed, I've had it; I just can't go on." "Good," Ed answered. "We'll work in our Christmas shopping today." The professor said, "Ed, Ed. It's January 3rd!"

This story shows the white heat in the quest of science, and the scientists who embody it. Now, that has to be distinguished from the expectation that science itself will reveal a world that is full of—saturated with, you might say—a kind of meaning that the myths proclaim. Take Steven Weinberg, the Harvard physicist, for example. In *The First Three Minutes* he says that the irony is that the more understandable—from the scientific standpoint—we find the universe to be, the more meaningless it becomes. Now, that's true too if you just hold entirely to what the sciences actually depict and lay out for us. But if we fold it into a larger vision, it fits smoothly.

Toms: I was thinking, as you were just giving that white-heat description about Ed Land and that professor of how the Vipassana [a type of mediation practice] teacher might dismiss the student with a wave of his hand, saying, "That's just another one, just another one. Go back and meditate." And I was wondering about how we do get caught up in our life in ways that perhaps remove us from what's real.

Smith: We do. But then there are many encouraging signs. You mentioned Vipassana. I was just last December with my wife at the Insight Meditation Society in Barre, Massachusetts. There it came over me again watching those 120 Western yogis sitting and walking for sixteen hours a day in silence, it came over me that this institution goes back uninterrupted for twenty-five hundred years, to the "rains retreat" that was instigated by the Buddha himself.

As you probably know, when Buddha formed his *sangha* [spiritual community], his community of monks, he sent them out on the highways and byways for nine months of the year to teach and preach the dharma [path of right living]. But then when the monsoons came along, slamming in and turning the subcontinent of India into a sea of mud, the monks would regather for three uninterrupted months of solid meditation in what they called the rains retreat.

I find it quite thrilling that to this day, twenty-five hundred years later, the rains retreat is intact in Barre, Massachusetts. And land has been purchased for a Western offshoot in California. This kind of extensive retreat and mind training is being seriously attempted right here in the West.

Toms: That's one solution, as it were, to getting off the merry-go-round. But I can hear the critique, "Well, how does someone get three months to go

*off and do this?" You know, how does one take time out of their busy
life? "I've got a family; I've got a career; I've got this, I've got that."
There are lots of reasons for not being able to do that in this day and age
and in this society. What is your answer to that?*

Smith: My answer is that somebody should tell me the answer! My
wife has actually gone for three years in a row and will be going
back for a fourth one. She manages her life to do it. I have not
succeeded in freeing such time myself. But the real answer is,
"Where there's a will, there's a way." To be sure, very few people
could just decide tomorrow that they'll go; but, if there is a will,
then one can begin with a day or a weekend. Then, from what one
learns and from the encouragement and the incentive one gathers,
one can begin to build it into one's life—ten minutes in the
morning, ten minutes in the evening. This is not at all to mini-
mize the difficulty of doing that in a busy world. But, again, when
we decide that we really want to do it, I think we can free up the
necessary space.

*Toms: Huston, I can't think of anyone more qualified to answer my next
query. Am I correct in thinking that Buddhism is the only major
religion that hasn't gone to war for its creed? When one looks at
Buddhism, one notices its incredible variety and diversity as practiced
in different cultures. It seems to adapt to the different cultures. We
had the phenomenon of Zen becoming very popular in the 1950s, with
the beat era. Now we're talking about Vipassana, but Tibetan
Buddhism has also become very prevalent as their people have been
spread across the planet after losing their country to the Chinese. As
we look at Buddhism, how would you describe the differences? And
also, are you aware of Buddhism ever having been in war for the
creed?*

Smith: Yes, but so incidentally that it's the exception that proves the
rule. Right now, in Sri Lanka, there's the conflict with the Hindus,
and I've been told by fieldworkers that some of those Buddhist
monks are becoming fierce politicians. But in the volumes of
Buddhist history, this is a small chapter. Basically, I would validate
your point. Buddhism seems not to have been violent to the extent
that the other religions have.

Toms: As I hear the Dalai Lama, it strikes me as very unusual and quite commendable that I've never heard the Tibetans say a bad word about the Chinese.

Smith: Nor have I.

Toms: One can look at Afghanistan as a relevant, contrasting example. When one looks at Tibet and China, the Tibetans—at least the ones who escaped Tibet—have dealt with that situation much differently than other peoples have dealt with the loss of their country or culture. I'm not suggesting we make a judgment about this, whether it's right or wrong, but just to notice it.

Smith: Yes, it does appear to be the case. It is both interesting and impressive.

Toms: I want to expand my question relative to Buddhism. As we look at the different varieties of Buddhism, there seems to be a substantive difference between how it's practiced in, say, Sri Lanka or Thailand, and how it's practiced in Tibet and Japan. What about those differences? How do they come together, or do they come together?

Smith: It presents indeed a remarkable spread and variety. As for the differences, I happen to have a personal theory on this, respecting the two major branches of Buddhism: Theravada, or southern Buddhism, which we find in Sri Lanka, Thailand, and Burma, and then Mahayana in China, Japan, Korea, and the like. Usually the two branches are distinguished according to whether the aspirant is out for his own enlightenment or postpones his own enlightenment until others are saved—that kind of thing.

There is something to describing the split in this way, but I think there is an underlying, deeper difference that the historians have missed. Southern Buddhism is the branch of Buddhism that adhered to the Buddha's vision of Buddhism as a total civilization, one that blueprinted an entire way of life—economics and politics included. Whereas Mahayana gave up the claim to being a total civilization and contented itself with being, you might say, simply a religion that could be fitted to any civilization and could take up its abode therein.

Original Buddhism presented the vision of a total civilization that was founded on the tripod of monarchy, monks, and the laity. Each of these had obligations to the other, and also was entitled to benefits from the others. Southern Buddhism has adhered to that ideal. This makes the monks more important, for they are one of the three legs on which society rests.

But when Buddhism entered China, China opened its arms to it, seeing that it had psychological and metaphysical resources the Chinese lacked. East Asians weren't strong on metaphysics or psychology. China's social structure, though, was solidly intact. The Chinese Empire was not about to change its ground plan for foreign import. So Buddhism entered, but compromised: "Okay, keep your social structure as it is, and we will deepen its religious component." Therein, I think, lies the fundamental difference between southern and northern Buddhism.

Toms: Tibet seems to be an exception to the Mahayana transfer, because there the religion actually became the politics.

Smith: You are quite right. In this respect it is more like the southern Buddhist model. This difference between the branches of Buddhism that you brought up is interesting. When Buddhism first significantly entered this country in the 1950s and 1960s, it was primarily in its Mahayana, specifically Zen, form; then, Theravada, through the Vipassana meditation, and Tibetan Buddhism have gained ground. I think that is healthy because Zen—although I have the utmost respect for it—depends on a *roshi* who functions as a kind of guru. Vipassana is something like a democratized Buddhism. It relies on its method more than on a teacher.

Toms: It's also interesting to note the seemingly limitless amount of scripture and documentation that the Tibetans have. Tibetan Buddhism has an incredible pantheon of literature behind it.

Smith: It does. And this makes surprising the effectiveness with which the Tibetans have spread their teachings in this country, given the fact that it is so technical and involved. And its meditation is unbelievably intricate. I've made stabs at both Theravada and Mahayana, but though I attempted Tibetan practice, I soon despaired. It seemed impenetrable because of the complexity of the teaching. Yet there are innumerable Americans—you know them as well as do I—who are drawn to that branch.

Toms: Yes. Three are also Tibetan teachers, who have come to the United States, that are perhaps less strict or less formal or structural—so that there's more allowance for a little informality.
Smith: Good point.

Toms: So, where do you think we go from here? What do you think the future of philosophy and religion is?
Smith: I have never been to Disney World, but I hear it has a section called "Tomorrowland." When I first learned of it, I hooted. We don't even know what "Todayland" is, and people are already scripting "Tomorrowland."

I don't know. I don't feel like I have much of a feel for the future. We all have our strengths and weaknesses, and personally I feel I'm pretty good with the past. At least I get some traction there. But the future? Who wrote the song "I Can't Get No Satisfaction"? [It was the Rolling Stones.] I feel like parodying it: "I can't get no traction on the future." Tomorrow a bomb might accidentally go off, or we may discover that we have burned too wide a hole in our ozone covering. Still, we've managed thus far. I'm not much given to prognosis. What's important is to see the direction in which we should move and to let the future take care of itself.

Toms: Well, there's certainly something to be said for the value of knowing the past.
Smith: Roots. Roots are important.

Toms: Who was it that said, "Those who forget history are condemned to repeat it"? [It was American philosopher George Santayana.]
Smith: Whoever it was, I agree.

CHAPTER 10 | **SCIENCE, FAITH, AND INFINITY**

Tracy Knauss and the Reverend Jack Young: In your book Beyond the Post-Modern Mind, *you suggest that we postmodern Westerners no longer know who we are.*

Huston Smith: I would like to quote Walker Percy, the writer, who is also a psychiatrist. He points out that in the West we no longer have a coherent view of the human self, such as was contained in the Middle Ages, or seventeenth-century New England, or in tribal societies today. Whether or not those views were correct, people believed them, and they provided models for human behavior. Now Percy says we no longer have such a model.

Actually, we have two clusters of ideas as to who we are. But the problem is, they stand in sharp contradiction with one another. On the one hand, from Monday through Friday, in our schools and universities, we're taught that we're the *more* that have derived from the *less*. That is to say, we are at the top of the evolutionary scale, having emerged out of slime or a bacteria or primitive forms of life.

But on the weekends, in churches and synagogues, why, just the

---

This exchange with Tracy Knauss and the Reverend Jack Young for *Chattanooga Life & Leisure* appeared as "A Cosmic Conversation with Huston Smith" in April 1989. Reprinted by permission of Tracy Knauss.

opposite is proclaimed—namely, that we're the less that have derived from the more, the more in this case being God. And we who have been created by God are obviously less than that infinite source from which we have come. So Percy points out that, simply by virtue of being Westerners today, all of us believe parts of each of these theories as to who we are. But the problem is, they do not cohere. As a psychiatrist, he sees this as a schizophrenic point of view about ourselves—a schizophrenic self-image.

Knauss and Young: You say that science—including Darwinism, Darwinian evolution, random selection, and the various mutations that lead evolution from the simpler to the more complex—is fine, but that it has its limitations. What is your view of Darwinism?

Smith: I think Darwinism is a half-truth. The half-truth is that we, as the higher form of organic life, have historically arrived on the scene later—not only later, but very much later, than the earlier or simpler forms. The evidence of the fossil record in that respect is conclusively established.

But there is another side of Darwinism that was already pretty well in place when Darwin entered the picture. He saw, and his successors have seen, the explanation of how we came into being. His claim regarding the engine of evolution, so to speak, what makes it advance, is natural selection working on chance mutations.

Now, we have virtually assumed that also to be true. But, in point of fact, that falls so far short of having been explained by the evidence that is deduced for it that I think it is a mistake for us to say that we know that is the device, the mechanism, by which we have come upon the scene. So in that second sense, you might say that evolution has occurred, that *that* side of Darwinism is proved. But *how* has it occurred? Darwin's claim on that second front has not been anywhere near established. We really do not know, from the scientific point of view, how we got here.

Knauss and Young: If Darwinism leaves a little bit to be desired in terms of the mechanism, scientifically speaking, what about its opposite, creationism?

Smith: My problem with that is that often they play fast and loose with the fossil record, claiming that—certainly in extreme versions of it—that we have been here only maybe six thousand years or so. In that extreme form (there are more subtle forms that would have to be dealt with individually) creationism, too, is a half-truth. Its claim that we are the less who have derived from the more, I happen, as a religious person, to believe. But then the other half—namely the way in which we have derived from the more—is literally and accurately and, you might say scientifically, spelled out in the Bible. That is the part where I think creationism goes astray.

Knauss and Young: You'll be coming to Chattanooga soon. One thing we'll prepare you for is that we're less than one hour's drive from Dayton, Tennessee, where the Scopes "Monkey Trial" was held. And we're a fairly fundamentalist group in Chattanooga. You will be asked if you believe that man came from, sprang from, a monkey. Are you prepared to answer that question in Chattanooga?

Smith: Sure. Well, oh, I don't think—if one takes that statement literally—I do not think that man came from a monkey. I think it's true that human beings came on the scene after monkeys arrived, but that phrase "man coming from a monkey" is shorthand for the Darwinian claim—and I've already indicated that I think it's half true.

Knauss and Young: You mentioned that you are a "religious person." How would you define a religious person?

Smith: There are many definitions, but the one I like is the one William James came up with. It is the opening sentence of chapter 3 in his book *The Varieties of Religious Experience*. "Were one asked to characterize the life of religion in the broadest and most general terms possible, one might say that it consists of the belief that there is an unseen order, and that our supreme good lies in harmoniously adjusting ourselves thereto."

Now, to that I would add one more sentence from James's book, but I'll paraphrase this. He says religion says the best things are also the most powerful things—those which say the last word and cast the final stone. So if we put these two quotations by James together, why, we have religion as the human relationship to a realm that is invisible and powerful and good, those three qualities combined.

Knauss and Young: Does the Bible have literal truth?
Smith: Certain things in it are literal—literally true. So I would say it has a literally true dimension. But Christianity, in its history, had worked out a very sophisticated—the going word, but it's a jaw-breaker word—hermeneutics of scripture. It's a fancy word for interpretation of scripture. And the literal is only the bottom rung of the ladder. In addition to the literal, there is the symbolic and the allegorical. And the last one has to do with the anagogic [mystical]. But—without going into the details about this—yes, there is a literal dimension to the Bible, and certain factual statements within it are literally true. But then these other principles of interpretation that Christianity has always held have also been introduced to derive the plentitude of meaning from it.

Knauss and Young: What about science and its attempt to prove and disprove order and meaning? It attempts to deal with and prove all types of concepts, but it fails to address our questions of purpose in this universe. However, religion attempts to answer the question of purpose but really fails to offer any proofs other than that kind that requires illumination of faith. Who are we to believe? Both? Neither?
Smith: Oh. I think we believe both. We believe science in terms of what it tells us about the workings of the visible, material world. That is to say, nature. However, it would be a gross mistake—and no one sees this more clearly than the really great scientists who are also great thinkers—to conclude that that's all there is to existence. There is the invisible. No one has ever seen life; we have seen living things. No one has ever seen consciousness, but we're conscious beings. So there's a whole realm of the invisible, the immaterial, and there we get into matters of values, meanings, purposes, and qualities—and none of these can science really deal with. So you're quite right. When they get into this other domain—I would call it a higher domain—then proof is not present. It's not available. But

that simply points out that we happen to be creatures who cannot live our entire lives on the basis of what can be certainly and objectively proven. In fact, were we such, we might be mechanisms pulled about simply by the dictates of fact and evidence.

We would not like that. We have more dignity by virtue of the freedom from not having the truth dictated to us all the way through.

Knauss and Young: You mentioned values. Are values relative, or are there absolute truths?

Smith: Oh, some are relative. Whether you prefer Cheerios or Bran Flakes is purely relative. And, of course, we can get into more significant relative values cross-culturally. But certain values are universal. Some of these we can spot by virtue of finding them in every culture that we have come upon—and now there are none hiding in the wings. We have encountered all of them. And others are more difficult to indicate in terms of their universality—and yet I think they are there.

Knauss and Young: How does Huston Smith define God?

Smith: The infinite power, meaning, and worth. Will that do? Or do you want it spelled out?

Knauss and Young: How about a little elaboration?

Smith: The infinite is an awesome concept. I just heard Stephen Hawking last spring say mathematicians—of which he is one—really don't know how to handle the infinite. I think that's an honest and sensitive realization. It's simply that which has no boundaries, no limits. But our minds cannot settle down with that. But God is infinite in every quality of value and criterion of value we can think of—and probably some that are as much beyond us as our rationality and use of language is beyond the capacity of a dog to understand. But just think of every virtue—goodness, compassion, intelligence, and creativity—and then let the mind go. Follow those virtues just as far as the imagination allows, and then that is God, adding that we have only tracked that reality a fraction of its actual immensity.

Knauss and Young: Is evil part of God if God is all-consuming, all-knowing?
Smith: Oh, evil. The truth of the matter is we *can* explain evil. And we can see a solution to this problem for a certain distance. But it only established a trajectory that our human vision is incapable of carrying through to the limit. The trajectory is that we can understand that certain things that seem evil in one context change their character in a larger frame of reference.

For example, a small child has broken a toy. In that frame of reference, this is unmitigatingly evil. The child, at the moment, can't see beyond it. And it may seem like and feel like the end of the world. But we, standing back with the larger frame of reference, can realize that there are learning experiences going on, and this is not the end of the world, and there will be more coming along that will put that in a very minor light.

And in ways like that, always moving to a wider frame of reference, we can accommodate more and more of evil—and see how, for example, it might be needed for the exercise of free will. And if it weren't there, we would again be automatons, rather than free beings with the dignity that goes with that.

But we can never, in our human state, complete that trajectory and explain to our own satisfaction how things like the Holocaust, or torture, or innocent children dying of incurable disease at an early age. And that's where the eyes of faith come in and take over—simply recognizing our human limitations in this regard and yet having faith that, if we were privy to the whole spectrum of reality, we would then see that, yes, even what looks like unmitigated evil to us has its place in the scheme of things entire.

Knauss and Young: Would you describe yourself as a Christian?
Smith: Yes. I go to church every Sunday that I can. And that means most Sundays.

Knauss and Young: What is it about Christianity that appeals to you? And in your personal view, was Christ prized as more than a man, more than Gandhi or Muhammad, or Buddha?

Smith: I would say more than Gandhi; and, yes, I would say more than Muhammad, too, who never claimed—and the Muslims do not claim—that he was divine. Buddha would be a more difficult question to answer.

You started out by asking why I am a Christian. And the simplest, most direct answer is because this is the tradition that I was born in, the one that feels natural to me. I certainly have found nothing in my studies to suggest that any other tradition is superior to it. So it is my tradition.

Now I happen to be, in ways, quite orthodox and conservative and, in other ways, quite liberal—to the point where some would consider me a "radical." My conservative and orthodox side is that I tend to take very seriously the revelation within Christianity, and I am emphatically supernatural. I do not believe that the natural world—which is basically the material and the visible, by whatever amplification is needed to get at it—I don't think that's the whole of reality. Whatever lies beyond the material and what is inaccessible to science, I simply call the supernatural.

Now, on the radical side, I do not make invidious comparisons between the traditions. I do not think I have the right or under-standing by which I can rank, in order, the world's great enduring traditions. Therefore, operatively, in my life I accepted them as alternate ways in which the single God spoke to the various civiliza-tions of the world.

Knauss: I have a young child now, and it's difficult for me to know which way to turn in terms of educating this child about religion. I feel I'm religious in certain regards but not traditionally a "Christian." And I like science. But my wife and I don't really know how to raise this child. I think a lot of our peers have this same problem: how to introduce religion to children. I know you're a father and grandfather. How did you address this situation?

Smith: Oh, that's such a difficult problem in our time. We have three daughters—and, needless to say, we love them to pieces and think they're splendid. But only one of them is within a traditional religious context, and she happens to have married a Jew and converted to Judaism. They have a traditional religious home. But the other two children do not, which is a way of disclaiming any wisdom on this particular matter.

I personally feel that the institutional churches of our day have a very difficult task on their hands. But part of the problem is that the institutional churches try to speak to a very wide cross-range of human individuals, in terms of their educational level and political persuasions and things like that. It's not easy to keep all these horses in line, and that affects the level at which Christianity can be taught. My own concern is that I think the wisdom in Christianity is bottomless—I mean topless, in the sense there's no limit to it. There is more than anyone in his or her lifetime can plumb.

But only a trickle of that wisdom gets through; because, in sermons, and even in part in the liturgy, people are busy and the churches are limited to third-grade presentations of higher mathematics. So some people just cut out because they don't like third-grade-level mathematics. They want go beyond that—and it's good if they go beyond.

I think the matter of the raising of children is so much of a contextual matter, as far as institutions being available in one's neighborhood, because the beliefs and convictions of the parents must be given priority in trying to come to a little wisdom in this very difficult question.

Knauss and Young: In Beyond the Post-Modern Mind *you make the point that we Westerners today think of our time as the time of great progress. Do you agree with that?*

Smith: I think that, in very impressive ways, we have improved—and I wouldn't restrict ourselves to medical technology, which has given members of the affluent nations a longer life expectancy, by far, than in the past. I wouldn't limit it to that and the decrease of drudgery.

I would say that in our knowledge of one another, in our knowledge of nature and the awesomeness of the physical universe in which we live, these are incalculable gains. There have been advances in civil liberties, too. And even though we have tremendous problems like race problems, we are more aware of these and are trying to act responsibly regarding them.

Knauss and Young: I was just wondering what important values, in your opinion, have been lost.

Smith: The values of understanding as against acquisition. The value of compassion as against power. You see, in our lip service, we give place to the values that I'm mentioning; but, in terms of the overwhelming practice of our time, there is an externality and an emphasis on external power, prestige, and status that is out of line and needs to be corrected.

Knauss and Young: A couple of months ago, you wrote an article in remembrance of Aldous Huxley in the Los Angeles Times Book Review. *At the end of his life, Huxley was one of the intellectual giants of our contemporary times. But he didn't really have much to say or suggest to people except, "Try to be a little kinder." What is your opinion of that with respect to your own observations?*

Smith: Well . . . I like Huxley's answer partly for the modesty of it—and that was one of the charms of the man, his enormous erudition and understanding. He had no "big head" about him. A good part of me would like very much to take refuge in that and say, "Me, too." But then that might be a cop-out on your question. I would add to that such things as, "Follow the light where it leads" and, "Do not underestimate the possibilities and resources in this human life that each one of us has been privileged to be given."

April Thompson: There is a Buddhist parable that says one won't find water by digging many shallow holes. What do you make of the claim that one must dedicate one's life to a single spiritual path?

Huston Smith: I don't think the cafeteria-style approach to religion works. Chogyam Trungpa, a great Tibetan teacher, put it very accurately. When you go to a salad bar, you pick out what you like. But, as Trungpa says, that's not necessarily what you need. If at the start of the "salad bar" to make your own religion you knew what you needed, you'd be at the end rather than at the beginning. At the beginning you just know what your taste buds tell you. I don't think such an approach has the depth of committing yourself to a tested tradition.

Christianity has been my central meal from the start, but I'm a strong believer in vitamin supplements, and what I have gained from these other traditions is tremendously enriching. I've been fortunate to make my way in the world by immersing myself in

This article by journalist April Thompson originally appeared under the title "Spirit over Matter: An Interview with Huston Smith." Reprinted with permission from the September–October 2001 issue of *The Other Side*. For subscriptions or more information call 1–800–700–9280, or visit www .theotherside.org.

these traditions. But I'm careful not to recommend it for everybody.

Thompson: Your latest book, Why Religion Matters, *deals with the battle between science and religion, which you call the two most powerful forces in human history. Can these two opposing forces ever come together?*

Smith: Science and religion will always be partners in the sense that the world will never be without both. The question is, Must they be in conflict, or can we stake out the rightful territory for each and respect those boundaries?

In modernity, we have been ravaged by science's immense power over nature and the physical world. We've slipped into the assumption that because it can do so well with matter, it can also speak to values and morals and the question of the afterlife and things like that. It absolutely cannot. Science is a very powerful instrument, nearly perfect for understanding the material world, but it cannot address anything other than the material world. I liken it to a huge balloon. The scientific method is like a powerful flashlight that can shine the light of understanding on anything within the balloon, but it cannot speak to where the balloon is in space or whether there is any space outside it.

In my book, I lay down the ground rules for coming to an agreement: science deals with the physical universe, and religion deals with the whole of things. That seems to give religion the advantage, because it is a bigger circle, but science can deal far more effectively and precisely with its subject than religion can. So that restores the clarity and balance between the two.

Our careless belief that science can give us a view of the entire world—when in fact it can only deal with the physical—has pushed the human spirit into a tunnel. But the human spirit is too important, too large, too powerful in the long run to accept the tunnel as its home. I believe there is light at the end of the tunnel—signs that we are finally ready to bring science and religion into a partnership, rather than the conflict that has existed for three hundred years.

Thompson: In what religious tradition do you find the most satisfying explanation of good and evil?

Smith: Evil provides the primary challenge to any religious view of life and the world. Philosophies have no explanation—evil is the rock of Gibraltar on which all rational systems eventually founder and end up in splinters. But religions have another recourse—vision. It is almost like a physical organ—the third eye, as the Tibetans call it, or the eye of the soul, as Plato called it, or the eye of the heart, as the Sufis call it—through which they see a reality in which good encompasses evil and transmutes it, showing its place in the total scheme of things.

William James said that if we were to take the totality of religion and condense it into a single affirmation, it would be this: the best things are the most powerful things—the things that cast the last stone and say the final word. The Book of Job is a classic example. An innocent man is visited by afflictions of innumerable kinds, ending with boils that put him in physical agony. His friends try to persuade him that this is a just visitation for evils he has done. But he won't accept that. He stands up for his integrity, asks them to show what has he done wrong, and argues them down. He is still left with these boils, but in the end, what solves the problem isn't an argument but an insight that takes the form of a whirlwind.

Job sees the place of evil in the total scheme of things. Near the end, he offers the classic line "I have heard Thee with the hearing of the ear but now my eyes have seen Thee" (42:5). So it is that intuitive vision solves the problem of evil for the believer.

If a two-year-old drops her ice cream cone, it's the end of the world for her. The question is, Can there be a vision of reality—not just a reality we see, but an all-encompassing reality—that places even the worst evils we can imagine, like the Holocaust or a huge plague, in the position of a dropped ice cream cone in the context of the total infinite perfection of things?

The lives of the great mystics and visionaries seem to suggest this. Some of them report great joy when they are experiencing the greatest anguish. St. Francis wrote his famous "Canticle to the Sun," one of the most glorious paeans to the divine in nature, when his eyesight was so weak that even the flickering light of a candle caused great pain for him.

St. John Chrysostom was the fourth-century Christian preacher and orator who ran afoul of the czarina of Russia because he stood up for the poor and denounced the monarchy for not attending to them better. He was sentenced to die by being dragged by a chariot. The poor who loved him reported his last words as "Praise, praise for everything . . . thanks, thanks for all."

That is the final word regarding evil from the religious perspective. When somebody is feeling the stones from the road bashing into his head and can still possess that degree of certainty, that carries some weight. Otherwise, it's just wheels turning.

Thompson: What has been your personal experience with suffering? Have you gone through the dark night of the soul?

Smith: I have had an incredibly blessed life compared with most people, but I have had two brushes with the dark night of the soul. In my mid-forties I spent three years in a very deep depression. I was still able to go about my duties in a minimal fashion, but I had absolutely no energy for anything beyond that.

Then five years ago, we lost our oldest daughter to cancer. It was an anguish that put the mid-life crisis in the shade. I am tempted to say I have had my share of trials, but I know I have been fortunate.

Thompson: You have written about spiritual masters finding peace in situations where there is no hope of resolution and experiencing grief and sorrow rather than transcending them. This is different from the notion of peace as a place free of conflict.

Smith: There is no such thing in this world, in this life, as coming to a stage where all will be sunny and happy. The possibility is to experience evil and suffering as present, yet transmuted into a different valence, a different order, by being penetrated. It's the light coming to shine within the darkness, not the darkness being pushed away. But this happiness is paradoxical, because the pain remains.

There's a story of a Zen *roshi* who liked to walk on the outskirts of his village. Returning from his walk one evening, he heard wailing in a household where a child had died. He immediately sat down and started sobbing with the family. The next day some of his disciples said, "You know, that behavior of yours was terribly unbecoming. We thought you were past all that." He answered, "It is because I have passed beyond that that I sobbed." He didn't mean he was just going through the motions of sobbing, but that he was overcome by tears. This is the paradoxical happiness of life in this world.

Thompson: It's true that faith can either transform or exacerbate suffering. But faith seems to be something people either have or don't have.

Smith: Faith is not like a faucet you can turn on and off, but it is something we can move toward and work toward the possibility of possessing. We can do things we know are wrong, but we cannot believe things we think are false. Faith is in that second category. It is not totally under our control, yet neither are we totally powerless.

We can ponder, for example, the three words "wiser than despair," which I find very catalyzing. There are so many problems—global warming, population explosion, the increasing gulf between the rich and poor. It's so easy to despair. But despair is not a creative stance toward life, and we must seek opportunities to put every ounce of our strength to use.

Thompson: And hopefully, by the grace of God, we have experiences that keep our faith going. Have you had personal encounters with God?

Smith: I have found my way to God through understanding. We all come upon thin places between this world and another—chinks between the parapets, where suddenly we see a ray of light or a little opening.

Yes, I have had those experiences, some of major proportions. The one I think of at the moment is my daughter's courage in facing a horrendous ordeal: seven months of cancer. There was no hope of recovery, but there was a buoyancy of spirit. There again, the light was shining within the darkness, and it was such an inspiration. During those seven months—on my birthday, her birthday, Father's Day—we went up to Santa Rosa to visit her, just in despair. How could I bear to have her wish me a happy birthday for the last time? How could I wish her happy birthday? And yet when we drove back, we felt this paradoxical happiness. We drew from our daughter's great courage and spirit.

Thompson: Before we close, I wonder if you would be willing to offer a favorite prayer.

Smith: It is hard for me to pick a single favorite prayer. I do have a favorite in each tradition. I will share a prayer that is a Hindu Sanskrit chant. The translation is "Lead us from the unreal to the Real, lead us from darkness to Light, lead us from death to immortal life. Peace, peace, peace."

*Richard Gazdayka: You have written that the most important thing you
inherited from your parents was faith. Is this faith in the Divine, in the
divinity of humankind, or faith that the human species will survive, if
not thrive?*

Huston Smith: I think that faith is a character structure, and therefore if
it's present, it's present more deeply than the specifics one has faith
in. George Santayana, the great philosopher from mid-century,
wrote a book, *Skepticism and Animal Faith,* in which he brings this
out. Even animals have faith. They don't articulate anything, but
they have faith that if they go out on this limb, the limb will
support them. I think faith is deeply ingrained in my stance toward
the world rather than in any specific belief. I can give you an
anecdote. When I was in college, I had a summer job and had to get
out of bed at 5:30 A.M. Fortunately, there was another fellow who
had an alarm clock. So all summer long he would come to my room
and shake me to wake me up. At the end of the summer, he said,
"In the thirty-nine mornings that I woke you, when you roused,

This interview with Richard Gazdayka originally appeared as "Huston Smith: Why Religion Matters"
in the magazine *East West: Events, Books, and Gifts for the Inner Quest* (July–August 2001). Reprinted
by permission of *East West,* Mountain View, California.

even before your eyes opened, your first word was 'good.'" I think that says something about faith, because who likes to be awakened, especially at that age? Faith is an affirmative stance toward life.

Gazdayka: You wrote, "Modernity's big picture is materialism or naturalism, which acknowledges that there are immaterial things—thoughts and feelings—while insisting that these things are totally dependent on the material." How has this view affected humankind?

Smith: Oh, adversely, because if our thoughts and feelings are epiphenomenal, the technical word in epistemology, then they depend on their material substructure. So when the material body dies, the picture stops; death has the final word. Of course, the great traditions all unite in saying the opposite.

Gazdayka: You wrote, "Nothing in science's universe is more intelligent than we are." What's the result of such thinking?

Smith: I think the impact of converting the scientific worldview, or escalating it beyond what it actually is—a view of nature as the physical universe—is like having been led into a cage and closing the door to another wider, better world around it. The results on the human spirit are subtle to discern, but they are major in their impact on our lives.

Gazdayka: If, as John Polkinghorn states, the chances that life could have evolved randomly is something along the odds of ten followed by forty zeroes, why don't we see more adherence to the intelligent design theory? Is there a fear of being branded "religious"?

Smith: It's sad I have to say this, but nothing is gained by sweeping things that are unpleasant under the rug. The truth of the matter is that there is a kind of war going on for the human mind. The biologist E. O. Wilson says that the struggle for the human soul in the twenty-first century will be between science and religion. He's absolutely sure, in his own mind, that science is going to win. Though I don't like the combative way he sets this up, nevertheless I think he's going to be wrong, because I think that religion has more staying power. To answer your question, science would have to admit there is an intelligence greater than ours, and since the tool kit of science can't get its screwdrivers into that, it means that they don't have the whole story; and yet they would, of course, omit that.

Gazdayka: If these two worldviews—the traditional and the scientific—will be competing for the mind in the third millennium, how can the traditional view survive, when nearly all traditional societies are extinct?

Smith: With great difficulty. Up until the last five years I was discouraged, because although it seemed to me that religion is an unstoppable force in human nature, it met the immovable object in scientism—science as a sacred cow. However, I now believe that scientism is not an immovable object. I think there are signs that it's giving way. Not science—but *scientism:* one of the reasons I believe this is the response my book *Why Religion Matters* received. I thought that because it takes on science, kid gloves off and so on, there would be far more outcries against it than there have been.

As it is, of the twenty-seven reviews my editor has sent me thus far, only one is negative, stating that I didn't treat science right. But twenty-six to one—I never expected that. And it's been on the *New York Times* extended best-seller list for eight weeks, and *Publisher's Weekly,* and the *San Francisco Chronicle* Bay Area best-seller list. None of my other books ever came close to this. Of course, over forty-three years, *The World's Religions* has topped 2.5 million, but in no single year did I come close. This is one of the reasons I feel very encouraged.

Gazdayka: You make a clear distinction between religion and spirituality.

Smith: I've gotten a little flack on that. The fear I have is that spirituality is trumping religion and is therefore indirectly replacing our confidence in religion with a confidence in spirituality. I think there is a place for both. Certainly in the popular New Age mind, the pendulum has swung toward spirituality. And one can see why. In my last years of teaching, I never met a student who didn't feel they had a spiritual side to them. *Spirituality* is a good word on campus; *religion* is not. When I would ask students why *religion* is not a good word too, they would say first, because religion is dogmatic: "We've

got the truth, and the rest of you are going to hell in a wheelbar-
row." Second, it's moralistic: "Don't do this, that, and the other,
especially not the other." I used to think, well, what's the difference
between spirituality and religion? Religion is organized spirituality.
It's institutional. And as such, it inherits all the problems that
institutions—people trying to work together—manifest.

*Gazdayka: Why would you say that it's important to be organized when
Jesus had just a couple of followers, and the Buddha—*
Smith: Because if he had not been followed by St. Paul, who founded
the Christian Church, the Sermon on the Mount would have
evaporated in a single generation. As it is, we have it today—and
the same thing with Buddhism. It is the oldest institution surviving
on our planet, twenty-five hundred years and still intact. Otherwise,
the Four Noble Truths [the basic teachings of the Buddha] and the
rest of it would have evaporated with the Buddha's death. Institutions give traction, give spirituality traction in history. So we have to
take on the burden of those institutions if we're serious. Just like if
you're serious about politics, you'd better join a party. I mean, is
there a perfect political party on our planet? The whole idea! But if
you don't get in there and get your hands dirty, then you're talking
to yourself and your friends.

*Gazdayka: What has a lifetime of studying and practicing the world's great
religions given you?*
Smith: The world—and I mean that quite literally. It has given me
another world to live in, comparably better than this pigsty of a
world that threatens to come zooming in.

Richard Smoley: How would you characterize the primordial tradition?
Huston Smith: It's a synonym for the phrase used by Aldous Huxley:
the "perennial philosophy." Both phrases suggest that a common
conceptual spine underlies all of the major religions. Crucial to that
"spine" is the distinction between the fully real and what is only
partially real. "This world" and "another world"—Mircea Eliade
called them the "sacred" and "profane"—have the same connota-
tions.

All religions start with that distinction and then subdivide both
halves. "This world" divides into its visible and invisible (or material and immaterial) components. As I look at you, I can see your
bodies but not your thoughts and feelings; no one has ever seen a
thought or a feeling. Yet these are an obvious part of everyday life.

As for the other world, it subdivides into the part that we can
describe—say, as *satchitananda:* "being, consciousness, and bliss" or
whatever—and its deeper recesses that language can't track: *Nirguna Brahman* (God beyond qualities), Meister Eckhart's Godhead,

This interview first appeared as "Tradition and Truth: A Gnosis Interview with Huston Smith," by
Richard Smoley and Jay Kinney, in *Gnosis*, no. 37 (Fall 1995). Copyright © 1995 by the Luman Foundation. Reprinted by permission of Jay Kinney.

"the Tao that cannot be spoken," whatever terms are employed. Theologically that comes down to the distinction between a personal God—a God endowed by our imagination with attributes such as creativity and love, in which we share—and the infinite abyss of God that the mystics speak of, which defies conceptualization. Here all the attributes of the personal God smelt down into an ultimate unity that we cannot imagine, though it is actually the only true reality.

There's a trap in all this, though. Some esotericists who anchor their faith in the Ineffable Mystery turn the conceptual spine I just mentioned into an independent religion—which it can't be, not an adequate one, any more than a skeleton is a human being. You can't love a skeleton.

Smoley: Over the past century there has been a trend toward making esotericism a religion, starting with Madame Blavatsky and the occult revival of the nineteenth century, and continuing in some strands of the New Age movement. Where do you place this trend in religious history?

Smith: There is no way one can confine the spirit and say, "You can manifest only in these structures and not in others." People are moving toward the New Age for a variety of reasons. Some turn to it in revulsion against the sins of traditional institutions; every institution abounds in sins. Sometimes it comes from a more egoistic impulse. If you start a religion, you are automatically its head, and some people like to have followers. Finally, when history brings new issues to focus—the ecological crisis, the rights of women and minorities—it's not surprising to find new religions arising that focus on those issues. There's some virtue in that.

Personally I distinguish occultism from esotericism, and don't have much of a feel for it. It doesn't grab me the way the historical traditions do. Great White Brotherhoods, history being masterminded by a clique of masters hidden somewhere in Afghanistan, if they haven't altogether dropped their bodies—I'm not into that kind of thinking.

There's another mode of offbeat spirituality that differs both from occultism and the New Age. I'm thinking of visionaries like Emanuel Swedenborg, Rudolf Steiner, and, in a way, Jacob Boehme too. These people possessed a distinctive spiritual talent: they could actually see spiritual realities. They were spiritual savants, so to speak.

I've agreed to write a foreword to a forthcoming book, *A Thoughtful Soul*, that is said to be the best exposition of Swedenborg's position that has ever been written. I agreed to do that, not because I know Swedenborg well but because I don't and welcome the chance to learn more about him. For some reason I don't feel the same inclination to explore Rosicrucianism or Freemasonry, even though their underlying concepts are very close to those of the primordial tradition.

Jay Kinney: You say the primordial tradition polarizes the sacred and profane. I've come across some critiques of that, particularly from people who associate themselves with a Goddess religion. They seem to view that kind of polarization as patriarchal and disrespectful of the material world. And they generally describe all the great religions as being part of the oppressive institutions that are at fault in the world today. I was curious about your take on these notions, as well as on the idea of an ancient matriarchy that preceded the patriarchy, and an ancient Goddess religion.

Smith: Your question has several parts. One is the notion of hierarchy, which is tagged to patriarchy. I consider the indiscriminate, *unnuanced* attack on hierarchies to be one of the most destructive moves that is abroad today; it has all but wrecked a once-noble word. The notion that hierarchies as such—all hierarchies—are oppressive is simplistic, misguided, and flatly untrue. We live in a hierarchical universe, in which gradations of size, power, and complexity confront us at every turn. In addition, the social world, animal as well as human, couldn't last a week without chains of command that are honored.

Besides, hierarchies can be empowering as well as oppressive. A loving family with small children is an empowering hierarchy, as is a well-run classroom. Beyond and above these stands the archetype of a benevolent, empowering hierarchy: God's relation to the world. Without hierarchies of worth we have nothing to look up to, no worthy role models, and nihilism results. Nothing is better than anything else, and anything goes.

As for patriarchy, prehistory is prehistory. That matriarchy preceded patriarchy remains a dubious claim, though there may have been pockets here and there. It may be a necessary myth for our time, but the factual basis is shaky.

There has been oppression; women have plenty of grounds for complaint. But I think we do better to stick to specifics—the concrete injustices that need to be corrected—and not wander into generalizations that weaken the case by being only partially true.

To cite the case I'm closest to: I happen to believe that, gender relationships to one side, the view of ultimate reality put forward by the traditional religions is more accurate than any that modernity has devised. But because that view took shape in a patriarchal age—and as I said, whether there have been ages of any other kind remains open to question—the traditional view gets tarred with the patriarchal brush. It is thrown into question, not because it is untrue, but because it was primarily men who gave voice to it. The question of its truth gets second billing.

Kinney: Traditionalism is a category associated with people like René Guénon, Frithjof Schuon, and Martin Lings. Do you pretty much agree with their perspective?

Smith: I do, and there's one point that needs to be stressed here. I, we, hold that the esoteric is more profound than the exoteric; however, it is not more salvific. That is, you can reach the goal just as well if you're an exoteric as an esoteric—if you're a good one. Therefore I would hold no spiritual advantage over an exoteric who was radically against the idea of universal salvation. People who think theirs is the only truth can be saved as readily as those who think otherwise.

On the other hand, if anybody says that the philosophies of the modern world—Hegel or Kant or Descartes or Marx or Freud or Darwin—have a better take on the nature of things than the traditional religious, why, I'm not going to accept that view at all. I'm going to debate it and critique it.

Smoley: Traditionalists like Guénon seem very pessimistic about the modern world. Do you agree with that position?

Smith: Not altogether. It's too one-sided. Actually, when I first came upon Guénon's *Reign of Quantity and the Signs of the Times,* I didn't finish it, because although he was making a very insightful critique of modernity, his tone was so uncompromisingly negative that I put the book down. Only later, after I came upon the more moderate statements of Schuon and Lings and Coomaraswamy—Ling's book *The Eleventh Hour* deals entirely with hopeful signs today—did I go back to Guénon.

Frankly, people's talents differ, and I have no talent for prediction. I don't have a futurist gene in me. What impresses me is how much the inward remains the same, whatever the historical period. That's where the real battle, the great jihad, as Muslims say, lies. It's the personal, private, internal issues that preoccupy me, and on that front it is always the best of times and the worst of times.

The worst of times today relates to our mounting ecological crises and the greater capacity for destruction that technology has given us. It's one thing to use a club for revenge and quite another to demolish a federal building with a homemade bomb. The best of times today relates to our new sensitivity to the rights of minorities. We have a long way to go, but in the early part of our century the Brooklyn Zoo exhibited an African behind bars like a gorilla. That could never happen today.

Kinney: You spoke of salvation earlier. Some of the great religions speak of salvation as going to heaven rather than to hell. Others speak of reincarnation and getting off the cycle of rebirth. Is there a primordial notion of salvation?

Smith: Yes. There's a common theme that underlies the variations. It's that the death of the body is not the end of consciousness, and that this consciousness can eventually attain beatitude.

The variations on this theme have to do with whether consciousness reincarnates on this plane to complete its agenda or accomplishes this work on other metaphysical planes—*bardos,* as the Tibetans call them. I don't take sides on that. It's even possible that if you believe in reincarnation, it will occur; otherwise not. That's a bit lighthearted, but what follows death is the final mystery. There's plenty of room for speculation.

Smoley: What interests you in the American spiritual scene now?

Smith: There's the whole New Age business and the paradigm shifts in science. I don't myself see any evidence that scientism is on the wane; anyone who thinks it is should read Bryan Appleyard's *Understanding the Present.* Appleyard is not a religious man himself; for twenty years he was science and philosophy columnist for the *London Times.* Even so, he sees science as colonizing the entire world, including its religions. It's the new colonialism. Taking off from Spinoza's insight that everything tends to enlarge its domain unless it bumps into something that stops it, he sees nothing strong enough to stop science, so its hegemony keeps expanding.

Kinney: I wonder if the Khomeini phenomenon isn't in fact the secular and scientistic perspective running into the brick wall of Islamic traditionalism.

Smith: Good point. I think the deepest cause of fundamentalism—Islamic or Christian—is the vulnerability its adherents feel. Fundamentalists see their traditional religious values threatened by scientistic, humanistic secularism. Of course their ways of reacting can be very unbecoming and very scary.

At the same time I think liberals shouldn't dismiss fundamentalists as simply fanatics and bigots. The climate of modernity and postmodernity is excessively naturalistic and scientistic, and liberal intellectuals have played a part in making it so. One enormity has given rise to another.

Kinney: Do you think there is some way out, some reconciliation possible?

Smith: This philosophical side of my work, summarized in the collection of my essays titled *Beyond the Post-Modern Mind,* has been devoted to precisely that end, to showing how the modern outlook, fueled by science as a privileged way of knowing, has created an abnormal condition for the human spirit.

Science is not a neutral methodology, now, as it is too often taken to be, the right way to get at truth. It is a very specific probe into the nature of things. In terms of our capacity to control the material world, it succeeds brilliantly. But at the same time it is a very narrow approach. It can't connect at all with the things that concern religion, like values, meaning, or beings that are superior to us, if such beings exist. Those things slip through science in the way water slips through the nets of fishermen.

I think we've made a start toward understanding this. The change from modernism to postmodernism involves realizing that science cannot give us the full picture, or a *metanarrative,* to use a word the postmodernists like. It's to the credit of postmodernists that they see this, but they make their own mistake. From the fact that science can't give us the big picture, moderate postmoderns conclude that no reliable worldview is possible. The extremists add that this is fortunate, because worldviews, by their very nature, oppress. Both these versions are only half-truths.

Smoley: The "new paradigms" often seem very obsequious toward science. Even the human potential movement seems to be trying to enlist scientism to prove its own validity. How do you see the whole "new paradigm" vision and its relation to science?

Smith: I find it a mixed bag. On the one hand, it *is* obsequious toward science. It assumes that science has the truth, so humanists had better scrounge from it such crumbs as they can find.

Even so, some scientific findings are suggestive for our thoughts about the human spirit. For example, the shift from discrete atomism to field theory seems to support a sense of greater interrelation. Second, the demise of Laplacian determinism leaves more room for human freedom. Also the etherealization of matter opens the door for the possibility that it may ultimately phase into spirit.

Having admitted these points, though, I want to retreat to a note of caution. It's a mistake to think we can prove spiritual truths by science, because science can't speak to the things that concern religion. Also, if we lean too hard on science, that very leaning will imply that we think it has the last word on truth. That puts us on the defensive again.

Smoley: Educated people today feel obliged to pay lip service to scientific cosmology, to believe in the Big Bang, for instance. Is this a mistake?

Smith: Not in itself. The issue isn't how the physical universe evolved in the way a cosmic videotape might have recorded it; the issue is the place of consciousness in the scheme of things. In the traditional view, consciousness is the inclusive sea, and matter appears as an island within it. Matter is like a tiny iceberg in consciousness's unlimited expanse, a chunk of frozen consciousness, we might say.

The scientific picture reverses the relationship. Matter—15 billion light years across—becomes the inclusive sea, and consciousness is reduced to a tiny speck within it. I think the traditional view is closer to the way things actually are than the scientific view, but there's no way to prove that. All we can say is that "absence of evidence isn't evidence of absence," as Stephen Jay Gould remarked in another context. Science doesn't find consciousness outside of organisms on our planet, but that doesn't prove it's not out there. Scientific instruments don't register consciousness anywhere, not even in us.

As for the sequence in which the physical universe evolved, I see no reasons to question the Big Bang, as long as we are mindful of how quickly scientific scenarios can change. Allan Wallace's book *Choosing Reality* points out that there are currently twelve interpretations of quantum physics, all of which lay equal claim to proven facts.

What interests me is the analogies between the primordial traditions and scientific findings that are currently coming to light. To mention only two, both say that things are more integrated than we normally suppose and that for the finite human mind, paradox has the last word. It's both interesting and encouraging to find metaphysical claims surfacing in science's backyard, but I would never try to tie a metaphysical claim too tightly to a scientific finding, because science can't consider things as a whole. Strictly speaking, a scientific worldview is a contradiction in terms. The most it can give us is an exquisitely detailed and exact picture of the *physical* part of the world.

Kinney: What do you make of Matthew Fox's Creation Spirituality?
Smith: Oh, I don't know. I find more of his views based in traditional Christianity than he does, so his message doesn't sound as new to me as it does to many people. I think he's wonderful on St.

Thomas; I think he's terrible on St. Augustine. I think his Rave Mass is an attempt to quicken the spirit by somewhat artificial means, rather than going to the cognitive ontological truth and letting it surface into experience. We're of different temperaments, on different wavelengths.

Smoley: You mentioned the proliferation of Eastern religions in America. Certain thinkers, like Jung, said that Westerners aren't geared for Eastern approaches; their psyches are quite different. Do you agree?

Smith: No. Oh, they might be mismatched here and there, but as a generalization I don't subscribe to it. Jung was unduly influenced by his friend Richard Wilhelm, the great Swiss sinologist, whose translation of the *I Ching* remains the standard one in English. During his career in China, Wilhelm was idolized for his erudition. But when he retired to Switzerland, he found that no one gave a hoot for China or for his remarkable understanding of it, and he became severely depressed. Jung generalized excessively from Wilhelm's case and seems to have overlooked that reason for his friend's depression.

Sure, there are dangers, but I think that the way in which the Asian traditions are moving in and taking hold in the West is evidence against Jung's theory. It's an overgeneralization.

Smoley: Do you think Buddhism will take root permanently in America?

Smith: I've already declined the role of a futurist, but in this case the signs are pretty clear that it will take hold. For one thing, the Asian population in the United States is increasing, and its background is largely Buddhist. Last year the Buddhists in California overtook the Episcopalians in number.

Smoley: Yet in San Francisco, for example, a lot of the most devout Christians seem to be Chinese, whereas a lot of the most devout Buddhists are middle-class whites.

Kinney: Someone told me that comparative religion is in the doldrums academically. Does it seem that way to you?

Smith: In theological seminaries, yes, but not in colleges and universities; there comparative religion is holding its own both in appoint-

ments and in number of courses taught. But perhaps your inform-
ant was thinking not of numbers but about the quality of teaching.
There he could be right.

There are two sides to the picture. In scholarship, the quality in
the study of other religions has risen and is still increasing. I'm
referring here to the number of teachers who know the languages of
the religions they teach and have mastered the tools of anthropological and historical research. But this means that they have, for the
most part, adopted the methodologies of the social sciences, which
are more interested in objective facts than in what the religions
mean to their adherents. Why, other than habit and social conven-
tion, do those adherents believe what their religions teach? What
difference does it make to their lives that they believe? Too many
teachers of religion accept the academic shibboleth that those
questions are too subjective to be objectively dealt with.

As for the question of whether what religions teach is true, that
tends to be avoided on principle. The assumption—which I'm
convinced is mistaken—is that that question leads to proselytizing.
The prevailing method in religious studies is phenomenology,
which systematically brackets the question of the ontological truth
of beliefs.

Off campus, this practice of concentrating on the objective and
visible externals of religion—its shells rather than the kernels they
protect—plays directly into the hands of the media, for that's what
can be photographed for the nightly news. And because the media
batten on atrocities, the sins of religion—religious terrorists,
Jonestown, Waco—get more billing than its virtues. The primary
work of religion occurs in the depths of the human heart: that's
where the switches of aspiration and hope are flipped. But it's
impossible to look into someone else's heart, much less photograph
what's there.

CHAPTER 14 | **COUNTERING**
SCIENTISM
By Marsha Newman

In every conscious attempt at either personal or social transformation, we need to begin by taking a clear, critical look at where we stand, and how we got there. Personally or collectively, this quest is affected by the assumptions of our times, which being constantly with us, are as little noticed as glasses in our field of vision. The life and work of Huston Smith, world-renowned philosopher, author, teacher, lecturer, and filmmaker, have been devoted to illuminating the buried assumptions of modernity to reveal errors that have drained our lives of meaning, releasing the "magic" from what Max Weber called "the enchanted garden" of earlier worlds.

Born and raised in China by missionary parents, Huston Smith has had the unusual opportunity, as an American, to look at the Western world from the outside. The contrasting picture Asia afforded has enabled him to see in sharper outline what to many of us is a myopic blur: that the Newtonian worldview—discarded by science but alive and well in the public imagination—is a wasteland for the human spirit. "I think

Originally titled "Huston Smith: Mediator of a 'New' Worldview," this essay by freelance writer and English teacher Marsha Newman serves as an exemplary overview of the life and work of Huston Smith. It is based on an interview with him that appeared in *New Realities* magazine (July–August 1988). Reprinted by permission of Marsha Newman.

it's a question," says Smith, "of whether matter, as understood by common sense and even the advanced, exact sciences, provides the wherewithal for a meaningful life."

At a time when there are an increasing number of conflicting voices prophesying both the end of the world and the beginning of a new utopian age, Smith, who refuses to wear the robes of prophet, watches thoughtfully from the sidelines. "I find myself," he explained in a recent interview with *New Realities*, "besieged on the one hand by the Cassandras and Jeremiahs who think we're about to go down the drain with Rome tomorrow, and on the other by the New Age prophets who talk as though the gates of paradise are about to open for two-way traffic any day now. I'm prepared to hold their coats and let them fight it out."

Yet it's clear that Smith thinks the issue is important, for he has poured enormous effort into looking deeply at what has brought us to this point of polarization. Through many of his writings, and particularly in the trilogy *The Religions of Man* [reissued as *The World's Religions*], *Forgotten Truth*, and *Beyond the Post-Modern Mind*, he has chronicled the progressive encroachment of what he has called "modernity," a mind-set framed by the Newtonian worldview, which virtually reduces reality to that which is perceivable. It is in the attempt to apply the methodology of science to realms of knowledge not accessible to the five senses that the modern age has, knowingly or not, all but succeeded in eliminating the transcendent from our worldview.

As a leading thinker of our times, Smith has upheld with exceptional rigor the minority view that the methodology of science, which relies upon prediction and control, is both misleading and destructive when applied to metaphysics. According to Smith, "The Western hunt for knowledge, analytic and objective to its core, has violence built into it. For to know analytically is to reduce the object of knowledge, however vital, however complex, to precisely this: an object." Science, operating out of its place, he asserts, turns demonic, like an angel that has fallen.

"It presumes to control too much and to disclose more of reality than, in fact, it does. To approach existence as if it were purely or even primarily physical and mathematical is to falsify it. The approach could end in smashing our planet, for if a hammer is the only tool one learns to use, it is tempting to regard everything as if it were a nail."

Smith affirms not only the existence of the transcendent, but the vital need for us to return to a worldview that upholds spiritual realities, for if we rely upon science to give us meaning, we can only despair at its inability to do so. "Strictly speaking," he says, "a scientific worldview is impossible; it is a contradiction in terms. The reason is that science does not treat of the world; it treats of a part of it only."

Yet Smith is no enemy of science. He is rather a seer with exceptional powers of discrimination who distinguishes between pure science and that muddle of science and metaphysics he calls "scientism." In *Forgotten Truth* he says, "With science itself there can be no quarrel. Scientism is another matter. Whereas science is positive, contenting itself with reporting what it discovers, scientism is negative. It goes beyond the actual findings of science to deny that other approaches to knowledge are valid and other truths are true. In doing so, it deserts science in favor of metaphysics—bad metaphysics, as it happens, for as the contention that there are no truths save those of science is not itself a scientific truth, in affirming it scientism contradicts itself." The real problem is that, unthinkingly, we do not attempt to see the difference.

One catastrophic result he sees of our presently truncated view of reality is that the transition from "tradition" to "modernity" has "impoverished our sense of what the world includes and what it means to be fully human. . . . We have lost our grip on the innate immensity of our true nature."

Should anyone protest that the churches are properly the custodians of the transcendent, Smith responds, "The mainline churches have a real problem on their hands. Bluntly stated, it is atheism." The churches, he explains, through their seminaries that ring the universities, have come under the influence of academia, which is dominated by the objectivizing scientific method. "The theological seminaries," he says, "feel the pull of this modern, reductionist worldview."

Nevertheless, despite this suffusion of scientific worldview into Western churches, and despite Vatican II's urging that scientific views be accepted along with religious ones, science and religion remain fiercely polarized on this issue of human origin. And nothing so profoundly affects how we see ourselves as how we see our beginnings.

As Smith describes it: "On the one hand, there is the view preached in our churches and synagogues according to which we are the less who have derived from the More; we are creatures created by God, who exceeds us by every standard of worth we possess. Concomitantly, our schools teach that we are the More who have derived from the less: we are organisms that have evolved out of inert matter through the play of mechanistic principle (natural selection) on chance mutations—from slime we have ascended to intelligence. There is no way to reconcile these opposing aetiologies, yet every denizen of the modern West schizophrenically believes parts of both of them. . . . The eclipse of transcendence has placed the evolutionary account alongside our fading theological account and confused us as to who we are. It has produced an identity crisis."

And it is an insidious one at that, since many of us do not recognize this schizophrenia in ourselves or our times. Yes we presently live in what has been called the Age of Anxiety, and Smith, feeling the pulse of the times, looks beyond symptoms to find the prime cause. It is not a simple matter of creationists, who take the Great Origins theory at its most literal level, versus the evolutionists, who accept without examination what Darwinians assert.

According to Smith, "An age comes to a close when people discover they can no longer understand themselves by the theory their age professes. For a while its denizens will continue to think that they believe it, but they feel otherwise and cannot understand their feelings. This has now happened to us. We continue to believe Darwinism, even though it no longer feels right to us. Darwinism is, in fact, dying, and its death signals the close of our age." Darwinism works fairly well as a description of an evolutionary process (what has happened), Smith says, but not as an explanation for why it happened.

He quotes Darwin himself as saying, "Geology . . . does not reveal . . . finely graded organic change, and this, perhaps, is the most obvious and gravest objection that can be urged against my theory." Evidence of evolutionary development is still missing, Smith notes, quoting David Kitts, professor of geology at the University of Oklahoma: "Evolution requires intermediate forms between species and paleontology does not provide them." Smith's point has been to show, as he says, "how little (in the way of hard evidence) has been allowed to eclipse so much (the Great Origins principle)"; and to assert that the Great Origins theory, the idea that man has emerged from a higher source, is inherently superior because, like the great myths of the world, it meets the fundamental human need to sense oneself as grounded in the cosmos and thereby oriented.

One antidote Smith sees to the effects of scientism and Darwinism is a return to what he calls the "primordial tradition." This "primordial tradition," like the Great Origins principle, restores to our worldview the critically missing element—a transcendent philosophy that allows us to see ourselves as part of a hierarchical order, restoring a sense of both worth and place in the universe. It is a universal philosophy that has infused the cultural traditions and belief systems of all times and all ages; it is thus a universally human perception, but one that has been lost—overshadowed by the great drama of scientific discovery. The main principles of this philosophy are that there is a divine origin for everything in the universe and, therefore, the divine order—and not mere mechanical causation—informs all being. In such a universe we find both meaning and value.

Smith believes the world to be in a state of transition at this time and sees a need for it to move from a polarized to a unified field of thought; from a three-dimensional perception to one that includes both dimensionality and spirituality. To do so would require a movement from a literal, reductionist trend of thinking to a more comprehensive view in which science has an important place but is not presumed to speak for the whole.

A key to this transformation, the return to the primordial tradition, lies in rekindling our capacity to see symbolically. "Symbolism," Smith says, "is the science of the multiple levels of reality. It is the science of seeing how something on one level, here in the material, sensible plane, actually transports our minds to a reality which is on a higher level. . . . Equally one could say that it is an opening on the sensible plane for the supersensible to enter into and infuse it. . . . To say that this mode of seeing is important is an understatement. It's the lifeline."

One way this transcendence is reachable is by means of art. Although in many respects art has flattened into a one-dimensional reflection of a one-dimensional world, it has the potential to take us beyond the limits of this prison. "All sacred art," Smith says, "is symbolic because it is not sacred unless it does transport the mind and heart to a higher level of reality."

What Smith calls this "one empirical contribution" to the history of religions is also a significant contribution to the world of art. A chance meeting with a Tibetan lama on a bus in India led to his admittance to a four-day *puja,* or worship ceremony, at the Gyutu Monastery near Dalhousie. There, much to his surprise, and the world's, he discovered a form of spiritual chanting that seemed impossible: amid much group chanting, occasionally a single lama would sing alone, not single tones, but chords! In an article recording this find, Smith notes, "He was singing, by himself, a three-tone major chord: a first, a third, and faintly audible fifth."

In another article co-authored by Smith for the *Journal of the Acoustical Society of America,* the symbolic significance of this chanting is explained. "The chord-like effects appeared when the words came to the holiest mantra (sacred syllables) of Tibetan Buddhism: *Aum Mani Padme Hum. . . .*"

Smith believes it is the overtones of these mantras that evoke deep feeling, sung in this special way. [Overtones, in a musical context, are acoustical frequencies that are higher in frequency than—while simultaneously produced with—the fundamental frequency or pitch being sounded.] "Overtones awaken deep feelings because, sensed without being explicitly heard, they parallel in man's hearing the relation in which the sacred stands to his life. The object of the lama's quest is to amplify life's 'overtones' that hint of a 'more' that can be sensed but not seen; sensed but not said; heard, but not explicitly. . . . The lama's chords place, as it were, a magnifying glass over the aural symbolism imbedded in the *Aum Hum* mantra. . . ."

Smith also thinks that it is natural at this time for the West to be looking toward the East to find a philosophy that "transports," since the mainline Western churches have become overly rational and moralistic. "We live in a Westernizing world, but there is a cultural lag; so Asia isn't yet as scientist as our Western styles of thought have become."

Smith and his wife, Kendra, have conducted several year-long academic trips around the world, studying civilizations on location. "Almost invariably," he says, "when we asked the students at the end of the year what country meant the most to them, they would name India, even though they got sick, and many had severe culture shock. . . . Why does India mean so much to people, even with all its poverty, squalor, and destitution? When people ask me for the secret of the magic it works, I find myself answering, 'It's a land where the name of God still floats in the air. Spirituality, one can still breathe there.' "

In a country where the name of God is all but excluded from the classroom, Smith has little hope that education can respond to our need for the sacred in our lives so long as the Newtonian worldview prevails at the popular level. His work *Beyond the Post-Modern Mind* examines this problem and potential. "In a university setting," he says, "any move to reinstate the enchanted garden will naturally be met by the question, 'How do you know it is enchanted?' If we answer that we experience it so, that we find ourselves ravished by its mystery and washed by its beauty and presences—not always, of course, but enough to sustain conviction—we shall be told that this is not to know, it is merely to feel. This crude response requires of us a choice."

The choice is either "to blow the whistle at once on this cramped and positivistic definition of knowledge" or to "let this restriction of knowledge to what-can-be-proved stand," but only as a foundation for insight that can discern spiritual realities. "What we must never, never do is make proof our master. . . . Even physicists, if they be great ones, see (as Richard Feynman pointed out in his Nobel lecture) that 'a very great deal more truth can become known than can be proven.' "

Yet this is not a call to abandon thought for feeling, Smith insists. "At this higher altitude the mind is, if anything, more alive than before. In supreme instances the muses take over and our minds go on 'automatic pilot,' that inspired, ecstatic state Plato called 'the higher madness.' We cannot here track them to those heights where myth and poetry conspire with revelation and remembrance, science joining them at those times when hunches strike terror in the heart, so fine is the line between inspired madness and the kind that disintegrates."

Even below the ecstatic level, there are suggestions, if not proofs, that if we were to approach it right, we would still find our "garden" enchanted. Interestingly enough, many of these hints come from science itself. Smith argues, "That reality has turned out to be quantitatively more extravagant than we had supposed suggests that its qualitative features may be equally beyond our usual suppositions. If the universe is spatially unbounded, perhaps it is limitless in worth as well." Smith places some hope in the new physics to pry us out of mechanistic materialism, for "it is the first of the empirical sciences to see through its subject to a glimmering beyond. It knows the derivative character of space and time; the unimaginably transcendent character of the real."

He also points to the unification of nature that science is discovering: "Matter and energy are one. Time and space are one—time being space's fourth dimension. Space and gravity are one: the latter is simply space's curvature. And, in the end, matter and its space-time field are one. . . . If we could be taken backstage to the spiritual recesses of reality, might we not find harmony hidden there as well—Earth joined to heaven, man walking with God?"

Many, including Smith, are feeling hopeful that the new physics will ultimately unlock the prison that scientism has created. "The Cartesian-Newtonian paradigm will not work for quantum physics. It's going to be very difficult to fashion an alternative, for the new physics is so strange that we may never be able to visualize it or describe it consistently in ordinary language. But this in itself is exciting." He cites the work of physicist David Bohm, whose idea of "the implicate order" identifies a different dimension of reality entirely, consistent with Bell's theorem and Karl Pribram's holographic model of mind.

Smith invited Bohm to Syracuse University for a few weeks while he was teaching there. All its physics professors had cut their teeth on quantum mechanics through Bohm's textbook and turned out in full for his first lecture, but were disappointed by what sounded to them more like philosophy than science. Smith finds it encouraging that science and philosophy are overlapping more and more, but sees a danger of lay[people] becoming confused or drawing hasty conclusions. "We must be careful here," Smith says in *Beyond the Post-Modern Mind,* "for science cannot take a single step toward *proving* transcendence. But what it proves in its own domain in the way of unity, inter-relatedness, the 'immaterial,' and the awesome makes it one of the most powerful symbols of transcendence our age affords."

It is exactly this ability to see objective facts as symbols that distinguishes the mystic, and it is because Bohm has this gift that Smith sees him as a mystic, one 'for whom almost anything can be symbol of the divine.'" Smith's most recent work has been preparation for a book on spiritual personality types, part of his effort to establish a coherent "middle ground" between extremist views.

"My New Age friends," he says, "often talk as if the human species is about to mutate. In a generation or so, everyone will be a mystic." But Smith's thesis is that "corresponding to the four levels of reality in *Forgotten Truth*—terrestrial, intermediate, celestial, and infinite—there are four personality types. . . . It comes down to the depth of the metaphysical vision of the person in question. There is no question of the representatives of one type being better persons than those of another type. It's just that people differ as much in metaphysical talent as they do in mathematical or musical ability."

To describe the differences in the human capacity to fathom the four levels of reality, Smith uses the analogy of one-way mirrors. Looking up, the materialist sees a mirror that reflects back to him his material world. Meanwhile, the polytheist, looking down from the next level up, which includes spiritual beings, sees the mirror as plate glass. Everything the materialist sees, the polytheist sees too, with other things added. On the third level, the spirits of polytheism coalesce in or under the Great Spirit—the God of monotheism. Finally, the monotheistic God gives way to the ineffable Infinite, the indescribable, unfathomable mystery, the Godhead of the mystics. The principle of one-way mirrors pertains throughout: from upper levels, the mirrors transform to window glass. What lies below remains in full view.

The way this scheme fits Smith's argument is by now clear: science, operating by a methodology that fits level one, cannot make statements about the other three realms. But this would not prevent a scientist, like Bohm, from knowing higher realms through means other than those of empirical science. Individuals can, in principle, outgrow their current spiritual type, but Smith doesn't think it is easy to do so. To illustrate what he means, he tells the following anecdote:

An interesting experiment was done on a colony of ants, and the scientist watching these ants day after day got to know and tag them all as individuals. He found that half of the colony worked harder than the other half. Half of them were industrious; the others loafed on their oars. So he decided to separate the two groups. What do you suppose happened? Half the industrious ones got lazy, and half of the lazy ones pulled up their socks and began to pitch in. Perhaps this suggests that there may never be a time when everyone is a mystic. Perhaps it takes—will always take—all kinds to make a world.

We cannot live without hope, and a worldview that excludes hope is not humanly viable. Smith's primary goal has been to restore hope for ourselves and for our future—not for the pragmatic reason that we need that hope, he insists, but because a hope-offering world is the world we actually have, could we but see it to its full extent.

For that extent to become visible, he says, we need to stop limiting truth to what science tells us and listen more seriously to the testimony of the world's great wisdom traditions. The new worldview toward which Smith points the way is simply a return to a primordial awareness of a living, meaningful, unlimited universe.

Phil Cousineau: How did your experience at the World Parliament of Religions in Cape Town, South Africa, in 1999, influence you? Are you any more optimistic about the future of religion than you were before?

Huston Smith: Cape Town exceeded my expectations. What were there—seven thousand people? This pilgrimage, a journey not for quantity, but for quality, and with the most important objective— the most important objective—peace and justice. For that many people to come together, during this time of terrible ethnic conflict, was a statement to the world that conflict is *not* the bottom line of religion. It's people working together; that's its real payoff. The conveners of the parliament were brilliant in where they located it. If there is a geographical symbol of oppression in the world it is Cape Town. To place it there underscores the leading social problem of our time, which is injustice. Then to have it climaxed by having Nelson Mandela giving one of the most moving addresses I have

This interview with editor Phil Cousineau is an excerpt from the documentary film *America's Shadow Struggle: The Native American Fight for Religious Freedom*. It took place in October 2001 at Huston Smith's home in Berkeley, California. Copyright © 2003 by Kifaru Productions. Reprinted by permission of Kifaru Productions.

ever heard, in which he said, "There can be no future without forgiveness"—it all came together to make it an unforgettable event.

Cousineau: I know you have limited patience with conventions and conferences. But would you like to speculate on the idea of a Religious Olympics? In many ancient Greek athletic festivals, the athletic competition was complemented by competitions in poetry, drama, and dance. Maybe someday it will be possible to have spiritual leaders meet for inspired talks about the spiritual life. Could it make a difference?

Smith: Well, a Spiritual Olympics is a new idea to me. But why not? If the participants came forward with not only their basic beliefs but reports on how they put their faiths into action it could accomplish something and would move things beyond one more gathering in which people just talked.

Cousineau: We've worked together on several documentary film projects about Native American issues, so I am interested in your transition from the great historical religions to what Jamake Highwater calls the "primal religions." When the Onondaga spiritual leader Oren Lyons introduced you to the ways of his people, did it produce a kind of epiphany—a moment when the truth about the power of the primal religions "shone through," which is the very definition of epiphany?

Smith: It did. In retrospect, it almost feels as if the hidden, secret reason for my decision to move to Syracuse for the last decade of my formal teaching was to add the entire dimension of the indigenous religions to my knowledge of the subject. I fault my teachers for causing me to ignore the indigenous religions before Syracuse. A half-century ago the university was still under the delusion of historical progress, in which early peoples are primitive and basically unenlightened. After all, they didn't even have writing, so what could they know?

My Syracuse decade demolished that delusion completely. The first step was to discover that the Onondaga Reservation was only five miles from the house and we bought. Well, interesting, so one Saturday afternoon we drove through it. That piqued my curiosity, so a couple of Saturdays later I went back by myself hoping to strike up some conversations. This proved easy to do—I found them less pressured than we whites and remarkably hospitable. So I kept going back, and with each visit my admiration mounted until by the time we moved to Berkeley I knew that the wisdom of their spiritual traditions was fully the equal of that of the historical traditions I had devoted my career to.

There was a specific moment when this realization broke over me like a thunderclap. I was driving home after spending a day with Oren Lyons and Chief Shenandoah when I suddenly found myself exclaiming out loud as if the voice were coming from another source, "Huston, for thirty years you've been girdling the globe trying to learn from other cultures and here's one that's been under your feet all these years, and you haven't given it the time of day."

Shall I continue?

Cousineau: Please.

Smith: So many memories, but I'll confine myself to two. One day Oren Lyons informed me that the next weekend there would be a gathering of the chiefs of the Iroquois nations who meet annually in the Onondaga Long House—"and I would like you to meet them." Needless to say, I jumped at the chance, and it lived up to my expectations. It was a lovely moment. We were chatting comfortably when Oren said, "Well, it's eleven o'clock. It's time to begin." Then looking me square in the eye, he said, "Huston, that means we are going into the Long House and *you are not*. We know you are a loyal friend, but the story of Handsome Lake is sacred to us, and we will be rehearsing it in our sanctuary. So it's not a time for profane spectators."

What I still find amazing is that I didn't feel at all rejected. Instead, I felt this surge of exaltation rising and coursing through me. The reason was immediately clear to me. It was just thrilling to me to discover that there are still people on our planet who think that there are things that are so sacred that they would be profaned by the presence of outsiders.

My other anecdote comes from something called the Youth Seminar, an ecumenical project in which one hundred college students from all the major religions pilgrimaged together for a summer to visit the world's great religious shrines. I was an advisor to that project and proposed that before they took off for the world, it would be appropriate to follow up their orientation session in upstate New York. The first of the religions they honored would be that of the Native Americans as representative of the indigenous religions of the world. The proposal was accepted, and I caravanned with three carloads of Onondagans—most of them college age—to the appointed site. When it came time to present their religion, their leader said, "We want to offer a prayer for the hopes of the seminar. I will say it in my own native language."

There followed a forty-five-minute prayer. The young man who offered it didn't close his eyes. To the contrary, he kept looking actively around in all directions, up and down, even turning around so as not to overlook what was behind him. Finally, he turned to his audience and returning to English, said, "Have you any questions about our religion?"

Not surprisingly, the first one was about what he said in his prayer. His answer was that in his religion everything is alive—they had no distinction between animate and inanimate. So by name he was calling on the spirits of the things around them to ask their blessings to the seminar that was then beginning. I found that to be immensely powerful.

Cousineau: Were your experiences with Native Americans instrumental in your decision to revise The Religions of Man?

Smith: The only religions I had dealt with until then were historical religions, which have sacred texts and recorded histories. But even together they are only the tip of the iceberg. The primal, oral religions are forty or fifty thousand years old. To omit them is even conceptually inexcusable, provincial, and narrow-minded. So when I stumbled onto the Native Americans I knew I had to fill that gap in *The World's Religions.* I added a chapter that did that, and I am so glad I will not go to my grave with that baseline of religion not covered.

Cousineau: Is there something about the primal religions that is uniquely important?

Smith: Yes, there are several, but if I were to single out one it would be that they never fell for the idea of historical progress which has been "the bitch goddess" of the modern West, with its simplistic notion that later is better. I heard a stand-up comic spoof our addiction to this idea by saying that he liked even his antiques to be of the latest genre. If anything, primal peoples reverse that notion—what's closest to the Source is better.

That's why tribal people tend to give a place of pride to animals over human beings—they are closer to the Source. Can you imagine Darwinians believing that? I, by contrast, think it makes a lot of sense. On the human level, primal people never lose sight of what is important, whereas, inundated as we are by the avalanche of information, we do lose sight of it. Primal peoples are ignorant of many things we know, but they are seldom stupid.

Cousineau: You may recall that the futurist and novelist H. G. Wells, at the turn of the nineteenth century, remarked, "History is a race between education and catastrophe." Those words seem to loom truer and truer as we move on down the log flume of time. I thought of them when I read your book Why Religion Matters. *I was struck by the tone and timbre of your latest book. It reads like a bold manifesto. But I was also struck by the parallels between that work and one of the last books by our old friend, the mythologist Joseph Campbell. The story goes that when Joe went out on book tour in the mid-eighties he was confronted time and time again by questions such as, "Mr. Campbell, why have you wasted your life writing about lies?" By the time he reached the end of the tour he was fed up with the level of intelligence of the average radio interviewer, and he told me, "I have been writing for fifty years trying to convey the fact that there is primal truth in myth." Moreover, he was so disturbed by this ongoing cultural misunderstanding about the truth of myth that he halted work on his* Historical Atlas *to write a book about the power of metaphor and the symbolic life, which he called* The Inner Reaches of Outer Space. *With this in mind, were you infused with something like Campbell's urge to write an apologia for mythology when you wrote* Why Religion Matters?

Smith: In part I was. Let me put it this way. Worlds weren't made for one another, so you can't map one onto the others without distortions. Take physics. It gives us three worlds—the microworld of quantum mechanics, the macroworld of everyday experience, and the megaworld of the astronomers and relativity theory. Human languages arose to deal with our everyday experience, where it works pretty well, but it breaks down fast if we try to use it to describe the quantum and relativity worlds. We run into paradoxes at every turn. The standard example in quantum mechanics is the double-slit experiment. Fire a photon at a shield with two slits in it, and it goes through both slits simultaneously *without dividing.* In relativity theory consider this. Two objects are traveling in opposite directions each at almost the speed of light, yet they separate from each other at no more than the speed of light. In our everyday world, almost one plus almost one equals almost two, but not so in the world of relativity.

Here is where myth kicks in. If ordinary language is useless in trying to describe literally what goes on in the micro- and mega-worlds of physics, are we to think that it can accurately describe the transcendental world, which is at least as mysterious as they are? Physicists have to use their technical language—mathematics—to get at their esoteric worlds, and myth is the technical language by which metaphysics and religion access Transcendence. *Myth is the way to get to those worlds in religion.* There's a problem here because the word *myth* is ambiguous. On the one hand we use it to refer to what is false, as in the myth of a super-race, while on the other hand we use the word to refer to what is false if its assertions are taken literally but true when used metaphorically to point our minds toward transcendence. Plato refers to myths as "likely tales," and Reinhold Niebuhr said, "Myth is not history, it is truer than history." Joseph Campbell did our century a great service in driving home the fact that they have this second, "truer" side. If I differ from him, it is in believing that myths' claims to being truer than history are accurate, whereas Joe contented himself with arguing with great persuasiveness that it is their descriptions of transcendence that gives them power. But you wrote the book *[The Hero's Journey]* about him. Does that sound right to you?

Cousineau: Yes, yes. It reminds me of the definition of myth he enjoyed at the end of his career: "Myth is a metaphor transparent to transcendence."

He also enjoyed a little gem I shared with him that my friend the psychologist Robert A. Johnson had heard from a five-year-old boy: "Myths are lies on the outside and truths on the inside." Campbell roared with laughter when he heard that and then asked me, "Can I use that?" I think he agreed that it pointed to what is ultimately real about myth, their revelation of psychological truths. So in this way your work dovetails with his; you both spent your lives in search of what is deeply real.

Coming back to Why Religion Matters, *I know that for the last couple of decades you have become increasingly frustrated by the needless, unproductive battle between science and religion. Did you decide to use this latest book of yours to set that matter straight by pointing out the confusions that have generated it?*

Smith: That was certainly one of my aims, and I used E. O. Wilson's *Consilience* as a case study. *Consilience* is an awkward word that means "bringing things together," and in doing that job I consider it the most important wrongheaded book of the last decade or two. The sweep of its net is staggering—all the way from the Big Bang up through frontier physics, Darwinian theory, the genome project, stem cell research, and the cognitive sciences. He knows what he's talking about, and he pulls this oceanic quantity of knowledge together to give us the most complete scientific worldview that we have ever had. His mistake—the wrongheadedness of the book—is that he includes culture in his scientific worldview, arguing that what transpires in politics, ethics, art, philosophy, and religion can be explained by what the empirical sciences have discovered. This, of course, is pure reductionism—trying to explain the more from the less—and it won't work.

Wilson may be right when he goes on to say that the battle between science and religion will be the twenty-first century's struggle for the human soul, but I don't think he's right in his confidence that science is going to win that battle. I side with Albert Camus, who said that the twenty-first century will be religious—or there won't be one. Science is only the tip of history's iceberg, whereas religion goes back as far as we can see. The earliest artifacts that archaeologists have uncovered are not utilitarian instruments, like spears for hunting. They are sacred objects, which is proof positive that this religious impulse is part of human nature. We know that human nature is flawed, so religion makes mistakes, but they don't outweigh its contributions. The media attends more to its mistakes than to its contributions, so I'd just like to point out that every historian agrees that the civil rights movement of the 1960s would not have succeeded without the help of the mainline churches. Robert Bellah, a great sociologist, goes on to say that if in the 1970s it had not been for the strong protests of the mainline churches, we would have had troops in El Salvador and Guatemala helping the CIA overturn democratically elected regimes.

Another problem I have with E. O. Wilson is that I don't like the way he positions science and religion as combatants. There's a lot of combativeness going on, as each side has vested interests it wants to protect. But religion and science are the two most important forces in human history, and as A. N. Whitehead said, the future of humanity, more than on any other single factor, depends on how they settle into relationship with one another. It is my hope and a major point in *Why Religion Matters* that they can settle down as partners, each respecting its own capabilities in certain areas and recognizing its limitations in others, and agree that there are areas where it does not have competence and look on its neighbor as a partner and ally rather than an antagonist.

Actually, in my appendix to that book, I adapted the key line in Chief Seattle's greatest speech—"We could be brothers yet" and changed it to "We could be siblings yet." That is the hope of the book, but it is also a stringent book because right now the power is on the side of science in our public domain, and there's not a level playing field.

As Lord Acton said, "Power tends to corrupt and absolute power corrupts absolutely." At the start of the seventeenth century, at was the birth of modern science, the church had the power, and it did not use it very wisely, trying even to strangle the infant sciences in their cradles. Now the power has shifted to the other foot. Our secular society isn't handling that power imbalance wisely either.

One newspaper reviewer of *Why Religion Matters* picked up my voice on that point very clearly. He said, "This is a book that is going to be very easy to *mis*hear because Smith is not putting the blame on either science or scientists, as it may seem. He is placing the blame on we intellectual moderns who have misread science into thinking that because its achievements in the material sphere are so great, it must be omnipotent—that it has the tools to deal with values, meanings, and purposes also. Give it time, it can deal with *the whole of life*. That mistake is what Smith is angry about—not science in its own domain or scientists doing what they can do well."

Cousineau: Do you believe there's a link between scientific materialism and the gross materialism that appears to be running rampant in our present culture?

Smith: Yes. Because scientists are the priests of our day. Therefore we look to them whether they are talking about their own specialties or speaking about things in general.

 I've also spoken of E. O. Wilson. He pontificates about culture and religion—and he doesn't know *beans* about the latter. But because he is a great scientist his words are taken seriously by public intellectuals.

Cousineau: Authors always want their books to do well in the world, but the favorable success of Why Religion Matters *must have taken you by surprise. How does the oracle interpret its success? Does it mean that there is hope yet for the culture because your book has been on the* New York Times *best-seller list?*

Smith: You are asking if I see hope, and my answer is that I do see hope in the surprising response to *Why Religion Matters*, for it is indeed a very controversial book. I come out swinging! It's an opinionated book! It's as though throughout my career—practically fifty years—I've tried to turn a pleasing, smiling face toward the public talking about good things. But you cannot live in this pigsty of a world without bumping into things that just annoy the *daylights* out of you! Over the years I have pretty much kept those things to myself and stuffed them into the duffel bag of my private feelings. You know how it is when you try to push a sleeping bag into its case; you push down hard, and it bulges back out on the other side and out, and so you push again. That was the way it was getting with me. My annoyance bag was getting very bloated with all these pet peeves. So I decided that I didn't want to go to my grave with all those peeves locked inside me, so I dumped them onto the world. And lo and behold, it was as if I hit a nerve. A lot of people recognize my peeves as theirs as well. So I'm glad I went that route. I feel lighter within and supported from without. That support encourages me to think that our ethos, our collective mind, has been moving in this direction more than I had realized.

Cousineau: I recall Vine Deloria Jr. telling you at his home in Tucson, Arizona, during your interview with him for America's Shadow Struggle, *that Americans won't truly understand Indian religions until they understand their own. If that's true, could the popularity of your work, along with the efflorescence of other spiritual books, workshops, and tours, be indicative of a genuine reaching out on the part of the American public to understand themselves in a new way? Perhaps you could address the cultural threshold we seem to be crossing with these attempts to delve deeper into religion.*

Smith: I think one of the indications to which you speak—and it is ambiguous—is the surge in the interest in spirituality. The word is almost replacing religion in our times. Organized spirituality is the traction that religion needs to take hold. Spirituality has the virtue of lifting out features of religion. One of the most interesting developments is the huge surge of emphasis on the dark side of religion that denigrates it and places spirituality above it. I know of no one who would deny they had a spiritual side to their being, but in our time *religion* is a bad word, while *spirituality* frees us from the horrors of institutionalized religion. So there is a sorting-out process today, which can give life and validation to our religious or spiritual side. As the discussion proceeds, the question becomes, Is there also a historical place for institutionalized spirituality?

Cousineau: Can a greater knowledge or experience of primal religions help us curb the excesses of scientism? Can cross-cultural studies and debates help us come into a sounder balance?

Smith: As I said earlier, having relieved myself and vented my spleen of some of my prejudices and peeves, I tend to be more cheerful, and that reflects here. I tend to be hopeful that, yes, we will come to see that science is incomparable and truly thrilling in its own domain. But we will come to see its limitations as well. The problem is that even though people who are leaders in our culture see this it never gets into the textbooks—that science has limitations. Recently, I attended a conference with a title that moved me: "Teaching Science with Awareness of Its Limitations." If only every textbook and every course in science would begin with a half-hour of putting this phenomenon in perspective, I think that the *eschaton* [ultimate destiny] would have arrived.

But there is no sign of that at present. So students who leave higher education and go out and become the cultural leaders of our world are taught—or it is ingrained into them—the staggering achievements of science, but no mention is made of its limitations.

Cousineau: I'm reminded here of the scholar Edwin Bernbaum's incisive take on myth, that it is the "unquestioned assumption" of a culture, the belief system that is absolutely taken for granted and rarely, if ever, questioned. To my surprise, both E. O. Wilson and Lewis Thomas have called evolution the equivalent of a modern myth. So if science has replaced religion as the mythic story of our time, than maybe religion is pounding its head against the door, as science did in Galileo's time. Have you ever thought of science, progress, and evolution as modern myths, in the sense of the overarching story of the times or, as Campbell called it, "the group dream"? And is it possible that religion is also up against the myth *of progress, the* myth *of evolution, the sense of the great and overarching story that becomes the collective story?*

Smith: Yes, yes. Let me restate this to reshape it in my own mind. One of the very plausible and accurate definitions of myth is that which we believe implicitly without question. From that the question arises as to whether science, including, very importantly, evolution as its account of how we got here, the less to the more, from slime to intelligence. All of this we believe and just absorb. The Romans had a good phrase, which we can carry on: we absorb it *cum lacte*, with our mother's milk. Just unthinkingly take it in. I think that is true, and I think that it is a great part of our problem because a myth, in that sense, is not even recognized as a construct. It is transparent truth.

Greg Easterbrook had a column in the *New York Times* that brought this out vividly. He was speaking of one specific point, namely evolution and Darwinism, and he said, "The situation today regarding Darwin and Darwinism can only be described by using religious language." Darwinism taken as *the* explanation—brooking no alternative as how we humans got here—is the dogma of our time, and dogmas in sacred history are not to be questioned. To question a dogma is heresy, and anyone who engages in heresy can expect to be excommunicated. That's exactly the situation regarding that theory, which has a lot to be said for it. But it certainly is not—in religious language *gospel truth*—which cannot be challenged.

Cousineau: James Joyce once quipped, "You can't teach an old dogma new tricks."
Smith: Let us hope that's wrong!

Cousineau: One of the most memorable things I have ever heard you say was in response to the charge that you are only interested in the past, only the nostalgic beauty of past religions. It was during your interview with Winona LaDuke at the World Parliament of Religions in Cape Town, South Africa, in 1999. You said that you were interested in what was true then, what is true now, and what will be true in the future. Which is to say that you are finally interested in what is timeless. Is this sense of timelessness the key to the religious life?
Smith: I'd never had put it to me that categorically. I would certainly say without a moment's hesitation that it is an aspect of it.

But now I may be very open and say things, so I'm now talking with my history of religions cap on. I am giving you my own belief and my own conviction, which is that there are *striking* parallels between science's twentieth-century discovery that there is another world than this everyday world. Namely, the quantum world, which is just incredibly different from this world. Yet, it holds the key in terms of its forces to what we're experiencing here in a way that's strikingly like that which the world religions have all said, too: "Yes, there is another world."

So there is a striking parallelism between science and religion on this point. It is my conviction that that other world is anchored in *eternity* and the eternal is different from everlasting. Everlasting goes on forever with changes, but eternity is beyond time. It includes time, but is beyond time. The second thing this other world is anchored in is spirit rather than matter, the matrixes of space-time and matter it is not subject to. The third thing is that it is perfect. Those points all converge in a mathematical point, which exceeds our capacity of our left brain to put into words, so it cannot be adequately articulated. Our articulations can be, as a Zen monk would say, fingers pointing toward it at the moon.

While Huston Smith believes that intriguing points of overlap exist between the worldviews of religion and science, he doubts that reconciliation between them is just around the corner. Figuratively speaking, it is as if we were in a bungalow in North India facing a window that commands a breathtaking view of the Himalayan mountain range. What modern science has done, in effect, is to lower the window shade to two inches above the sill so that, with our eyes angled downward, all we can now see is the ground on which our bungalow stands. That ground stands for the physical universe, and to give credit where credit is due, science has shown it to be awesome beyond belief. Still, it is not Mount Everest, which we can view any time we decide to lift the shade.

The concluding part of this book comprises nine interviews illustrating several approaches that Smith believes can help lift the shade. The conversations in part 3 range from a personable discussion with Jeffrey Kane about the potentials of education when it lives up to its highest calling to, in a discussion with Timothy White, vivid descriptions of Smith's encounters with what has been called the "ecstatic technologies" of mind-altering entheogens. In his talk with Jeffrey Mishlove, Smith compares the relationship between mysticism and psychotropics (literally, "soul-turning"), which led Smith to study them seriously. With Richard Scheinin he connects the potential revelations one can gain from ingesting entheogens to the possible epiphanies awaiting those who step outside Plato's cave, a metaphor that recurs frequently in Smith's work. The discussion with filmmaker Bill Moyers revolves around Huston's personal philosophy, including his conviction that in their mystical reaches, which constitute their "highest common denominator," the world's wisdom traditions speak with a single voice in describing "the way things are." All these traditions testify to a happy ending that blossoms when life's difficulties are faced with courage and determination.

These interviews reveal the last stage of Smith's pilgrim's progress, from Paradise Lost to Paradise Regained, a progress powered by the belief that faith is wiser than despair and by the conviction that religion is a kind of tropism drawing the human soul toward the divine light. Responded to by enough people, this tropism could lead to the re-enchantment of the world. At its best, religion *is* the response to that tropism that stretches our souls toward the mysterious Spirit whence we came. In the end Smith sides with religion, because it gives courage to the human soul and lights up the path it should follow.

Jeffrey Kane: Holistic Education Review *begins with the idea that there is a spiritual dimension to reality and that it should make a difference in the way we educate children. The first question I'd like to ask you is, As you walk down the street, or as you eat your meal, or as you go to bed at night, do you see a spiritual dimension which pervades everyday existence?*

Huston Smith: If I answer honestly and personally (it's a personal question), the answer is some days I do, and some days I don't. But let me say immediately that on the days that I don't, I feel unwell, you might say. It is as if I have the spiritual flu—something like that. When you have the flu you feel rotten, and when you have the spiritual flu the world seems drained of meaning and purpose—humdrum and prosaic. But I've lived long enough to be able to say when those days roll 'round: okay, this is the yin and yang of life—ups and downs. This is one of those dark days of the ego. Most of the time, though, meaning and purpose are discernible, often to lyrical heights. Those moments are privileged; they are gifts. Even

This interview by *Holistic Education Review* editor Jeffrey Kane took place during the summer of 1993 and appeared in *Holistic Education Review* 6, no. 4 (Winter 1993). Reprinted by permission of Holistic Education Review.

when my happiness isn't at a rolling boil, I tend to know that there is a spiritual dimension to all things.

Kane: When you think about the spiritual dimensions of reality, is it in the everydayness of the world, is it in a glass of water, or in the air that we breathe?

Smith: It's everywhere. Everything is an outpouring of the infinite that is spiritual in essence, so everything reflects that spirit. Blake is famous for having said that if the doors of perception were cleansed, we would see everything as it truly is—infinite. For him infinitude was also perfection. Limitations exist in us, not in the world.

Kane: Would it be going too far to say that everything is truly sacred if we see it rightly?

Smith: Not too far at all. As the Thomists say, *esse qua esse bonum est:* "being as being is good." Of course the evil in the world tests that principle, but I think it can be defended.

Kane: I remember back to C. S. Lewis, in the beginning of The Screwtape Letters, *where he explains that the devil must consume souls because he has no being himself.*

Smith: That's a good way to put it. There's another route to the same point. Heroin is horrible, but at the moment of the high, that high itself isn't bad. It's the toll it takes that is bad. Even cancer cells aren't bad in isolation. It's only the way they prey on other cells that's evil.

Kane: Do you think we might actually have here a very quick first inroad to educating children? Would it be too much to say that one of the most fundamental things we need to do if we are to educate children is to help them see all things as sacred?

Smith: It would be wonderful if we could do that. Education is more your province than mine, but I've always thought that if I stop teaching university/college students I'd like to teach preschool. Somehow it's two ends of the spectrum that attract me.

Kane: Incidentally, Rudolf Steiner made a point of saying that people who teach the youngest children should be the oldest teachers. Such matters aside, do you believe Emerson offered a signpost to the sacred with his contention that the invariable mark of wisdom is to see the miraculous in the common?

Smith: He's right. I wonder if tribal peoples, being closer to nature than we are, do better at that—seeing everything aglow with the sacred. That may be only a myth that we somehow need today, but I think it's more than that. Unencumbered by the busyness and humdrum of contemporary life, tribal peoples seem able to hold on to the shining world that children are heirs to.

Kane: Do you think that the "doors of perception" can be cleansed through aesthetic experience—through experiences of nature, for example?

Smith: Definitely. Just this morning I wrote something on that subject because *The World's Religions* is coming out in an illustrated edition that will include the world's religious art. In writing the preface for this new edition, I found myself saying that the function of sacred art—and indeed beauty of every sort, virgin nature emphatically included—is to make easy what would otherwise be difficult. If one is viewing an icon (in a way, all sacred art is iconic), then the icon basically disappears by offering itself up to the divine. The energy of the divine pours through it into the viewer, one consequence being that the viewer's heart is expanded and becomes uplifted by a great work of art. Note that word *uplifted*. Can you imagine performing in that state a despicable act? It's often difficult for us to act compassionately, but sacred art eases the difficulty by ennobling us. So your point is well taken, including your emphasis on virgin nature.

Kane: Might nature be considered the greatest of sacred art?

Smith: That's interesting. I do think of sacred art and virgin nature as two of the clearest apertures to the divine, but I've never thought of rank-ordering them. I think of Plato's statement that "beauty is the splendor of the true." I like that because it gets us beyond thinking of nature and art simply as pleasure giving. They do far more than that. They offer insight into the true nature of things.

Kane: Beauty wouldn't then be simply in the eye of the beholder?

Smith: Not ultimately, though there's partial truth in the saying that when a young man falls in love with a girl, he sees something in her that others don't see. The romantic illusions that color his perception don't alter the fact that at that moment he is closer than any other human being to seeing her the way God sees her. When I hear someone say, "I don't see what he sees in her," I feel like responding, "Don't you wish you could?" I don't think it's naively romantic to think that romantic love opens a window to the inner nobility of the beloved, one that is closed to ordinary eyes.

Kane: Would it be fair to say that beauty is something one is open to, rather than something that someone creates in the act of perception?
Smith: Yes, that's the case.

Kane: Could we rightly look at beauty as a matter of impression, as well as expression? Normally we think of art as expression, as subjective expression.
Smith: Something of the artist figures, but the accent is on what comes to him or her. It's imprinted, as you say. I like your way of putting it.

Kane: Perhaps we've reached a second education implication here, and I wonder what your thoughts are. If we are going to educate children rightly, perhaps we should spend a good deal of time in nature study and art (again to use the phrase)—as impression, attempting to open children to the beauty in the world.
Smith: I am sure that is true.

Kane: There was once a teacher who taught me about Shakespeare. He said that Shakespeare pointed to various aspects of human existence and the human condition, and that he pointed beautifully with great accuracy. He (my teacher) said what we often do in school is we say, "Look how nicely he points. You see how his eye is lined up with his finger? He's pointing very directly." But this overlooks what he's pointing toward. I wonder if that isn't true as well—a flower unfolding, or a cloud passing in the sky, again, opens a door, or provides a lens into something beyond itself.

Smith: The notion of pointing, of course, suggests the Zen adage of the finger pointing at the moon. If we obsess over the finger, we overlook the moon. It's very true. Much of education falls into that trap. In higher education I am distressed by the proportion of attention that goes to methodology rather than content.

Kane: *When we begin to think of there being sacredness, or when we recognize this sacredness in the everyday, does knowledge have a different "shape" than we normally think of knowledge having in the West?*

Smith: I think it does. My favorite book on this subject is Seyyed Hossein Nasr's *Knowledge and the Sacred*. He speaks from a traditional point of view. To fill in the background, in the hundred of years of the Gifford Lectures—the most prestigious humanities lecture series in the West—Nasr is the only non-Westerner ever to have been included. His thesis is that knowledge is not so much that which discloses the sacred as that which is sacred in itself for partaking in the knowing source from which intelligence derives. Human intelligence is a reflection of the intelligence that produces everything. In knowing, we are simply extending the intelligence that comes to and constitutes us. We mimic the mind of God, so to speak. Or better, we continue and extend it.

Kane: *So knowing and being are intimately related?*

Smith: In the end they are identical. That probably holds for all positive attributes. The closer to their source we draw, the more we find them converging.

Kane: *I think it is a particularly important point that, in the West, the concept of knowledge is impersonal and detached. We take out being, and say it has no place. What you are saying here is that knowledge is imbued with being. It is a direct experience. Knowledge cannot be detached as such. Would you say that knowledge of that sort is what helps you on those days when you see the sacred in the everyday?*

Smith: I am sure that is the case. To linger for a moment on this issue of detached, objective knowledge, writing—whatever its virtues, and I think there are some—is especially vulnerable to becoming detached, because writing can be disconnected from the writer. There it is in print, dead and frozen. Speech, on the other hand, is not only alive, it *is* life, because it cannot be separated from the living person in one mode of his or her own being. Exclusively oral cultures are unencumbered by dead knowledge, dead facts. Libraries, on the other hand, are full of them.

Kane: To quote Emerson once again, "To the wise, fact is true poetry." Would poetry present the same dilemma?

Smith: No, because poetry is art, and we've already talked about that. Poetry is a special use of language that opens onto the real. The business of the poet is truth-telling, which is why in the Celtic tradition no one could be a teacher unless he or she was a poet.

Kane: Would you say if someone has learned and has become inwardly active through learning, then the knowledge gained becomes part of his or her being? Would he or she be a different person than he or she was prior?

Smith: We have to differentiate between life-giving learning and kinds that deaden the mind. I think of a TV program around mid-century (there have doubtless been other since) that featured savants, essentially. They were amazing—veritable walking encyclopedias—

Kane: —what was the day of the week for January 1, Year 1, that sort of thing?

Smith: Yes, and, Who won the Oscar for best supporting actor in 1952? I was living in Saint Louis at the time, and the national champion in that particular series turned out to be a Saint Louisan. People knew him. He was unemployed. Couldn't get a job as a postal clerk because he couldn't pass the civil service exam. So when we talk about knowledge and learning, we have to distinguish between useless kinds and kinds that are useful—practically useful, but more important, useful in raising the stature of our lives.

Kane: Please forgive me if I ask you an unfair question: If we follow this through, is it possible that we educate whole generations of savants, just in the sense that you use the term?

Smith: More than possible, I suspect. And that's what turns off kids from learning, of course—when it seems like rote memory, and what's it for? We give them hoops to jump through, keeping the destination—purpose and the point—clearly before them.

Kane: *Many educators have recognized the limitations of a positivistic model of knowledge. They know that rote learning no longer works, or perhaps that it never did. The new paradigm that drives education is based upon a computer analogue wherein we storehouse individual bits of knowledge, discrete and separable. These bits can then be put into motion, as it were, through a program in critical thinking, for example. It often seems to me that we are trying to put the pieces in motion artificially without, again, reference to the content itself, without reference to being. So you might say that readers of this interview could argue, "Well, the fact of the matter is that we are teaching children how to put ideas together, how to think." But I wonder if that still doesn't miss the point.*

Smith: I think it does. I've heard about this issue; I am not in close touch with what actually goes on, but I share your skepticism about teaching critical thinking in the abstract. It doesn't work because thinking never proceeds in a vacuum. So to be effective, thinking must adapt and be faithful to the context in which it works. My skepticism here ties in with my earlier skepticism about method in general. We always know more than we know how we know it, so we get farther by attending to the "what" than to the "how." The trouble with trying to work out a method for knowing is that it will rule out resources that don't conform to it. Every method is, in ways, a straitjacket, a Procrustean bed. True, we all do have methods, and when we run into problems, it might be well to try to spot and revise if need be the course that brought us to the problem. But to put method first is putting the cart before the horse.

Kane: *If I am following you correctly, and tying it back to what you said before, it is being that animates knowledge. It is not the method that animates knowledge.*

Smith: Yes. In the final analysis what we know derives from our entire being. Historians of knowledge are providing us with detailed examples of breakthroughs where frontier scientists, say, simply discarded oceans of evidence because something deep lying in them generated a "gut feeling" that the truth lay elsewhere. Had they toed the line of the so-called scientific method, the breakthroughs wouldn't have occurred.

Kane: E. A. Burt—

Smith: —he was a dear friend of mine.

Kane: —in his classic work, The Metaphysical Foundations of Modern Scientists, *maintained that if Copernicus had presented his thoughts to thorough-going empiricists, he would have been laughed out of court.*

Smith: Exactly.

Kane: I wonder if this might not be a good place to familiarize some of our readers with the modern Western mind-set that you've written about in a good many places. At this point in our discussion, you have begun to rout out some of the assumptions that we make (one being relative to "method") that might limit the knowledge that we gain, or perhaps again, our openness to being. What are some of the other assumptions that have characterized knowledge in the West and might keep us from cleansing those doors of perception?

Smith: Science works effectively on things that impact more complicated things—cancer cells devastating human bodies, for example. If we call this upward causation, science is good at that. What it's not good at is downward causation—the way the superior impacts the inferior—and when it comes to things that are superior to us, we human beings, it draws a total blank. Because the technological spin-offs from science are so impressive, we slip into assuming that upward causation, more from less, is the name of the game. The universe derives (exclusively) from a dense pellet. Life derives (exclusively) from inanimate elements. "Hydrogen is a ubiquitous substance which, given time, gives rise to intelligence," as one scientist has put it. But as another scientist, Stephen Jay Gould, has pointed out—one wishes that in practice he paid more attention to his aphorism—"absence of evidence isn't evidence of absence." On balance, the wisdom traditions assure us, things proceed more by downward than upward causation. If science doesn't show this, it is because it is locked (as it should be, this being the key to its effectiveness) into a technically competent but metaphysically impoverished method—the issue of method again. The latest good book on this point is Bryan Appleyard's *Understanding the Present: Science and the Soul of Modern Man.*

Kane: Does this approach to understanding create particular problems when we apply it to understanding human beings? In education, we work with children all the time, and we often have positivistic models of knowledge when we conceptualize who the children are in themselves. Do you think this is particularly problematic?

Smith: I think poor self-images cripple children—and adults as well, for that matter. Moreover, our modern Western self-image is the most impoverished human beings have ever devised. We do not think well of ourselves, Saul Bellow observes, and Marshall Salins, the anthropologist, fills in the picture: "We are the only people who think we derive from apes. Everybody else assumes that they are descended from the gods."

If I can bring this discussion back to children, there's much talk today about the wounded child within. I won't say that's all bad, but it runs the danger of encouraging self-pity. How about the struggling adult within—more attention to that, and how the fragile adult might be strengthened? I hope it's clear how our over-reliance on the scientific method has been the (indirect and unwitting) cause of our impoverished self-image. It is as if the top of science's window stops at the bridge of our nose, so that in looking through it, we see only things that are beneath our full stature.

Kane: As I listen to you, I am thinking that physics, which we often think of as the most complicated, most difficult of all sciences, is, indeed, the simplest in its own way because it deals with things that are essentially lifeless. The mineral world, the physical world of atoms, I don't know if I would call the cosmos dead, but the way we view it certainly is.

Smith: You're right. The hard sciences deal so effectively with their objects because those things have no, or negligible, freedom.

Kane: Science seems to lose some of its power when it turns to animate objects. I am thinking now of the Chinese notion of chi, that there is a life force which we cannot explain in terms of physics or chemistry. More power is lost when it turns to the animal kingdom. And regarding the human self, little of importance admits to scientific proof.

Smith: I think that's exactly right. To pick up with the second level where microbiology enters, R. C. Lewontin has noted that "despite the fact that we can position every atom in a protein molecule in three-dimensional space, nobody has the slightest idea of the rule that will fold them into life." Microbiologists appropriately seek that rule, but I wonder if it exists on a plane they can access.

Kane: I have read of biologists who have synthesized protein compounds which, when given electrical charges, do begin to self-replicate, but then you still end up with the more primary question: Who is putting the electrical charge in to begin with? Where is it coming from? I think we're going to find in the ultimate that there are questions we ask that cannot be answered by modern science. I once found myself writing that we need to elevate our concept of science to meet the reality of the world, rather than to lower the world to meet the limitations of earth science.

Smith: I agree in principle but wonder how much the scientific method can be altered—elevated, expanded—without compromising its power. The power of science comes from its controlled experiments, and the nobler things in life can't be proved. We don't have to expect science to do everything.

Kane: I know that there have been a great many people (I am thinking of Martin Heidegger, for example) who see a split between meditative thinking and calculative reason—reason being closer to science and thinking (as he uses the word) to meditation. But I can't help think that Goethe, through his understanding of art and aesthetic perception, might actually have a key to how they can both be combined. I'm not sure.

Smith: I'm not sure, either, but it is interesting. Wolfgang Goethe, Rudolf Steiner, and Emanuel Swedenborg—all three were visionaries who connected science to the human spirit in original ways. But I haven't studied them enough to say more.

Kane: In another vein, can religion or ceremony bring us to the deeper dimensions of reality, or can they close us down to them?

Smith: Both, I think. Just as the world is religiously ambiguous in the sense that both theists and atheists see it as supporting their position, so too is religion itself an ambiguous enterprise. It is made up of people, and as we well know, people are a mixed bag. When they congregate in institutions, it is not surprising that we find both good and evil results. Religions do horrible things because they reinforce in-group–out-group feelings. At the same time, they nurture the transcendent urge that has compassion as its wake. In this mode it shatters existing social structures. The Book of Jonah shows the Jews expanding their theology to include even their enemies, the Ninevites. This was radical. We have to be sensitive to the two faces of religion: conservative and progressive. But that's true of almost anything. A while ago we were talking about art, but bad music as well as good has been written. The important thing is not to be cynical—realistic, yes, but not cynical. By functionalist criteria alone, religion would not have survived if it were not doing something right.

Connecting this to education, can religion contribute the empowering kind of knowing we have been talking about? I think it can. Why do I say that? First, because the noblest human beings that I personally have encountered have been shaped by religious traditions—His Holiness the Dalai Lama and Mother Theresa jump immediately to mind. Second, when I look at the sacred texts that inspired these people—and the commentaries that have been written on them by giants such as Shankara [Indian philosopher and theologian], Dōgen [thirteenth-century Zen master], Nagarjuna [Indian founder of the Madhyamika school of Buddhism], Augustine, and Meister Eckhart (not excepting Plato and Plotinus, who write in the same vein)—I find no alternate texts that are far beyond the public schools that we have been talking about. All I am saying is that the wisdom is there to be drawn upon and calibrated to the minds teachers seek to nurture.

Kane: Would you think that religious ceremonies have a place in educating children generally?

Smith: I do, though in this context I don't want to get into the complicated issue of church/state and the public school. Rituals help us celebrate, and at the other end of the spectrum they help us to connect deeply with people in times of sorrow. The repetition that ritual always involves sets the present moment in a larger context and infuses it with wider meaning. It's difficult to invent rituals. The Unitarians are trying, but for the most part rituals, like myths, emerge spontaneously.

Kane: Then a myth must be what it is and cannot be made different?

Smith: It must grow out of a deep historical experience like the Exodus, or from deep, unconscious layers of the psyche.

Kane: As I listen to you, I am wondering if ceremony doesn't provide a set moment in time for you to be silent and listen. Ceremony may be a way of blocking off the everyday—one must pay the water bill, and run to the store, and all that. Ceremony might just set apart moments of time in which you can get in touch with deep parts of one's self and the other dimensions of existence.

Smith: That is well put. You used the word *silence.* I wondered when you said that whether you mean literal silence or an inner silence even when there is chanting and litany.

Kane: In this instance, I was using the word to mean there is no nonsense running around in your mind, in your head, you have no inner dialogue for a moment, you're actually quiet. You're receptive, rather than working daily things through.

Smith: Sounds right. What I am not sure I had thought of before is that this apartness can come even while you are chanting or singing, for because the material is memorized, your conscious mind doesn't have to be attending.

Kane: Do you think that meditation in any of the great traditions, whether it be a Buddhist meditation, or Hasidic meditation, or Rosicrucian meditation, has any place in the education of children?

Smith: I don't really know. Questions of age would enter, and the kind of meditation. If we think of silent meditation, I find myself saying yes. It would probably be very good to encourage even small children to sit still and shift their minds into a different gear.

As I get into the subject, I once received an invitation from a third-grade class in a parochial school in the Boston area while I was teaching at MIT. It was so cute, I remember it verbatim: "Dear Prof. Smith: We are studying religion. We do not know much about religion. Will you please come and teach us about religion?" Signed, "The Third Grade." So I went, but it turned out to be last period on a Friday afternoon, and you can imagine the blast of restless energy that met me as I stepped into the room. I heard a clear inner voice say, "Don't try to talk to these kids. Nothing you can say could possibly hold their attention. They've got to do something." So I said, "You asked me to teach you about religion, so I am going to tell you about religion in a different part of the world. In Japanese religion, they sit on the floor, so we have to move all the desks against the walls." Instant pandemonium—everybody pushing things and bumping into one another. So we got the floor cleared, and I said, "Okay, everybody on the floor. When Japanese sit religiously they sit in a special position." I demonstrated the lotus position. "Can you sit that way?" A few show-offs could. "Also they sit in silence. Can you do that?" Heads nodded vigorously. "How long?" "Fifteen minutes," a voice sang out. "Are you sure? Without making a sound?" "Five minutes." We finally settled for two, and even that was too long for them. But we were off to a great start, and they gave me a bag of jelly beans as my honorarium—

Kane: You should work with young children!

There is often a distinction made between learning by doing and learning through detachment. There are many Hassidic stories which end with the conclusion that one learns through doing. Was what you did simply a pedagogical device, or do you think that it might have illustrated that one can learn most about life's spiritual dimension by being engaged in some kind of activity, a practice?

Smith: Perhaps the latter was involved. I find it difficult to rank-order modes of learning, because when I think back over my own experiences of learning, they have been so different—all the way from the

Zen monasteries to sitting spellbound before gifted teachers who just lectured. I find if difficult to prioritize learning situations.

Kane: I guess part of me likes to say one thing is more important than another, but it's important to step back. I wonder if we might now move a bit to the question of moral values. Do you see religion, or aesthetics, or beauty, or any of the things we have discussed as having an impact on the moral development of children?

Smith: All of them. Certainly, if what we were saying was true about beauty having an elevating effect—but let me be concrete. I don't think I've ever spent three or four hours in a great museum without the world looking different in a way that somehow purifies my motives. So there is beauty. As far as religion, we have to distinguish in the history of religion between three periods. In the "pre-axial" period of religion, before the rise of the great prophets and sages, around the middle of the first millennium B.C.E., religion was occupied mostly with time—death and the perishing of existence— and ethics didn't much enter. People were living in tribes and got along pretty much the way normal families do. In the post-axial period, though, populations began to be citified, which meant that a good part of one's dealings were with people who were not in one's primary group. Ethics needed bolstering, and from the golden rule to the prophets, religion shouldered the job. The modern period adds social ethics to religions agenda, for we now realize that social structures are not like laws of nature. They are human creations, so we are responsible for them. So to beauty we must add religion with its post-axial ethics and concern with social justice. So always, if we look back, concern for face-to-face morality, and its modern emphasis on justice as well, have historically evolved as religious issues.

Kane: To pursue this central theme here, I wonder if you see moral ideas as humanmade or as human replications, or human manifestations of a higher order of law? In other words, are they subjective, circumstantial developments, or are they reflective of something higher and more universal?

Smith: Something of both, but more replicas than constructions. Morality always aims at harmony or unity, and unity is a great idea, but not only an idea. It's great because it is a mirroring or reflection of what ultimately reality is. Reality is one. In an esoteric sense, the number "one" is beyond the entire numerical sequence, not just the first in an order of integers. It is qualitatively of a different order. If it had remained that, though, it would have been finite because it would have lacked multiplicity. And since the ultimate is also infinite, it must include the multiple in some way. It is not a relation of parity, because the one has a dignity beyond the many. Still, it requires the many for it to be infinite. Multiplicity poses a problem, because for things to exist they must have centers and boundaries.

Yet something is there that doesn't love a wall. Boundaries have their downside. We have this centripetal urge, but it can be narrow and confining, so we have to live with the tension to be ourselves and also identify with others. How can we, at the same time, be ourselves and embrace others? That is one way of defining life's project. As Aldous Huxley put it, "The problem of life is to overcome the basic human disability of egoism." This is a roundabout answer to your question, of whether morals are humanmade, but what I want to say is that to some extent they are—there can be silly, mistaken, and even pernicious judgments that individuals and even societies fall into. But it is also the case that this is a moral universe, and through lots of trial and error, history is trying to discover what its moral laws are.

Kane: *Would you say that there are certain universals that one would find through many of the world's religions?*

Smith: Yes. Two levels need to be distinguished here. The one which is the more explicit is what we should do, but beyond that is the question of the kind of person we should try to become. Now, on the first level, what we should do, there are four problem areas in human life that have to be dealt with. These are violence, wealth, the spoken word, and sex. In lower forms of life these problem areas are monitored quite adequately by instinct. Man, though, is an animal without instincts, so these problem areas can get out of hand. Moral precepts are devised to secure appropriate, life-sustaining behavior in the four areas, and they are remarkably uniform across cultures: don't murder, don't steal, don't lie, don't commit adultery. These are the basic guidelines concerning human behavior.

As for the kind of person we should try to become, the virtues point the way. In the West these are commonly identified as humility, charity, and veracity. Humility has nothing to do with low self-esteem; it is to recognize oneself as one and fully one but not more than one, just as charity is to look upon your neighbor as fully one (with all the rights and privileges pertaining thereto) just as you are one. Veracity begins with not being deceitful, but it ends in the sublime objectivity that sees things exactly as they are, undistorted by our subjective preferences. These are the virtues in the West. Asia, interestingly, has the same three but enters them by the back door, so to speak, by speaking of the three poisons—traits that keep the virtues from flourishing in us. The three are greed (the opposite of humility), hatred (the opposite of charity), and delusion (the opposite of veracity). To the extent that we expunge these three poisons, the virtues will flood our lives automatically. The convergence of East and West in these areas is remarkable.

Kane: If you were to look at these in an educational context, what is the meaning of what you just said for someone who now steps into a classroom filled with children?

Smith: This is your turf, and it would be presumptuous for me to pontificate. So I'll content myself with a single point. The most powerful moral influence is example. There's a saying, "What you do speaks so loud that I can't hear what you say." That's what makes it so difficult—we have to aspire to be models for our students. At the same time, what nobler goal could we set for ourselves?

CHAPTER 17 | DEMYSTIFYING
SPIRITUAL PRACTICE

The loss of wealth is loss of dirt,
As sages in all times assert;
The happy man's without a shirt.

—JOHN HEYWOOD

Now in his eighties, the eminent religious scholar Huston Smith, author of The World's Religions *and other books, is skilled at giving voice and language to big questions. I once heard him liken the human ability to understand and communicate with God to a dog's ability to know its owner. By comprehending a few of its owner's commands, and by sensing his presence even when it cannot see him, the dog has a real, if very limited, connection with the human world. We, too, can periodically sense the presence of something larger, but are about as capable of communicating with it is as a dog is with us. Just to know the little we know, we have to stop, listen, and watch or we'll miss the miracle, however fleetingly it may occur.*

I also heard Smith say once that as a spiritual human being he felt he had a responsibility to the past, present, and future. He never mentioned how he managed to fulfill that obligation, to find a harmony among all three states in a single gesture, so recently I asked him. His wise, touching response reveals how all of us, no matter how remote we may feel from cosmic truth, are capable of investing the simplest rituals and duties of our daily lives with eternal significance. —Sarah Ban Breathnach

This essay by Huston Smith, with commentary by Sarah Ban Breathnach, was published in *A Man's Journey to Simple Abundance*, edited by Michael Segell (New York: Scribner, 2000). Reprinted by permission of Huston Smith.

It began nineteen years ago when a six-year-old granddaughter paid us a week's visit in Syracuse. Some six-year-olds are content to watch television, but not this self-starter. She wanted projects. Some were quickly dispatched—an hour here, a half-day there—but this is the story of one that has lasted nineteen years thus far and has affected my spiritual journey.

At one end of our vegetable garden there was a compost heap. For the most part it enjoyed benign neglect, as the saying goes, but occasionally I would poke at it indifferently. One brisk morning we vigorously attacked it together and turned the whole heap over, whereupon her active mind wanted to know why we were doing that. What was the purpose? What did our shoveling accomplish? That extracted from me a short lecture on composting. Vegetation decays to become once again the earth from which it sprang, I explained. The cycle repeats itself and is, biologically speaking, everlasting. Air—scientists call it oxygen—speeds up the process, which was why we were turning the pile over: to work more air into the moldering grass, leaves, and vegetable matter, and accelerate its turning into humus.

She was fascinated. Part of the heap was ripe, but it contained stones and various kinds of bric-a-brac, so we seized on a wooden crate that was lying around, covered it with chicken wire, and sifted out the intruders. The result was, well, remarkable. I didn't know what the word *friable* meant until I ran my hands through that pure, black dirt, felt it crumble in my hands and then sift through my fingers when I spread them apart. A product of this order called for a name, and one was soon forthcoming: Perfect Dirt. It turned into a trade name. Much of the rest of the week was spent packaging Perfect Dirt in plastic bags, which we hand-delivered to friends I knew to be fellow gardeners—office secretaries, neighbors, and (on the last afternoon of my granddaughter's visit) passersby who took us up on our sidewalk poster, "Free Perfect Dirt." The project was a smashing success—she, totally absorbed in the project itself, and I absorbed in the pleasure of working alongside my visiting granddaughter.

She went on to greater things, among them becoming a marine biologist, but the project she set in motion survived her departure. Nineteen years and three geographical moves later, I am still making Perfect Dirt. With unexpected, life-enhancing consequences, it turns out, which is the point of this story.

The consequences crept up on me. At first I sensed only that I was riding the wake that she had set in motion; the day wasn't quite complete without my taking a look at our compost pile and seeing if it needed a bit of attention. But then it started to feel as if the project was assuming the initiative and drawing me into its act. I remembered Woody Guthrie's song that begins, "All my life is turning, sunup and sundown," and every turn of my spading fork phased me into nature's untiring gyrations—the wheeling of its planets, the circling of the seasons, the rhythms of its daily round.

And in time a second realization dawned. In retrospect I realize that I had been experiencing this second entry for quite a while before words took shape to give it a voice.

The first word that came to mind was *participation*—in composting I was participating in nature's rounds. Then, though, an adjective moved in to underscore that word. I was *consciously* participating in nature's rounds. Willy-nilly, everything participates in nature's gyrations—"ashes to ashes, dust to dust"—but we human beings are the only creatures that can choose either to enter the feedback loops intentionally or sit back and freeload on the ride.

That realization takes me from my garden to my study, where hangs one of the most treasured artifacts that I have gleaned from the world.

It is a bark painting of an emu that I acquired while I was spending a summer—its winter—in Australia. It was found discarded in the bush, but was in such good condition that it made its way into the hands of an anthropologist at the University of Melbourne who—I gasped at his generosity—gave it to me. In doing so he explained its history.

The artist belonged to the emu clan, and was about to set forth to hunt down an emu, who, at his approach, would voluntarily sacrifice its life to provide the sustenance that the members of the clan needed. But not if the hunter had not assured its replacement by painting its successor. Painting equaled creating. That there are still people on our planet whose minds work that way, I find one of the most astonishing (and moving) facts of our times. But my reason for mentioning the anecdote is this: it shows us active, intentional participation with nature at its zenith—the most vivid instance of such participation I have encountered. To our way of thinking, Mother Nature creates the emu that will replace the sacrificial victim. Not so with the aboriginal hunter. Nature required that he get into the act.

The more I reflect on that aboriginal mind-set, the more I find myself envying it, for it has things exactly right. All life has its active and passive poles, and by painting/creating his emu the hunter was giving rein to his active side. Nature needed him, and that need built him into its picture decisively and increased his sense of belonging.

That is why, in an act of imitation, every afternoon that I am at home finds me in my backyard for fifteen minutes tending to what has become the fourth component of my daily spiritual practice. For as long as I can remember that practice begins, on arising, with hatha yoga for the body, a reading from a religious classic for my mind, and a blend of prayer and meditation for my spirit. Those three practices remain in place, but it helps to have them grounded, and that is what the addition of composting accomplishes. Being physically anchored to the earth helps us to keep my ego from bobbing along mindlessly on the sea of life. In Kyoto there is a bridge named the Half-Dipper Bridge. Its name derives from a practice of the thirteenth-century Zen master Dōgen. As an act of gratitude, whenever he would drink from the river that the bridge spans, he would pour back half of the dipper of water he scooped from it for his needs. That gratitude is half the story, but composting adds to it the element of creating what you return.

There are some who will want to raise the issue of quantity. Of what account are my wheelbarrows of Perfect Dirt in the face of global ecological crisis that threatens to extinguish life on this planet? They miss the point, as this next Buddhist reference attests.

Alarmed by the thousands of sentient beings that a raging forest fire was killing, a tiny bird flew some distance to a neighboring lake, scooped up a beakful of water, and emptied it on the flame. It kept shuttling back and forth between the lake and the fire until it collapsed from exhaustion. It knew how little its ministrations would accomplish. Still, it continued to the end because it found that that was the only thing it wanted to do.

To conclude my own story, it helps to set it in perspective if I add that I am married to an avid gardener. The arrangement is that I create the dirt—with a little help from above, to be sure—and she can then do with it as she pleases.

There are feebler contracts on which to prolong a marriage.

How many times have you wondered about some aspect of your life that ended in bitter disappointment despite all your best efforts: What was the purpose of that? And what exactly did all that shoveling accomplish? Diddly, that's what. Squat. Thanks very much.

What I loved about Huston Smith's gently provocative essay was that he finally answered questions I've asked of heaven many times, only to come to think of them as rhetorical. But with the idea of composting as a spiritual metaphor, as well as a practice, then the shoveling starts to make sense. All of those mysterious times when we seem stuck, we're meant to just gently turn the pile (pain, remorse, regret, guilt) over, work a little more Spirit into the moldering parts of our broken dreams. Next, with a little loving attention, carefully pick out the stones and bric-a-brac no longer necessary. And then wait. The season will come to sow again, but this time, instead of our seeds falling onto rocky soil, they will find their home in Perfect Dirt. The most that we can do, then, when we are emotionally, creatively, or spiritually stuck, is all Nature asks of herself: participate in the regeneration of our own destiny.

Jeffrey Mishlove: It's a pleasure to have you here. Your background in religious studies and philosophy and psychology is very extensive, and the topic that we're going to discuss is so very broad in some ways; there are so many religions and they're so diverse. And yet ultimately they all seem to reflect the mind of humanity. Would you say that as a scholar of religion you've become a more religious person yourself?

Huston Smith: I certainly don't feel that I've become less religious, and I also feel that these studies have deepened and broadened my understanding of religion. But whether that has made me a more religious person in the best sense of the word, I can't say. I'm too close to the question to be the judge, besides which, I don't know what I would be like if I had gone a different route.

Mishlove: I suppose it's always a little delicate for a scholar, who is supposed to be objective, to study something as intense and passionate as religion can be.

Smith: Some see it as a problem, but I've been fortunate that it's never been a conflict for me. It seems to me that the opposite would be very difficult—that if you were studying something you were not really in love with, or you felt it could not bear the light of careful analysis and added information—now, that would be a real tension, a real conflict. But it's been one of my blessings, I think, that I've been able to spend my professional life working on precisely what concerns me most.

Mishlove: My first encounter in a personal or a deep way with the psychology of religious experience came from, of course, reading William James's classic, The Varieties of Religious Experience—
Smith: A wonderful book.

Mishlove: —in which he described his experiments with nitrous oxide and other drugs at the time.
Smith: That's right, yes. Very courageous, adventuresome mind.

Mishlove: And also in the mid-sixties, reading a book by Timothy Leary and Ralph Metzner [and Richard Alpert] called The Psychedelic Experience, *in which they attempted to create the analogy between the pantheon of gods in the Hindu and Buddhist traditions with the dynamic forces working in the subconscious mind.*
Smith: Yes, yes. That was a very interesting and indeed important— what shall I say?—happening of our time, because this correlation and connection, it's a very delicate one, as we all know. But between artificially induced paranormal experiences and ones that come naturally, they can have, and do at times have, a great deal in common.

Mishlove: An overlap, at least.
Smith: A huge overlap. The discovery of these substances is actually a rediscovery, because knowledge of them goes back at least three thousand years, and perhaps much further than that. But the fact that we now know how they work on the brain has opened this up as a field of study that it had not been before.

Mishlove: You were involved in some of the early work at that time.
Smith: Actually I was right at the eye of the cyclone. That was 1960,

and I was teaching at MIT and had arranged to have Aldous Huxley come there on an endowment program that enabled luminaries in the humanities to come to MIT. So I was his host for the fall of 1960 at MIT, and of course he had written the book *The Doors of Perception,* which was one of the opening books in this area.

Mishlove: Describing his experiences with mescaline?

Smith: Mescaline. Well, it just so happened that when Aldous Huxley arrived at MIT that September, Timothy Leary was also arriving at Harvard from Berkeley. And on the way—you know the story; it's part of history now. On his way, he took a vacation swing down into Mexico, and on the edge of a swimming pool one afternoon ingested—what?—seven mushrooms, which opened up his mind in ways that totally startled, took him by surprise.

Mishlove: Psilocybin mushrooms, I presume.

Smith: That's right, that's right. He had arrived at Harvard with a blank check. He was a research professor, had accepted an appointment as research professor in the Center for Personality Study, and he could pick his subject, whatever he wanted to work on. And the moment he had that experience, he was of course absolutely fascinated and mystified by how mushrooms could cause that kind of impact upon his mind, but he didn't know what to do with it. But he had read Huxley's book. So I actually had a part in getting the two of them together, and it's true, for that fall the three of us were very much in the ring in this matter.

Mishlove: This was a time, of course, when these drugs were perfectly legal.

Smith: Not only legal, but this was respectable. It was research at Harvard University. One of the first things that Leary did was to mount an open study in which people would simply report their experiences, but he found so many of those experiences had a mystical cast to them that he began reaching out for someone who might know something about mysticism. And that's where he tapped me and involved me in the project.

Mishlove: You had been studying mysticism long before this, I presume.

Smith: That's true, right.

Mishlove: Had you thought about the relationship between mysticism and drugs prior to your encounters with Leary and Huxley?

Smith: Well, only academically, in that I had read descriptions in *The Doors of Perception*. As he points out there, phenomenologically, which is to say descriptively, if you match descriptions of the experience, they are indistinguishable. I actually conducted an experiment on that in which I took snippets of paragraphs from classic mystical experiences, and then descriptions of experiences under the psychedelics, which were mystical. Of course not all experiences under those have that character, but those that did. And then I shuffled them up and gave them to people who were knowledgeable about mysticism, and asked them to sort them in what they thought—

Mishlove: Which came from the real mystics and which came from the drug users.

Smith: Exactly. And there was no reliability in their predictions.

Mishlove: That sounds similar to a more recent piece of work I know Lawrence LeShan did, where he took statements of mystics and statements of physicists and compared them, and they seemed almost indistinguishable as well.

Smith: That's right. I'd like to add one other thing. Phenomenologically, which again means simply descriptively, one cannot tell the difference. But I think I would want to say that that's not the only dimension, because religion is not simply an experience; religion is a way of life. And experiences come and go, but quality of life is what religion is concerned with. So one has to ask also, not only do they feel the same, but is their impact on one's life the same?

Mishlove: Well, I think especially now that we can look back after twenty years from the original psychedelic experiments of that type, you can see distinct differences between psychedelic cults and real deep religious traditions.

Smith: That's right. So I think it's important that, having touched on this subject, we not leave the impression that the two are identical in every respect. Simply descriptively they are indistinguishable.

Mishlove: What about the original insight that Leary seemed to have in The Psychedelic Experience *that the gods really do exist within us? I think what he was saying in effect is that the pantheons of gods from the ancient pantheistic religions are real active forces, even of a paranormal variety, within our own minds, even if we're Jews or Christians.*

Smith: Yes. Well, that's another very interesting development in our time—that in the religions of the West, up to this point divine forces have been imagined externally from the self. But when one comes to think of it, when one talks about things of the spirit geography falls away; the spirit is not bound by space and time. Therefore the distinction between out there and in here, which in our everyday life is very important—once one modulates to matter of the spirit this whole framework of space and time and matter sort of drops away. What we are now coming to see is that this talk about "out there" has a certain naturalness to it, but also certain limitations. One can just as easily turn the tables and talk about the divine within. If I can put it one other way, when one looks out upon the world, value terms—that is, what is good, are imaged as up there. The gods—

Mishlove: Heaven.

Smith: Heaven. And the gods are on the mountaintops, and angels always sing on high. They don't sing out of the depths, the bowels of the earth. But when we introspect—and by the way, that imagery is natural, because sun and rain come from on high too—but when we turn our attention inward and introspect, then we reach for the other kind of imagery, of depth. You know, we talk about profound and deep thought. All this is leading up to the fact that in point of fact this distinction between out there and in here is artificial and only metaphorical when we're talking about things of the spirit. And now I think in our time—this is one of the changes—having worked in imagery of the divine being out there, now there is a move toward realizing or exploring ways in which the same reality can be discovered within oneself.

Mishlove: Another related notion, I think, is the one originally developed by Èmile Durkheim, the French sociologist, in which he suggests that religions are really representations of the group mind of a society, and that the god of each culture is an embodiment of what he called the group mind. He almost described that in ways that seemed quite paranormal to me, when you begin talking about group mind— something like a Jungian collective unconscious.

Smith: Again, I think it's very useful. For one thing, we are too much given to the notion that the mind is simply attached to the brain, and therefore because the brain has a given geographical locus, then the mind must too. But I remember in a weekend conference down in Tucson a few years ago with Gregory Bateson, he posed to the psychologists Rollo May, Carl Rogers—all those people were there—he said, "Where is your mind?" And it sort of took everybody aback. But what he was leading up to is it's quite wrong to think of the mind as lodged inside the skin—encapsulated ego, as Alan Watts used to call it—that the mind reaches out as far as one's environment extends, in Bateson's notion.

Mishlove: And of course we can always go back to the argument of Bishop Berkeley that the entire physical universe, that everything we experience—your TV sets, for example—exist only in your mind.
Smith: Right.

Mishlove: There's no other way to identify them.
Smith: And we talk about ecology of nature now, but the ecology of mind, we're just beginning to get used to that idea. And yet it's an experience. One can walk into the room, and in current terminology, feel vibrations. You can sometimes feel like a wall of anger or hostility, but one can also sense an ambiance of peace, and now the physicists are realizing phenomena really float on networks and webs of relationship. So we're only now coming to see that our minds too

derive, they sort of factor out and congeal out of the psychic medium that Durkheim, I think, was quite right in identifying.

Mishlove: I notice, though, in contemporary religions, particularly among the evangelistic Christians who are experiencing such a revival, they're very concerned about certain errors that people fall into—you know, the notion that one might identify oneself with God in an egotistical way. How do you feel about that?

Smith: I think they've got a point. I mean, if someone comes along and says, "I am God," it's perfectly reasonable to say, "Well, your behavior doesn't exactly exemplify that fact." God, by definition, is perfect, and what human being can make that claim? So I think the ministers that you refer to have a good point, but it doesn't annul the concept of the divine within, which remains valid. The distinction can come even if we think of "the divine within," as Hinduism puts it. They have been perhaps the most explicit of all the great traditions in saying that ultimately, in the final analysis, in their terminology, Atman [the self] is Brahman [the Absolute], Atman is the God within, and Brahman is the God without. But then they deal with the point you're raising by saying, well, a lantern may have a functioning light within it, but it may be coated not only with dust and soot, but in egregious cases with mud, to the point where that light does not shine through at all. So both things are true, but both need to be said in the same breath. Namely, I believe that it is true that in the final analysis we are divine and are God, but we should immediately acknowledge how caked and coated we are with dross that conceals that divinity. It is, one is tempted to say, an endless quest to clean the surface, to let the light shine through.

Mishlove: We were discussing earlier in the program some of your experiences with some of the very primitive peoples, such as the aborigines in Australia. In their, I suppose, naive native religions, they are having a real sense of contact with this level of reality.

Smith: They do, in two ways, Australian aborigines. One is that they distinguish between our everyday experience and what they call "the Dreaming." The Dreaming is another level of experience, in which they participate in the life of their ancestors and indeed the creation of the world, in what we might call a trancelike state. But that doesn't quite do it, because even in the midst of their ordinary life, half of their mind, you might say, is still on or in this dreaming state. But then there's another way in which they're in touch with it, and this has to do with parapsychology as we know the word—telepathy, specifically. I was in Australia, basically giving a series of lectures at all the universities there but using my spare time to come in touch with the aborigines, and so I sought out at every university the anthropologists who introduced me and put me in touch with them. And I did not in that entire swing meet an anthropologist who was not convinced that the aborigines had telepathic powers. They simply told me story after story, of being with them, and suddenly one of the persons would say, "I must go back to the tribe; so and so has died."

Mishlove: That's a strong statement coming from anthropologists, who tend to be quite skeptical.

Smith: That's right. Their theory was, insofar as they had a theory, the presumption was that these are normal human powers, but like any power it can atrophy if unused, and also can be short-circuited if our conceptual mind doubts that it is real.

Mishlove: So would you say there are some religious traditions that encourage the development and the cultivation of the psychic side of human beings more than others?

Smith: It's interesting. I'll put it the other way, slightly differently. That is to say that most of them believe that these powers are there and that they do increase as spiritual advancement occurs. However, they also warn against it, and say if you make this the goal, why, you're settling for too little. And also there are some dangers; for one thing, this is treacherous water where one is not totally benign, but also there's a strong temptation, as these *siddhis,* as the Indians call them—

Mishlove: Powers.

Smith: Powers, yes. As powers become available to you, people's heads get turned, and they become egotistic in their abilities. And so in that way it can be counterproductive to the spiritual quest. So the greatest teachers are quite unanimous in saying they come but pay no attention to them.

Mishlove: But aren't there traditions—the shamanistic tradition, the Tantric tradition—which really emphasize these powers?

Smith: That is certainly so. Now, I guess I tipped my hand a little bit in excluding them from the most profound spiritual masters.

Mishlove: Perhaps you do have some preferences.

Smith: Shamanism is immensely fascinating, and extremely important in the history of religion. But sanctity one does not associate with shamans. They have immense power, and it can be misused as well as used. I think on balance it's been used. So I value them, but they're neither—what shall I say?—saints nor philosophers.

Mishlove: Well, perhaps we might liken the psychic abilities in this sense to musical ability, or to any other natural talent that could be used in different ways. And some religions cultivate music, I suppose, more than others.

Smith: That's right, that's right. Most shamans are very much linked with the people, in helping them with practical problems of life. But the aspect of religion that has to do with virtues and compassion and loving-kindness, now, this kind of thing is when I speak of profundity, getting into those waters. The shamans, that's not their forte. They have a different role.

Mishlove: As our program is beginning to wind down, I wonder if you could comment on two things. One is a little bit more on how your exploration of religions has affected you personally, and perhaps we can tie it to our viewing audience a little bit. Is there some message that you would have for those people who would be viewing us right now, in terms of what your studies might convey to them?

Smith: Yes. Like any term, *religion* can be defined as one's wishes. If one links it to institutions (and I think religious institutions are indispensable), they're clearly a mixed bag. We've had the wars of religions, but I tend to think this is the nature of institutions and people in the aggregate. What government has a clean or perfect record, you know?

Mishlove: We're running out of time.

Smith: In one sentence, I think if one takes a basic religious worldview, this is not only important but it's true, and we need to keep our ears open to those truths.

Mishlove: In spite of those problems. Dr. Smith, it's been a real pleasure having you with me today. Thank you very much.

Richard Scheinin: You write that peyote, like the other entheogens, can be a moral compass. Will you explain?

Huston Smith: The typical entheogenic experience or vision is of another world. Just like Plato tells us: the world outside the cave is a more significant, momentous *other* world. And once you have had a glimpse of it, compassionate behavior is the natural response.

Scheinin: How come?

Smith: Say you were in the presence of Mother Teresa. Can you imagine following her for a day and then going off in the evening and getting drunk or doing abominable acts? Well, these visions lay the same foundation—when we see human life in a broader, and a more true, a more *veridical* light, we see ourselves as more than we had thought we were. And that "more" never leads in the direction of evil or sin.

Scheinin: You write that mescaline acted as a psychological prism that expanded the bands of your own perception. How?

Smith: I still knew who I was, that I had taken the mescaline, and where I was—in Timothy Leary's house. And I could bring myself down to that level, if I wanted to. And occasionally I would touch base with it, and could hear my friends' voices in the next room, and could understand what they were saying.

But then, colors and light had *depth*, spatial depth. And patterns on the carpet undulated. More important, *time* was very paradoxical. A moment could be both just a moment and all time, pressed into that moment. You experience what Blake described as "holding eternity in the palm of your hand." You are seeing things *more* like they actually are than when we are in our normal state of consciousness.

Scheinin: So the entheogenic experience "opens" the brain?

Smith: Oh, yes. And we bring something back: we realize that there *is* another world. Now, I think that realization is the heart of all religion. There is our mundane, everyday world, and then another world, which is incomparably superior to this one. But in our materialistic, skeptical, reductionistic, scientistic society, why, we're in danger of losing our confidence that there is another world. But once you've had the *authentic* entheographic experience, you can't be the same as before.

Scheinin: But religions use all sorts of tools to find that other world: meditation, drumming, chanting, abnormal breathing. Why write about the entheogenic visions—which some would call "hallucinations?"

Smith: I did not publish this book *[Cleansing the Doors of Perception]* lightly. The opening sentence of the preface says, "Is it possible today, in the climate of fear created by the war on drugs, to write a book on the entheogens . . . ? And is the reading public ready for such a book?"

I still do not know whether the public is ready. It's not an easy book. So the danger is that the reader makes a short-circuit and thinks, "Here is perhaps the leading popularizer of the world's religions . . . speaking up for drugs."

If anyone, just seeing the cover of this book and my name, took it as a come-on for taking drugs, I will be very sorry that I published it. Because there are risks in taking any kind of mind-altering substance, including the entheogens. Many drug experiences are just cacophony and may be delusory.

The corollary is that there can also be gains. And I begin the book with quotations from William James and Aldous Huxley. These are Huxley's words: "The mescaline experience is without any question the most extraordinary and significant experience available to human beings this side of Beatific Vision."

The issue for my book is that there can be gains: the direct experience of another world, which is better, and which is our eternal home. Now, the possibility of having a foretaste of that can give something precious to the religious seeker—can boost their confidence so that they do not simply take these teachings of the religions as hearsay or on faith.

Scheinin: Still, if you walk down Telegraph Avenue [in Berkeley, California], there are burnouts all over. How can you establish the groundwork for responsible, religious use of entheogens?

Smith: This is an important point. But mine is not a programmatic book. I am a historian and a philosopher. The *practical* problem I delegate to a group, right here in the Bay Area, that calls itself the Council on Spiritual Practices. Can we devise the equivalent, for the entheogens, of seat belts in automobiles? The council is working on that.

Scheinin: What were the circumstances leading to your first entheogenic session at Timothy Leary's house in 1961?

Smith: I had brought Aldous Huxley to MIT in 1960, and he landed there the very same week that Leary landed at Harvard, a mile and a half up the Charles River. So Leary got in touch with Aldous, and I was serving as Huxley's social secretary.

I had put in twenty years on meditation. I don't knock it; I still meditate. But I'm a flat-footed mystic, in the sense that meditation never created *thumping* mystical experiences for me. . . . I was *hoping* for a mystical experience. And I didn't get one. I think my ego boundaries are unusually firm. . . . So, I of course volunteered for the experiment. At this time the substances were not only legal, but respectable. We were involved in a Harvard research project!

Scheinin: You write about returning home after taking the mescaline and finding your "precious" children asleep in bed. Did you ever feel that you had opened yourself to influences that might harm your children?

Smith: No. I felt a depth of delight in seeing them—which most parents sense and are aware of, in our better moments, when we're not too busy. But it took on a new dimension. They seemed, even if it seems prosaic to say it, *infinitely* precious to me. And for about three or four days after that, when the spell was still sort of lingering, I didn't want to do anything practical. And fortunately it happened on New Year's Day, so we were on holiday. I just sat around in wonderment and wanting to be with those I love and shut out the rest of the hectic world, sit in the garden, just mulling over and drinking it all in.

Scheinin: But it didn't really change the course of your life. You didn't turn on or drop out, as Leary recommended.

Smith: It didn't change my thinking at all because my worldview of the mystics was already solidly in place. What it did was enable me to experience what I had long believed to exist.

Scheinin: Has it undermined you over the years, or been a negative?

Smith: Not negative. But let me say that I only had a handful of entheogenic experiences during those years. About a decade ago, I got involved in the Native American cause, and I gave two years of my life to that. I had four overnight vigils in the teepees with members of the Native American Church, and I took the peyote. But that was "in the line of duty."

I have a tremendous awe of these substances. And awe is not fun. For awe is that unique religious experience which combines two opposites, fear and fascination. Fascination, because realms of existence are opening that you didn't even know are there. Fear, because these are new realms, but can you survive them? Often there come times when you are afraid that you'll be crazy for the rest of your life.

I hold these substances in fear, and that's one reason I don't want to repeat it. The other is that I have things to do and don't want to be interrupted!

Scheinin: Some scholars say the ancient Greeks ingested an entheogen during secret rites known as Eleusinian Mysteries. What might these have been like?

Smith: The Eleusinian Mysteries held in place for two thousand years, and the top philosophers—Plato, Pythagoras, and so on—were initiates. It was the elite intelligence. And in two thousand years, no one ever violated their order *not* to tell what went on or what was disclosed to them in that months-long initiation. Boy, that is fidelity to the promise of secrecy! On the climactic night, we know they drank a potion, and it was an entheogen.

Now, I am going to make a little diversion. These visionary experiences can come about through the ingestion of maybe five substances—the entheogens, taken by the right people in the right settings. But they are also brought on by two other things: physical exhaustion (including fasting) and water deprivation.

Think of Buddha under the bodhi tree: he has one of the world's earthshaking visionary experiences, and the austerities that he goes through—according to the accounts—fifty days motionless and not drinking. So Buddhism was *kicked off* by an experience occasioned by brain chemistry alteration.

Christ, after his baptism, goes into the desert for forty days and nights. Where is the water coming from? Where is his food coming from? I can't prove it, but it seems to me very likely that his brain chemistry underwent certain alterations as a result of exhaustion and ordeal.

Scheinin: What's the difference between insight and delirium? There's some relationship.

Smith: Absolutely. And I am sorry to tell you this, but there's no litmus test to separate the two. Plato, who had undergone the Eleusinian

Mysteries, said that there are several kinds of madness. And in fact, I quote him saying, "The greatest truths are those that come to us through divine madness." Now "divine madness" seems like an oxymoron. It seems mad to the world. And yet it opens the door to truth.

Aldous Huxley told me, "Never say that these experiences are caused by mescaline" or whatever substance it was. "Say they are *occasioned* by" the ingestion of these substances. He saw the distinction, and how they are enabling, but they are not the sole cause. I think they direct our awareness by certain configurations that happen—neuron firing—which let revelations come through to us. But they do not generate those revelations. They *cleanse* the doors of perception.

I am wrestling with the thought of one more essay that will squarely face this question: Can we hold on to the conviction that these disclosures about the mystical experiences are true—not just trumped up by scrambling neurons in the brain?

Scheinin: Why do you have such faith in their truth?

Smith: Because they have shown me what I already believed was true. They didn't change my worldview. They just fleshed it out with direct experience.

One more thing: the important thing is not altered states, but altered traits of life. If the experience doesn't in the long run make you more compassionate, reduce the clamoring ego so that you can give attention to others—why, then it's for the birds. Experiences come and go. In fact, this is one sign that people are on the wrong track—that they keep on wanting more and more experiences. They ought to get down on their meditation pad and start meditating to bring what they discover into their daily life.

Timothy White: I understand that you once defended R. Gordon Wasson's theory that soma—the plant that inspired the ancient Rig Veda—was probably the psychoactive mushroom known as fly agaric or Amanita muscaria. *Do you think that it is possible that other early religions could have been inspired by entheogens?*

Huston Smith: I think it is more than a possibility. I definitely wouldn't say that all early religions arose from chemically induced theophanies, but I think there is clear and undeniable evidence that psychoactive substances have played prominent roles in some religious traditions.

In 1972, I wrote an article for the *Journal of the American Academy of Religion,* which basically endorsed Wasson's proposal that soma was most likely the mushroom *Amanita muscaria.* Most scholarly reviews of his book *Soma* endorsed his conclusion. Of course, it is important to remember his case is built on circumstantial evidence, not irrefutable facts. Nevertheless, until someone makes a better

This interview is excerpted from "Understanding Psychedelic Mysticism: An Interview with Huston Smith," by journalist and artist Timothy White, published in *Shaman's Drum: A Journal of Experiential Shamanism* 49. Reprinted by permission of *Shaman's Drum.* Copyright © Timothy White 1998. Published by the Cross-Cultural Shamanism Network, Williams, Oregon; 541–846–1313.

case for an alternative, I assume that the soma of the Rig Veda was the fly agaric.

Almost a decade earlier, in 1964, I wrote an article titled "Do Drugs Have Religious Import?" which appeared in the *Journal of Philosophy,* the house organ of the American Philosophical Association. Although we have learned a lot about psychedelics in the ensuing thirty years, the points I made in that article have weathered the ravages of time pretty well. Just last week, I got another request for permission to reprint that article in an anthology. The managing editor of the *Journal of Philosophy* tells me that it has been anthologized more than twenty times—more than any other article published in that journal.

The basic drift of that essay still seems valid today. First, there is ample historical evidence that psychoactive substances have been implicated with a number of religions. It is clear that soma was a psychoactive plant, and that *kykeon,* the secret drink that the classical Greeks consumed during the Eleusinian Mysteries, contained some type of psychedelic substance. Scholars may continue to debate which psychoactive substances were used, but in both cases it is hard to avoid the conclusion that psychedelics figured importantly in those religions.

There are also the many contemporary examples of psychoactives being used in religions. Thanks to R. G. Wasson, Blas Reko, and R. E. Shultes, we know that the Mazatecs of Mexico still ritually consume "sacred mushrooms," as did their Aztec ancestors, who once called the mushrooms *teonanacatl,* or "God's flesh." As you well know, the psychoactive cactus peyote is at the heart of the Huichol Indian religion and culture in Mexico. In North America, there is the well-documented example of the Native American Church, whose members consume peyote as a religious sacrament during their all-night ceremony, or "prayer meeting."

The second major point I raised in the article was that from a phenomenological or descriptive point of view, psychedelic experiences are indistinguishable from traditional mystical religious experiences. In the article, I mentioned several studies that support this view.

Let me briefly describe one of the most interesting studies of substance-induced religious experiences: Walter Pahnke's famous doctoral experiment, which is sometimes referred to as the "Miracle of Marsh Chapel" or the "Good Friday Experiment." Pahnke drew up a typology or checklist of mystical religious traits, based on the descriptions of mystical experiences compiled by Walter T. Stace in his classic book, *Mysticism and Philosophy.* Then, he arranged for twenty theology professors and students to participate in a psychedelic experiment. Half of the group was given capsules of crystalline psilocybin and half were given placebos as a control group. The psilocybin was administered "double blind," meaning that neither Pahnke nor his subjects knew who was getting psilocybin and who the placebo. Then, the students all attended a Good Friday church service held at Marsh Chapel.

Following the chapel service, the subjects wrote descriptions of their experiences, which were later rated by independent reviewers against Pahnke's checklist of mystical religious traits. Pahnke's study showed that the subjects who were given psilocybin experienced religious phenomena, which were indistinguishable from, if not identical with, the typology of mysticism.

Stace, a philosophical authority on mysticism, was once asked whether he agreed with Pahnke's view that the psychedelic experience is similar to the mystical experience. He answered, "It's not a matter of it being similar to mystical experience; it is mystical experience." After observing several decades of psychedelic usage, I would qualify Stace's statement: some, but not all psychedelic experiences may be mystical or religious in nature. We now understand that psychedelic experiences can range from ecstatic euphorias to terrifying hells and bum trips, from transformative revelations to meaningless hallucinations.

Based on the fact that the same psychedelic substances can produce varied responses, researchers and users in the 1960s arrived at the now-famous axiom that psychedelic experiences are influenced by three primary factors. These are the pharmacological effects of the psychological makeup of the individual, the setting, and the social and physical environment in which the psychedelic is taken. I began to wonder if certain sets and settings might predispose one toward religious mystical experiences.

In the *Journal of Philosophy* article, I cited several psychedelic studies supporting my thesis that the set and setting were critical to producing a psychedelic religious experience. When psychedelics are given to people under benign, naturalistic conditions—yet without any attempt to influence the outcome—approximately one-fourth to one-third of the participants will have religious experiences. Among subjects who have strong religious inclination to begin with, the proportion having religious revelations jumps to three-fourths. In the case of Pahnke's Good Friday Experiment, where religious-oriented subjects took psilocybin in a religious setting, the ratio soared to nine out of ten.

Of course, there is a great deal more to religion than mystical experiences. Religions try to provide answers to the mysteries of life, but they are also concerned with enhancing the quality of life. The great religions encourage and promote compassion and loving-kindness.

From my perspective, the litmus test of religious revelations is whether they enhance a person's life and whether they enhance the lives of others. Although there is ample evidence that psychedelics can trigger mystical experiences, there is much less evidence that they produce religious lives.

The same observation could be applied to religious revelations. Many religions recognize that even "legitimate" mystical experiences can easily come to naught if they are not grounded in discipline. Zen scholar Philip Kapleau once observed that even the vision of oneness attained in Zen satori can, in time, become clouded and fade into a memory if it is not supported by *joriki,* a particular power developed through *zazen* [seated meditation] and other meditations.

By now, it should be obvious that I do not believe that ingesting chemicals will automatically lead people to enlightenment and to lives of compassion. Nevertheless, I do believe that when psychedelics are used within a religious context or by a religious person, they can lead to revelations that make a significant difference in that person's life. I would also caution that psychedelics can turn into crutches if we assume that psychedelic ecstasies are a substitute for doing our spiritual work. I like Ram Dass's dictum "Once you get the message, hang up."

The examples of Ram Dass and Tim Leary may provide some insights into the usefulness of psychedelics. Ram Dass explored psychedelics within a religious framework, and his revelations inspired him to dedicate his life to helping others. He has made a significant difference in the lives of others. Leary, in contrast, had no religious worldview, and he had difficulty grounding and manifesting his psychedelic revelations. I think Jack Kerouac was correct when he commented to Leary—after their first trip together—that "walking on water wasn't achieved in a day."

White: To give Leary a fair shake, I must say that his use of psychedelics seems to have inspired a spiritual perspective, at least in himself. During the last months of his life, while he was struggling with terminal cancer, he certainly showed a spark of spiritual wisdom in his approach to dying. But I basically understand what you are saying.

The difficult part of any mystical experience is bringing back the revelation of manifesting it in our lives—"on Earth as in Heaven," so to speak. Based on my own experiences, I would observe that entheogens can provide one of the easiest doorways to heaven, but I have also noticed that psychedelic revelations can sometimes be fleeting. Do you think that the maxim "easy come, easy go" may apply to religious revelation in general?

Smith: Not necessarily. Christian history is filled with countless revelations that occurred not through extended effort but through the grace of God. I don't even think that psychedelic experiences are inherently fleeting in their impact.

One of the best examples of how a single psychedelic experience can transform a person can be seen in the life of the nineteenth-century educator Cardinal John Henry Newman. Newman's book on higher education is still considered one of the best ever written, and his idea of the university has had a profound influence on Western education—it's not by chance that nearly every major university in this country has a "Newman Center" for its Catholic students.

Now, many people who are familiar with Cardinal Newman's life story may find it difficult to believe that this respectable nineteenth-century cleric would have had a psychedelic experience, but I think the circumstantial evidence is very clear that that is what happened. I'm not suggesting that Newman took psychedelic substances, only that he had a psychedelic vision. Let me explain.

It is common knowledge that John Henry Newman was a psychological mess in his early twenties. He suffered from a crippling fear of failure that had become an insurmountable obstacle in his life. It is also common knowledge that he was transformed by a religious experience—a revelation that God had singled him out for leadership. I can't prove it, but I am convinced that the revelation that prompted him to pull his life together was stimulated by a psychedelic experience.

Part of the credit for discovering the evidence should go to Hilary Jenkins, whom I met at the Salzburg Seminar on American Studies in 1972. As chance would have it, I was giving a talk about the connection between psychedelics and religion, and Jenkins had been researching his forthcoming biography of Cardinal Newman.

At the time, some religious scholars were refusing to accept the authenticity of psychedelic revelations, purely on the philosophical grounds that religious experiences could not possibly be triggered by taking chemical substances. Because of my interest in psychedelics and religious mysticism, I had been reading the research of medical anthropologist Raymond Prince, who co-edited the book *Do Psychedelics Have Religious Implications?* Prince's research had shown that starvation, extreme physical exhaustion, and certain infectious diseases—such as smallpox and typhoid—produce neurochemical changes that are similar to those caused by psychedelics. Because such conditions were quite common before the advent of modern medicine, Prince suggested that they could have induced countless psychedelic visions, which may, in turn, have played a prominent role in shaping religious experiences through the ages.

In my talk at Salzburg, I posed a rhetorical question: If Prince was right about infectious diseases and starvation prompting psychedelic experiences through involuntary changes in brain chemistry, should theologians summarily discount the many historical revelations associated with diseases and fasting? After my talk, Jenkins approached me and told me that he had uncovered an interesting fact: Newman's religious calling had occurred during a near-fatal bout with fever—a fever that appears to have been typhoid. Newman had experienced three days of delirium, and it was during that period that he experienced God calling him and telling him that he had a special destiny.

Based on Prince's research and the likelihood that Newman has suffered from typhoid fever, I became convinced—and Jenkins agreed with me—that Newman had probably experienced a biochemically induced vision. Assuming that was the case, Newman's vision provides an excellent example of how a single psychedelic experience can have transformative power. Newman certainly emerged from his mystical experience a transformed person, and he went on to become one of the intellectual giants of modern times.

Newman's case history raises some interesting questions. What would have happened if he had known what we know about biochemical stimulation of the brain, and he had assumed that his brain's chemical wiring had gotten messed up? Would he still have accepted his vision as a revelation, or would he have discounted the experience as a hallucination? If Newman had dismissed his vision that God had a purpose for him, it is quite possible that he might never have developed the drive and perseverance that turned him into a powerhouse.

White: Your example of Newman's transformative vision reminds me of the near-death experiences—or NDEs—studied by Raymond Moody and others. As you know, NDEs have resulted in ecstatic visions and personal revelations that have profoundly changed many lives. I suspect that there may be more to such experiences than mere changes in brain chemistry.

Several researchers have observed that NDE survivors often come back with enhanced psychic abilities and, sometimes, healing abilities. That intrigues me, because there are many examples of Native American shamans—such as Wovoka and Smohalla—who have claimed that they received their shamanic powers through dying and coming back to life. I think these parallels between NDEs and shamanic ecstasies may be more than coincidental.

I can't help but wonder if shamanic and mystical technologies may have developed from spontaneous situations that took people close to the edge of death and induced NDE visions. Obviously, it would be impractical for people to expose themselves to typhoid fever or other deadly diseases in order to induce visionary states. However, it is easy to see how some of the other psychedelic catalysts cited by Prince—such as prolonged fasting and extreme physical exhaustion—could have evolved into shamanic and mystical technologies.

Do you think that ecstatic technologies, particularly those that seem to mimic near-death experiences, could be used to induce transformative visions comparable to those that have inspired earlier religious mystics?

Smith: I can accept experiential practices as one of the tools of mystical traditions. It may be true that some religions even say, "Do X and Y will follow." However, I think that science has conditioned us to look for cause and effect, and that people today consequently place too much reliance on the efficacy of reductionistic technologies.

White: I agree that it is counterproductive to reduce religions and shamanism to one-dimensional, reductionistic technologies. In my experience, shamanic traditions—which tend to be very practical and result-oriented—seldom use just one or two technologies in isolation. Even in shamanic traditions based on potent entheogens, shamans often use a variety of secondary technologies—such as drumming, fasting, and chanting—in conjunction with the entheogens to achieve shamanic states.

As you noted with psychedelics, technologies used alone have their limits. Nevertheless, when technologies are linked with appropriate sets and settings, they do seem to generate mystical religious revelations. Take fasting, for instance. Famines won't automatically turn people into mystics, yet fasting does seem to enhance both spiritual and shamanic experiences. The early Irish Christian saints, such as Saint Brendan, certainly relied on prolonged fasting and vigiling to induce mystical visions.

Smith: Technologies and methodologies may work marvelously for some people, but there is historical evidence that they haven't worked as well for some others.

Catholicism has tended to teach that God can be approached through the use of technologies such as fasts, vigils, and other austerities. Those methods may have helped produce some great Christian saints, but they didn't work very well for Martin Luther.

In his early years, Luther gave his all to following his order's monastic rules and technologies—fasting, praying, meditating—but those practices didn't work for him. Then, one day, a statement in the Creeds, "I believe in the forgiveness of sins"—one that he had recited hundreds of times before—broke over him indelibly. Thereafter, he didn't pay much attention to technologies, and most Protestants consequently teach that salvation is a gift of divine grace.

There have been ongoing debates in many religions over whether salvation or enlightenment can be achieved by grace or through one's own effort. In Japan or China, there is the division between *jiriki* [self-effort] and *tariki* [other effort]. In India, the gurus speak of the way of the cat and the way of the monkey. In the way of the cat, it is as if the mother cat picks up the kitten by the nape of its neck and the kitten doesn't have to do anything. In the way of the monkey, the infant monkey must cling to the mother's neck. Sometimes the debates between these schools of thought get positively vituperative.

White: I can attest that visions and revelations can sometimes come as unsolicited gifts from the gods or spirits. I have also seen that even rigorous vision quests don't necessarily result in visions.

Nevertheless, I have always found it interesting that Moses, Jesus, Muhammad, and Gautama Buddha all received some of their principal revelations during shamanistic quest experiences. Moses received several visions while fasting and praying on a mountain. Jesus spent forty days fasting alone in the desert. Muhammad was visited by angels while he was out fasting and meditating in a desert cave. The Buddha underwent eight years of extreme physical deprivation and long periods of meditation leading up to his enlightenment.

Doesn't it make sense that if the founders of the great religions found it useful to engage in ecstatic methodologies, others might also benefit from exploring those same practices?

Smith: It does. Your examples carry real weight. We have both affirmed that mystical revelations can happen in a variety of ways. Gratuitous grace may be one way. Psychophysiological technologies—like raja yoga—may be another. Ingesting psychedelics is another. I would like to champion one approach that we haven't talked much about but that I personally resonate with—revelation by way of direct discernment.

I think rituals have a very important place in all religions, including, of course, oral religions. These rituals provide an envelope for carrying and protecting the message. In many cases, the message and the rituals derive directly from an integrated mystical revelation. For example, in the Lakota Sioux vision of Buffalo Calf Woman, there was the initial visionary encounter with the holy woman who changes into a buffalo and offers her revelation. Then she takes the sacred pipe to the people and teaches them the seven sacred ceremonies that go with the pipe.

As long as religious rituals have power, they serve as containers for the truths, and the truths are carried down. Unfortunately, when the rituals lose their power, they become dead weight. I think that, to some extent, that has happened to the rituals of mainline churches in this country. Some of their rituals still work, but many of them have lost their power.

White: There is one more subject I want to discuss before we run out of time. I know that you were involved in the struggle to secure the American Indian Religious Freedom Act Amendments of 1994 (AIRFA). So I assume that you are aware of the recent Supreme Court ruling in the case of Boerne vs. Flores, *which struck down the 1993 Religious Freedom Restoration Act (RFRA) as unconstitutional [as applied to the states]. Does that decision affect the Native American Church?*

Smith: No. *Boerne vs. Flores* leaves AIRFA, which Congress passed a year after RFRA, untouched. And this leaves us in the interesting situation that the Church, which the Supreme Court outlawed in

1990, is today the one Church in the United States that is explicitly protected by law.

White: Unfortunately, that protection may soon prove fleeting. Since the Boerne vs. Flores decision essentially restores the Smith decision, it may be only a matter of time before state governments challenge AIRFA as an unconstitutional establishment of religion. Do you think that state governments may start enforcing state laws still on the books against peyote?

Smith: I'm not a legal scholar, so I don't really know what will happen. Having said that, let me review my understanding of the sequence of events that led up to the *Boerne vs. Flores* decision.

Quite apart from its specific impact on the Native American Church, the ultimate impact of *Employment Division vs. Smith* was that it lowered the threshold of proof that the government needs to amass before it can intrude on religion. Before that decision, common law—the accumulation of prevailing decisions—had established the principle that the government had to demonstrate that it had a "compelling interest" before interfering with a religious practice. After the Smith decision, all the federal or state governments have to do is to claim that they have a "rational basis" for interfering.

Justice Sandra Day O'Connor, in her dissenting opinion on the Smith case, argued against throwing out the "compelling interest" phrase. The Court could have gotten what it wanted by keeping the test and saying the NAC flunked it. As it was, by allowing the government to infringe on religious practice with flimsier reasons, the Supreme Court sent a shock wave through the country.

The day after the Smith decision came down, the largest coalition of religious groups ever to come together in U.S. history formed. Through several years of hard work, it secured the passage of the Religious Freedom Restoration Act. That act wrote the compelling interest standard into federal law—it stated that governments may not "substantially burden" a person's free exercise of religion unless they can show that the law being proposed is the least restrictive means of furthering that common good.

In my opinion, the Supreme Court used a rather minor case to strike down the RFRA legislation. The City Council of Boerne, Texas, which had created a preservation plan to preserve historic landmarks, had denied the application of the St. Peter Catholic Church to enlarge its building. The Catholic archbishop went to court and won an exemption under RFRA, and the Supreme Court responded by declaring RFRA unconstitutional. The courts said that Congress has no right to legislate the level of proof required for government interference in religion.

White: My understanding is that the Supreme Court justices viewed the Smith case as a states' rights issue, and they consequently resented Congress setting national standards for the protection of religious rights. In the Flores case, the Supreme Court ruled that RFRA was unconstitutional because Congress had exceeded its constitutional powers under the Eleventh Amendment, when it gave religions special rights and protections that weren't afforded to atheistic or nonreligious groups.

Smith: The Court did say that Congress had exceeded its powers in passing RFRA, and Justice O'Connor's dissenting opinion stated clearly that the key issue was who sets the level at which government can intervene in religious affairs. My question is, Why did the Supreme Court take the initiative to lower the threshold for government intervention? I see the Smith and Flores decisions as the unfortunate culmination of a movement that has been happening over the last several decades—the secularization of society.

When the separation of church and state was originally built into the First Constitutional Amendment, the intent of the framers was to protect religions from the tyranny of state-run religions. The authors of the First Amendment had come out of centuries of religious oppression in Europe, and they were concerned that the establishment of a state religion would result in the oppressing of other religions.

In this century, the courts have reinterpreted the no establishment clause to mean that religion should be kept totally out of secular life. Now, by throwing out the compelling interest principle, the court is saying that secular laws can take precedence over religious rights.

White: I find it ironic that a conservative court—swept into power by the religious right—has ruled in favor of secular convenience over the protection of religious rights. My concern is that by legislating and enforcing so-called neutral laws, local and state officials could easily harass minority religions. Antidrug laws could be used to strip the Native American Church of its sacrament, and fire regulations could be used to ban Native American sweat lodge ceremonies. Do you think we could be heading toward a sort of secular Inquisition?

Smith: I don't think the recent Supreme Court decisions were aimed at persecuting minority religions, but they seem to be another step toward the secularization of modern society. There is a growing tendency in government to view religions as spoiled, problem children who get in the way of implementing rational secular policies.

Despite the religious rhetoric of some politicians, most of the people who currently control our economy and our government were educated within a predominantly secular, proscientific educational system. Let me explain how this came about and how it impacts our culture.

I have had a long-standing interest in the interface between science and religion. The philosopher Alfred North Whitehead called these the two most powerful forces in Western history, and he went on to say that the future of humanity will depend on how these two forces settle down into relationship. For five hundred years, the relationship has been a nightmare. For several centuries, the Christian Church abused its power, trying to strangle science in its cradle. Once science gained the upper hand in this century, it went on the attack, trying to retire religious beliefs to the old folks' home.

For several centuries, scientism assumed that matter was the only thing that mattered and that everything else was an epiphenomenon. That view gradually led to the denial of spiritual experience and the rejection of much religious wisdom. Western science was quick to challenge sacred myths and religious traditions as unfounded superstitions, but ironically it has often replaced those myths and traditions with new, untested theories—which are essentially scientific myths.

It is important to remember that the word *theory* comes from the Greek word *theoria*, which was originally a theatrical word that had to do with presenting an idea on stage so that it could be seen. Theories may be useful starting points for further testing and study, but they should not be mistaken for facts or laws.

For most of this century, most Western schools have taught that science is the ultimate path to truth. The problem is that our schools have worshiped science as an impartial oracle of truth for so long now that many scientific theories have been turned into "scientific" dogmas by the popular culture. For example, biology has adopted a Darwinistic perspective of human evolution, which is not fully supported by scientific fact. There are so many missing links in the archaeological records that the debate over human evolution may never be resolved.

Recently, Alvin Plantinga, a distinguished philosopher and former president of the American Philosophical Association, and I noticed that the National Association of Biology Teachers defines evolution as holding that "life appeared through impersonal and chance happenings." The truth is that those two conditions are theories that have never been—indeed, can never be—scientifically shown; they are scientific speculations—not scientific facts.

Because such wording perpetuates an unnecessary schism between science and religion, Plantinga and I sent an open letter to the director of the National Association of Biology Teachers suggesting that it would be helpful to remove those terms. The director of that association responded, thanking us for the letter and saying that he would present our suggestion to the board of directors at their next meeting.

I believe it is only a matter of time before the ruling elite acknowledges the bankruptcy of materialism. The lives of the rich and famous have shown us that materialism doesn't necessarily bring happiness. Life without an awareness of spiritual reality becomes existentially meaningless. I think that is why so many people today are in search of spiritual experiences—we seem to have an innate need to experience and celebrate the spiritual dimensions of life.

White: Considering that it has taken several hundred years for scientific materialism to become the dominant paradigm of reality, how long will we have to wait for science to find common ground with religious mysticism?

Smith: Cultural lag can be devastatingly slow, but life is speeding up. Revolutions in science and education are happening far more quickly than they did in the past. I expect that by the first decade of the next century there will be a discernibly different ethos—one that is more open to spiritual realities than the scientism we have today.

One of the chief reasons I see light at the end of the tunnel is that many cutting-edge physicists have begun to recognize that the one-dimensional view of physical reality may not be the whole of reality. While I was teaching at MIT, I developed an interest in quantum physics, and I am still in touch with several world-class physicists at the University of California, Berkeley. Some of these physicists are now saying, "Everything we now know about nature points to the fact that the fundamental process of nature lies outside of space and time." That sounds very mystical and transcendental.

Science can't prove that there is another reality, but we're beginning to realize that science may be incapable of pronouncing on that issue. This has momentous implications because it suggests that we may need to look elsewhere for answers to life's ultimate questions.

Bill Moyers: Is God an objective reality to you?
Huston Smith: Yes. I would want to qualify that because it doesn't—my
   conviction does not stay on even keel all the time, and there are
   desert periods of the spirit. But by and large, my answer to your
   question is, "Yes." Was it H. G. Wells of whom somebody asked the
   same thing? He wasn't overly pious. He once said that the only two
   things that matter are sex and God. But somebody asked him, "Do
   you believe in God?" He groaned, and said, "What else?"

*Moyers: If anything characterizes the modern era, it seems to me, it's a loss of
   faith in transcendence, and yet, here you are, having spent your whole
   life teaching religion, and teaching about transcendence. I wonder if
   you sometimes have the impression that you've been going the wrong
   way on a one-way street?*
Smith: No, I don't think I have ever doubted that I was going in the
   right direction, because from early childhood on, by virtue of my
   upbringing, which was in a believing family (and it was a positive

This interview is a transcript of the conversation between Bill Moyers and Huston Smith for the PBS
television series *The Wisdom of Faith*, part 5, "Personal Philosophy," which aired April 23, 1996.
Reprinted by permission of Public Affairs Television.

experience) it "took" for me. I have not wavered in the most basic sense the way they saw reality—and the emphasis was absolutely on transcendence—that there is another reality that is more real, more powerful, and better than this mundane order. That has never wavered in my mind. Now, how it is to be conceived has changed all over the map in the ensuing years.

Moyers: And by transcendence, you mean . . . ?

Smith: By transcendence I mean there is a perfect being that embodies all the positive qualities that we experience in this life. Let's tick them off: intelligence; compassion; creativity; the classical virtues of beauty, truth, and goodness. All of these virtues that we experience are like fingers pointing at the moon, the moon being that transcendence. Now, the finger never reaches the moon, but it's very important in pointing in the right direction.

Kendra, my wife, just came home with a book of Flannery O'Connor's shorts stories, which reminded me of the title of another one of her books, *Everything That Rises Must Converge*. That just struck me because these fingers pointing at the moon with these various virtues that I've listed all converge and come together, and in transcendence they're not separate. They're smelted down so they are all present in an undivided unity, which our minds, of course, just smear when we try to imagine.

Moyers: Of course, the experience of the this transcendence is—

Smith: Not provable. The world is religiously ambiguous, and to my lights, always has been and always will be.

Moyers: And what do you mean by that?

Smith: I mean that the world comes at us whether we are ready for it or not. The Spanish philosopher José Ortega y Gasset said life confronts us point-blank. It doesn't ask, "Are you ready to be married? Are you ready to face suffering?" It just comes at us, and it's up to each one of us how we pattern this experience. For some, there is no meaning. I mean, it's randomness. For others, they see experiences that don't quickly, clearly fit into a pattern, and yet, on balance, they think that there is a pattern there which, as they come to understand its complexity, will become gradually and incrementally known to them.

That's what I mean when I say life is religiously ambiguous. It does not tell us what we have to think about it. Now, some regret that. They would like to have an answer given to them. Søren Kierkegaard is very good on this. He said, "That's what we think we want, but if we had it we would realize that's not what we really wanted, because if it told us the answer it would take our freedom away from us."

Moyers: If life *told us the answer?*
Smith: That's right. Then we would be like puppets, and we would just passively accept the answer. So the ambiguity of the world, religiously, dignifies us by forcing the choice, the decision, upon us.

Moyers: Well, it dignifies us in that sense. I can see that. But it also leaves us having to find our own answer. For those who don't find the pattern, who don't find the meaning, who don't discover the purpose of it all, it can be a forlorn discovery.
Smith: I think those people need—well, if I say our compassion, that patronizes them. They need our full respect, because if we experienced life in the way that they do, why, we would very likely be in the same position. On the other hand, I know people who have lived very creative, interesting lives who would think, at least in explicit terms, that the religious quest was an illusion. So I wouldn't say they haven't had very good lives. But I think on the average it is an enormous help, or it would not have existed. There are those sociologists who say that if an institution doesn't serve a function in society, it will drop away. The fact that anthropologists have found no society without it just suggests that it's doing something right. I think what it's doing is what you've just put your finger on—it provides mass and guidelines, which people perpetually fall away from, and don't live up to. But it sets a goal in the right direction.

Moyers: Is it true that archaeologists have found no founding city of a civilization that doesn't have a sacred center?

Smith: There are pockets in modern, contemporary Western civilization where the dominant mood is atheistic. But prior to the rise of modern secularization, modernism, in the traditional world, it's absolutely clear not only that every society has a religion, but the anthropologists cannot sort out what is the religious compartment because it just pervades the whole.

Moyers: *You make me think of a plant leaning toward the light—*
Smith: Wonderful.

Moyers: *—because the light is there. The light is real. What do you think a human life leans toward?*
Smith: Well, in minimal terms, it leans toward something more—and transcendence could come in there—something that transcends anything we have mastered and experienced up to this point. There's a little piece of doggerel that I learned very early on, by Rudyard Kipling. It's not great poetry, but it makes this point so vividly. I'll see if I can remember it. It's called "The Explorer":

> There's no sense in going further, so they said, and I believed them,
> Built my barns and strung my fences in that little border station
> Tucked away among the foothills where the trails run out and stop
> Til' a voice as bad as conscience
> Rang interminable changes on one everlasting whisper,
> Night and day repeating, "Soul,
> Something hidden, go and find it,
> Go and look behind the ranges,
> Something lost behind the ranges,
> Lost and waiting for you.
> Go."

I may have been twelve years old, and yet I still remember that because, whatever you think of it as poetry, it sounds the true note that there is something that lures us.

Moyers: *I once heard you say that you were teaching your students about another world to live in.*
Smith: Yes.

Moyers: Is that what you mean? This quest, this journey, this search for "more"?

Smith: Yes, yes. Oh, it is, and let me put it in a bit of context. My students, through their science courses, are also learning that there is another world. There is a quantum world, which is very strange and doesn't conform to our ordinary notions. I won't take time to elaborate on that. But they are taught, systematically, that there is a quantum world and a classical physicist world that underlies this experience that we have. But when it comes to our direct experience and the world of values and meanings and purposes, we have been so ravished by the scientific worldview, which, with all its magnitude and size and space and power, unfortunately cannot deal with. . . . Alas, the assumption is that when it comes to value, meaning, significance, our ordinary, mundane view of things is what there is.

Now, these great wisdom traditions that I have—and I'm so grateful—chosen to steep myself in for my career say the same thing, really, about this quantum world, *but on a value dimension.* The quantum physicist will tell us about a world of size, which we could never have dreamed of if we had to rely on our ordinary senses. And it's awesome when we think about how fast light travels, how long a billion years is, and so on. But what the great wisdom traditions speak to is the *vertical* dimension, which is the dimension of *worth.*

Moyers: Of worth?

Smith: Worth. Value, value and importance. And what they say is that the access is as much beyond our worldly, ordinary experience as the physical world of the cosmologist is beyond our sensory world. Science didn't have to struggle to free itself from religion when it— in the sixteenth and seventeenth centuries—earned its own autonomy, which is quite right. But since then, now, with the burgeoning of our confidence in the scientific point of view which, by and large, in the modern West overshadows the confidence in the religious point of view. Certainly on campus. Now, there is a disciplinary rivalry between science and religion, and the university, grounded in science, is in that camp and they do not want to release their claims to being the pipeline to truth through their methods. So there's a kind of built-in professional competition going on.

Moyers: And your understanding of religion, as you spent your whole life studying it and teaching it, is that it is another kind of truth? It is not a competitive truth or an alternative truth—it's another kind of truth.

Smith: That's a fair statement. In one sense, in the broadest sense, there is only one truth, and we have two windows on that. But the windows to it are very different.

Moyers: The one truth is reality?

Smith: Yes. Things just as they are.

Moyers: And science tells us the constituent nature of that reality, insofar as it is measurable, identifiable, weighable—

Smith: Quantifiable, in the end, and that it should be honored and validated as the near-perfect way to understand nature. But we should add calculatively so that we can use it, because the Taoists understood nature, too, but not calculatively. So the scientific method is the near-perfect way to understand a region of reality, but as a probe to the whole, it has shown itself—it has taken us three centuries to see that the scientific method, with all its power, is at the same time a radically limited instrument.

Now, again, a qualification. Science does deal with the invisible insofar as it can be definitely proven from the visible. If you sprinkle iron files on a sheet of paper and put a magnet under it, the files will straighten up, in line—proof of magnetic fields. Magnetic fields are invisible, but we know they're there because we can strictly infer their existence from the visible. But anything invisible beyond that you cannot infer logically, conclusively; science can't deal with it.

Moyers: But here's the difficulty. We can measure the truth of science, we can test the truth of science. We can measure the speed of light. But how do you test the truth of religion?

Smith: You cannot—not in the laboratory. You cannot test it in the way that delivers objective certainty in the way that the scientists can. To perform a laboratory experiment, the first thing you have to determine is what the relevant variables are. But we're talking about an intelligence that is greater than ours, as great—much greater—actually more—than our intelligence is greater than a dog's. Just as a dog would not know what would be the relevant item in terms of our mental framework, there's no way, since a superior intelligence lives in a wider world, that we're going to know what are the relevant variables. And so, in principle, it is impossible to prove or disprove the existence of God by the scientific method. Now, let's quickly add that the fact that we can't prove or disprove is no proof that it exists, but it is a knock-down proof that if God exists, there's no way that God is going to fit into a laboratory experiment. It would be like dogs getting together and saying, "We've heard about mathematics, let's just see if mathematics exist. We'll submit it to the sniff test." It would be something like that.

Moyers: If, by your own admission, you can't prove the truth of religion, what claim can you make about its plausibility?

Smith: The fact that all the enduring traditions make the same claim on this point, and the claim being that everything proceeds from an absolute perfection. Now, let me pause on that. You know, the Taoists believe there is a being, wondrous, perfect, how quiet it is, how mysterious it is. Everything comes from it. But it does not ask to be recognized. They say, I do not know its name, so I call it the Tao, and I rejoice in its power. One can go from that to India, where Brahman is infinite awareness, infinite bliss, and then one can go all the way over to the Semitic traditions where the ulti-mate—call it Yahweh, God, Allah—is a perfect being in which all power and virtue unite. You know, that's a remarkable unity to have occurred, independently, to the human mind. And why are we still quoting them today? That view has lasted.

Now, my own personal view is that it is so at odds with our daily experience, with its humdrum and dreary routine of obligations, that it's almost like Saul Bellow says of Mozart's talent: "All we can say in the end is that it comes from somewhere else." The religious word for that is: this truth is revealed. And I so hold it to be.

But now let me make a concession to modern thought. We can think about revelation as coming from outside. God tells people, plants it in people's minds. But we can also think of it as bubbling up, this insight bubbling up from the deepest unconscious of the spiritual geniuses of humankind. Now, in either case, it's a revelation. We've just switched our spatial image from coming from outside, or coming from the inside. But when I say bubbling up from the deepest, in either case, it's an incursion. It's an implosion into the conscious mind.

Now, I find that supporting evidence for the claim being true. But let's not deviate from what was said. There is no objective proof of this.

Moyers: I agree with you that all the religions entertain and are informed by this notion of perfect source, a perfect being. But whereas Mozart's music arrived flawlessly, beautifully, as an act, a gift of God, Amadeus, the work of this creator, the religious creator, has not arrived perfectly in the world. It is a very imperfect consequence of a perfect source. This is why the religions are silent. They are affirmative and assertive on the question of being and source, but they're confused and discordant and uncertain and ambiguous themselves over the consequences of that being's creation, and over the connection between the perfection of the source and the imperfection of the consequence.

Smith: Well, I don't think they are confused, and I don't think they are ambiguous. But I think on the basic theme of why the world is imperfect, I think they're basically saying the same thing. They're saying that it has to be imperfect in order to allow, Bill, you and me, to be here because we're not perfect. And this perfect source, let's just say it had the option to keep being existence to itself—or to share being with other kinds of creatures. If it wanted to share its being, it had to create creatures that were not perfect. Now, you would probably agree with it, but does it have to go this far in imperfection? St. Augustine says, "I came to see that the greater and the lesser, taken together, was greater than the greatest alone."

But that's where we have to realize, Bill, that we have no view of the whole. Take the matter of the analogy of our sight, how little we see. We see a few feet, a few yards, a few miles, and with our telescopes, something more than that. But when you take 15 billion light years, we have no experiential sense of that whole. Figuratively speaking, the things that immediately concern us constitute the "hot spot of being": How is it going in my career? How is it going in my personal relationships? and so on. And these are the hot spots of being that encompass, flood, almost the entire horizon. Those things are far removed. If we are aware of them at all, it's with a kind of cold indifference. They just do not figure.

What the wisdom traditions insist is that if we could understand and comprehend the whole of what seems to us, in our heart's hot spots, as being irreducible tragedies, it would be like the learning experiences that a one-year-old child encounters that we understand are necessary for the growth of that child. But we see it in a very different perspective and light than the child does.

Moyers: St. Augustine said that faith is essential for understanding. If you start with disbelief you won't get it. You've argued that in order to understand one of these faith traditions, one of the wisdom traditions, it's essential to get inside it. But how do you get inside it without subscribing to the belief? And if you subscribe to the belief of every faith tradition, are you just a relativist?

Smith: That's a problem in any area of understanding. The Sufis have the saying that there are three ways to understand fire. The first way is that you can hear about it. Somebody tells you, "Hey, there is this something like fire; it leaps around." The second way is to see fire. And the third way is to be burned by fire.

Moyers: Have you been, as the Sufi Muslims put it, "burnt" by that fire?

Smith: Yes. And what I would call being burned is those rare, just intrinsically wonderful moments when one feels that everything is in place and that life makes perfect sense, and then there is that sense of elation and joy and gratitude that comes with it. So doubts are just banished as irrelevant in those moments of disclosure. But, of course, we can't stay in that state. That's not our lot in this life. We're not here to be "blissed out" all the time, and so we come back to it. But they do offer moments of encouragement and a kind of verification. But, again, not of a public nature.

Moyers: There's a character in one of John Updike's novels who says, "Not even the worst atheist in the world denies that people have been religious." Everybody admits to that. But you don't stop there with just teaching your students the bare facts of religion. There's something else uppermost in what you're trying to do, whether it's talking about prayer, or talking about perfect being, or talking about the need for unity. There's something else going on in your teaching of religion that makes me wonder if you aren't considered an academic heretic, despite having spent your whole life at universities, from MIT to Berkeley. Some people might say you've become an evangel, or a missionary, not a professor.

Smith: I'm a maverick in the sense that I do not think that I can do justice to my material if I leave out what is most important. That means not making primary the objective facts about festivals and rituals and texts, and so on. It means leaving in the heat. The *essence* of what inspires all this is what happens in the human soul when someone *really* is in a religious moment.

Moyers: What your critics say is that the modern study of religion should be descriptive, and that the question of truth should be bracketed. They say that it's okay to teach about the human enterprise of religion in the academy, but that if you go beyond describing it and teaching about it, you have stopped teaching religion and started preaching it. There's a danger in which the professor and the scholar become apologists for and advocates of what reason, alone, is silent about.

Smith: That's a perfect statement of what the critics say. And why should religion be isolated as the only candidate for that criterion, when the whole university is riven with fanatical controversies as to truth in their particular field? If a music teacher didn't love music, what is he or she in the profession for? And I feel like I have the same love for my subject matter that they do.

Moyers: But to be fair to them, most scholars are afraid to "get inside" the thing that they're studying because they're afraid that they'll lose their objectivity. And just as many believers of a particular faith are unwilling to get too deeply into another's faith out of the fear that they'll lose what makes them unique. You seem to have avoided both fears—the fear of getting inside, and the fear of losing your own faith by coming to understand other faiths.

Smith: Yes, well, I'm not afraid of losing my objectivity, as it goes, because, Bill, my heart is pure! What I mean is I think it's transparent to the student from the first class. I don't want to indoctrinate them, and I'm honest about that. I haven't thought of it in this way before, but I really try to make myself a plateglass window, so they're not listening to me, they're not looking at me, they're looking at these wisdom traditions and what they say. And if you give students, with all their busyness, something to put before them, something of worth, they will see it, and they will move toward appropriating it. I admit I'm a proselytizer in one sense for the wisdom traditions. But if somebody is uninterested, I'm not a missionary in the sense of seeking them out. I'm a Buddhist, in the sense of the Buddha's opening gambit: "How are things going?" If the answer is, "Quite well," he said, "I'm very happy. I have nothing to say to you." And I think that's the way it should be. So there has to be an interest. If everything is going along swimmingly, including the fact you're not even curious about whether there are other things in this world than you know about, why, there's no reason for me to seek you out.

Moyers: Have you borrowed from all these religions to compose your own daily journey?

Smith: Not consciously. I certainly didn't set out to create my own religion, just right for Huston Smith. It doesn't go anything like that. But as I ventured out for basically a decade at a time in this tradition and the other, so much of enduring worth came through to me that I just was reluctant to leave some of those practices.

Moyers: You've said that religion calls the soul to confront this reality of the world. In what way?

Smith: To understand it in its deepest meaning, and to sense what that calls us to by way of response to it.

Moyers: And does religion help master the self?

Smith: Yes. Never perfectly. I'm a heretic among the Hindus in questioning the reality of what they call a *jivanmukta,* a completely enlightened soul within this body. I do not think this happens. I think our mortal coils are too firm and too binding to allow that complete attainment within this life, but incrementally. *Incrementally.* One can move toward that.

Moyers: So how do we comport ourselves in a pluralistic, materialistic, scientific world that is riven by both sacred and profane passions?

Smith: Yes, well, by keeping our wits about us. It's very difficult to do. I love Walker Percy's line "These are curious times, when you don't know who the enemy is, and you can't stand your friends." These are very troubled and turbulent times. I know of no formula that will do it, other than keeping our wits about us, trying to think about everything.

Moyers: It seems to me that the larger issue is that modern people no longer are confident that God created them.

Smith: Right.

Moyers: That we're even created in the image of God. What does it mean that human beings who once lived in the cosmos saturated with the sacred now simply scrape to find a crumb of meaning in existence? What does that mean to you?

Smith: It means that we live in a very troubled time in which we have stumbled into a frame of mind which has great potentialities in certain respects. Either there is meaning and purpose in this world (and in life) which eludes us—and it stands to reason we're just children in the face of that—or there is none. But if there is none, the alternative is randomness, and that is not a fulfilling answer. It's not much of an answer to live a life by. Now, even as I say these words, Bill, I know the objection: this is wishful thinking; that is the charge. Okay. One cannot prove that it is not, but as one moves into it, I think one sees more and more clues as to its being right.

Moyers: *My own understanding is that the meaning that each religion announces to the world is a meaning that has been wrestled from the world. Whether it's in a religious sense, like Jacob wrestling with the angel, or whether it's in the long pilgrimage of the Buddha to come to a sense of what the random patterns can be arranged to express and articulate; or whether it's Jesus in the wilderness discovering his mission, and then on the Cross finding his vindication or his purpose, or feeling in the lostness of the Cross his being born again; the meaning of each religion is not that transparent.*

Smith: What the religions say is that there is a happy ending that blossoms from difficulties that must be surmounted. I think these intellectual difficulties with seeing transcendence and perfection is part of the necessary groping and grappling and overcoming. Again, because then we have a part in the achievement. It isn't just handed to us.

Moyers: *There's this wonderful line in* Wuthering Heights, *Emily Brontë's novel, where Cathy says of Heathcliff, "He is always in my mind as my own being." As my own being. That presence for which there is no other word that I have. That presence is what I have come to appreciate most closely to be the experience of God. One and the same mind. Does that make any sense to you in your own experience?*

Smith: It makes absolute sense. Perhaps the greatest symbol in most lives of glory is the bliss of the divine. But as C. S. Lewis put it—I just came across this passage—"It is only an intimation." It is as if, and I'm now putting it in a personal theistic term, God needed to plant in this life an experience which would be the closest to joy and bliss. The moment of sexual union when it's absolutely complete and total love on each side is the closest manifestation to the divine, the joy, that God and bliss. But this is our clearest window to what the inner life of God is like. Affectively—in feeling.

Moyers: *Your understanding of God has changed through the years, has it not?*

Smith: Well, let us hope.

Moyers: That's part of the wrestling, part of the—
Smith: Yes, yes.

Moyers: —arguing with yourself and with—
Smith: With others, yes, it's part of it, and there's joy in it. In Herman Melville's novel *Billy Budd*, the main character says at one point when he's being goaded, baited into a fight, "I like a fair fight every now and then." So I too like this discussion with unbelievers.

Last evening when I reported in to Kendra, she asked, "How did it go?" And I said, "Now, the first day of filming was great, but I'm getting pretty sick of talking about spiritual matters in this degree of concentration. I'm beginning to feel like the person that the Zen people describe in their wonderful line 'He stinks of Zen.'"

But, Bill, we're picking up on important things. This reminds me that there is often a moment when I've been in joyful conversation, as I've been in with you for the last several days, when I think of some lines by the poet Robinson Jeffers:

> A little too abstract
> a little too wise
> It's time to touch the earth again
> and let the leaves rain down from the sky.
> That the rich life can run
> through the roots again.

Moyers: Thank you very much.
Smith: You're welcome.

CHAPTER 22 | **WHY RELIGION**
MATTERS NOW
MORE THAN EVER

Phil Cousineau: For many years you have written and taught that religion has always mattered, through human history. How has your belief that religion matters been affected by the tragedies of September 11, 2001?

Huston Smith: Well, there has been a shock effect, and people have been drawn up sharp, and that's very understandable. However, there has never been a time in our history when clear thinking was more important than it is today. This is at the heart of the matter. Let's get one thing straight right at the start. There are many things here that must be taken into consideration.

Now, every social institution conforms to that adage. You can never find a really pretty institution because there are lots of people involved, and it's not easy for them to get along well. Also, wisdom is limited. The ideal of the United States is wonderful, but my, how many flaws there are in our national life. Does anyone think it doesn't make mistakes and does bad things at times? It's the same with regard to religion.

This is an edited transcript of an interview with editor Phil Cousineau and filmmaker Gary Rhine that was conducted especially for this book. It took place in May 2002 at Huston Smith's home in Berkeley, California. Copyright © 2003 by Kifaru Productions. Reprinted by permission of Kifaru Productions.

I published a book, a few months before 9/11, and I titled it *Why Religion Matters.* I wrote it intending to show why religion matters for the good. But since 9/11, when I see that title, I find myself wincing—and I can all but hear people saying, "Of course religion matters—it causes trouble. It's divisive, it causes ethnic conflicts, which can escalate into terrorism and all-out war."

But that line of thinking misidentifies the cause of 9/11. The cause was not religion. Religion wasn't at the bottom of it. Those suicide bombers couldn't care less what Americans believe. It's the bad things that, in their view, we have done to them, that provoked the toppling of the trade towers and produced the Pentagon attack.

I can make this very graphic. At the heart of the Bosnia conflict several years back, I happened to catch a brief news clip. A journalist was interviewing a Serbian woman in a village: "Are there any Muslims in your village?" "No." "What would you do if there were one?" "We'd tell him to leave—and if he didn't, we would shoot him." And the interlocutor asked, "Why?" Her answer was, "Because that's what they did to us four hundred years ago."

That's what causes these horrendous conflicts. It's not the difference in religions. It's atrocities *unavenged* that's at the heart of the conflicts.

So we come back to the basic issue, Does religion matter *for the good?* I think that I was right in arguing in *Why Religion Matters* that on balance it matters for the good. To begin with, anthropologists have found no society without it. That in itself means that it must be doing something right, or it would have failed the Darwinian test—and disappeared from history. What's important is to see the contribution religion makes to life, to think through what religion does that is *positive,* and also to acknowledge the *sins* that it commits in the course of trying to realize its ideal.

Cousineau: That's very helpful, Huston, especially after what happened last fall. You may recall that I flew into New York on the morning of September 11 to begin a book tour. I landed in New York City around 8:50 in the morning, just minutes after the first attack on the World Trade Center and got trapped for hours in the chaos at La Guardia Airport. I was scheduled for an appearance at Rizzoli's Bookstore in the

Trade Center that very morning, at 11 A.M. The next day my publisher sent a car for me and somehow got me into Manhattan, and after our meeting where we spoke about the mythic implications of what had just happened, I wandered down to Washington Square Park, a mile or so from Ground Zero. I was struck by how many shrines had already emerged there—spontaneously—in honor of those who were missing. Hundreds of people were milling around the arch in the center of the square, just numbly staring at photographs of the missing that hung on the chain-link fence that surrounded the arch.

As I looked at the "Missing" posters, bereft with grief, someone wandered up next to me—a complete stranger—and together we wept. Then the stranger said, out of the corner of his mouth, with a kind of sneer on his face, "This is what we get for still being religious." The implication being that religion is a kind of medieval manifestation, a horrid or superstitious way of thinking, and that we should have advanced far beyond such irrational behavior. Then he said, rhetorically, "Well, what do you expect?" Again, implying that the terrorist attacks are what we get for not moving beyond religion.

Huston, I've heard you describe this kind of view as a "third-grade understanding" of religion. What would you say to people who are embittered or have an angry view of religion? Or what do you say to those who rightly point out how easily debased religion can be by those who abuse it for political purposes?

Smith: I'm glad you asked that. I would try to get them to think about this monstrous twentieth century that we lived through that witnessed more destruction than the innumerable centuries that preceded it. Possibly excepting the Holocaust, the greatest crimes were perpetrated by the only two avowedly atheist nations that history has ever seen. The Soviet Union, which had its Museum of Atheism, was one, and Maoist China was another. Both were militantly atheistic. And what did they do? Between them they killed 70 million of their *own* people. Why is it that we never hear that this is what atheism produces? Something's cockeyed here. Why do we come down hard on the sins of religion (which we should) while overlooking the sins atheists commit? They are conveniently overlooked by the secular society in which we live.

We can come at your questions from its other side by asking what we would lose if we throw the baby out with the bathwater. The bathwater is there. It's dirty and should be discarded, but it would be an incalculable loss if it we threw out the baby with it. What is the baby a metaphor for here? In a word, religion, but what makes it precious is its insistence that there is a reality other than the materialistic universe in which we live. Religion is important because it is the standard-bearer for this incalculably important idea that we human beings are not at the top of the hierarchy of intelligence in the total scheme of things. Heaven help us if we are. Religion insists that there is a reality that is wiser, more powerful, more compassionate, and more mysterious than we can possibly imagine. I think it is right in this claim, and that is why—again, on balance—I'm for it.

Let me, for a moment, put on my historian of religions cap and give you a quick "Cook's Tour" of what the great wisdom traditions, as I have come to think of them, say on this point. In East Asia, there was heaven and earth. Earth is this physical universe, and heaven is what transcends it, and, as Confucius said, "Only heaven is great." In South Asia we have samsara [repeated cycles of birth, misery, and death], again, this everyday world, and we have nirvana. I mean, what a signal that this is not all—there is something more to aspire to. And of course in the Abrahamic traditions of Judaism, Christianity, and Islam there is this physical universe, its creator, Yahweh, God and Allah.

The opposite of all this is materialism. Just last week I came upon an aphorism that states the contrast tellingly: "Materialism is a belief that is starving for ideas." The point of this assertion is subtle, but if you spell it out logically, materialism reduces ideas to their physical underpinnings—neuron firings. In technical parlance, an idea is an epiphenomenon—something that derives from what is less than it is, which makes them significant in the nature of things. They're like foam on the beer, unimportant compared with the beer itself, metaphor for the physical universe. Materialism is a deflating move. If we follow it to its logical end, there is no alternative to spiraling into cynicism and despair.

Cousineau: Is it possible that that downward spiral can be described or imagined as the modern version of Plato's cave? That we are where we are today because we are trapped in the world of scientific materialism or we've become convinced—or been hypnotized into believing—that the shadows on the wall are all there is? And if so, do you think Plato's allegory is still relevant today?

Smith: Absolutely. When I was conducting the Cook's Tour, I was going across the vast Eurasian continent, where all civilizations originated, and I included their philosophies along with their religions because in traditional cultures, there is little difference between the two. But in the West they've become bifurcated. I am so glad that you referred to Plato's cave because that allegory has been one of the two foundations of Western civilization, the other being the account of Moses on Mount Sinai. Both of them involve an epiphany, an incursion, of something greater than the mundane into history.

The outline of Plato's allegory is very simple, which belies its profundity. Plato asks us to imagine prisoners chained inside a cave in such a way that they can only face the wall, and that's the way their whole lives have been lived. All they have seen are the wall and the shadows, but behind them are puppeteers who parade puppets and different objects, and the sun outside the mouth of the cave throws the shadows of the puppets on the wall. All of this leaves the prisoners thinking the entire world is black and white and two-dimensional.

Plato then says, what would happen if one of those prisoners—just imagine with me—if one of those prisoners were to be un-chained and turned around and led toward the opening of the cave? What does he see?

First, he sees not just black and white, but Technicolor. Hey, there's color, color in this world! And not just shadows but light! Light? What's that? Then he goes out into the enchanted garden of the world, and he understands that this light is coming from a source—the sun that fills the world with light.

"Would he not be astonished?" Plato asks.

Fair question, I would say. But now suppose he is led back, and he wants above all to share this world with his fellow prisoners. "This isn't it at all," he says to them. "*It's out there!*"

Plato winds down the story by asking, What would they think? They would think he was crazy, and if he persisted in his opinions they would *kill* him. Plato was not imagining this because that's exactly what they did to Socrates, who was his teacher, and had opened his eyes to realities greater than those of the mundane world. If I may, I would like to move to the present and add an anecdote to this.

This came my way only this last spring. One of the great gratifications of a long teaching career is the many lasting friendships with students that can develop, and this concerns an MIT student who was passing through Berkeley and told me something that I had never known about himself. He told me *his* story of the allegory of Plato's cave, which took place back when he was a kid of about fourteen, in the Bronx, and as he put it didn't know beans. One afternoon he was in Manhattan, and passing its public library, and decided to step in. He walked inside and was amazed how many books there were in the world. All these stacks. He wandered down one, and his eye fell on the *Dialogues* of Plato. Plato? Who's he? Something prompted him to reach for the book and he took it to a reading table, where the book fell open to opening of the Seventh Book of the *Republic,* which begins with the Allegory of the Cave.

He found himself reading the story, and when he came to the end of it where Socrates asks, "Would not someone who had seen the outdoors and gone back into the cave—would that person not realize that the basic point of education is not to communicate facts and figures, but to open student's eyes to vaster worlds they hadn't known existed?"

When he came to that rhetorical conclusion of the Allegory, my student said he found that tears were streaming from his eyes. He said, "You know, Huston, this was evidence of the longing inside me that there be something more than the streets of New York and the skyscrapers. *Something more than that.*

Cousineau: That's a beautiful story, Huston, a remarkable example of the timeless aspect of great myths. It doesn't matter when they were written or compiled; when we find them it's as if they were recently written just for us. If it's true that it is the function of religion and philosophy and

art to help us turn our eyes from the shadows on the wall to the true
light, the divine light of the sun, then what is the contribution that
Native American religion has made toward showing us a glint of that
holy light? Are they showing us something of that original source? You
might remember our friend Gary Rhine asking, "With all our centuries
of history and accumulated knowledge, what is left for Indian people to
tell us?" Is there something about turning toward the light that Ameri-
can Indians can still teach us?

Smith: Not having been taken in by modernity's reductionism, Native
Americans survive as a living witness to the transcendent that is
hidden in the ancestral memory of the rest of us. When I say
ancestral, I have in mind this Turtle Island that is America's geographical ancestor. Let me put it this way. Earlier I was talking
about materialism as a philosophy that is starving for ideas. Native
Americans were never materialists. It would have seemed crazy,
crazy to them. For them, the Great Spirit has always been the
ultimate.

The Winnebago medicine man Reuben Snake was my preeminent teacher from the Native Americans. I recall one of the
things he taught me. He told me, "Huston, our teepees pointed
east, and when we stepped out of them in the morning we would
throw up our arms and shout *Aho!* when we saw the sun. Huston,
you should do that, too." And I do. At my first glimpse of the sun I
raise my arms and shout, "*Aho!*" I did it this morning. The first
time I see the sun it infuses me with this inspiration, just like the
sunlight brings the vegetation and the beauty and all life.

I also remember what the Sufi mystic and poet Rumi once said:
"Knoweth thou not that the sun that thou seeth with thine eyes is
but a reflection of the sun behind the veil." So even the sun is only a
symbol and a metaphor for a deeper transcendent invisible source
from which even it springs, and it relays to us the glories of that
source.

Cousineau: That's beautiful, beautiful, and yet it seems to be very difficult
for many Western audiences to understand the power of the primal, the
aboriginal religions. Is it helpful to people who are unfamiliar with

these ideas to look for equivalents or find comparisons between different religious traditions, let's say between Jesus, Buddha, Muhammad, and Wakan Tanka [The Great Spirit]? Or does it muddy the waters?

Smith: Your last comment, "muddy the waters," is important, but I am going to swing around to say at no time in history, at least for this country, was there greater need for clear thinking. With regards to this issue, yes, it enriches our lives *enormously* to see how other peoples independently have come to the same basic conclusion. The danger, which you have captured neatly, is in your phrase "muddy the water," is if finding equivalents blurs or erases the boundaries between them. Then they just lose all their identity and fail to be a resource for us. We have to be as wise. You've just come back from Ireland, haven't you?

Cousineau: Yes, I've just returned from leading one of my annual literary tours or pilgrimages to Europe. It was a joy, especially to return to Ireland, which I feel is one of the last bastions of what you might call "everyday mysticism." Ireland has that timeless quality in what they call the "thin places" that I've heard you emphasize as being at the heart of the spiritual life.

Smith: Do you know the story about the Irish tailor who characterized trousers as singular at the top and plural at the bottom? I think that's wonderful because, after giving a lifetime's study to these wisdom traditions, that's exactly it. He beat me there. At the top, the mystics all speak the same language because the mystics are "singular" at the top, right? But at the bottom they're plural, and that's good, too. We would have an awkward garment if there were not that also. And that is like the different angles onto the single truth. Each of the traditions has fingers pointing to the moon.

Cousineau: One last question regarding the current mood of the times. Due to some unfortunate interpretations surrounding the events of September 11, there appears to be some suspicion of other people's religious beliefs.

Before September 11, there had been some progress toward granting native people some of their lost religious rights, and yet the mood of the times is chary about granting more religion because of the consequences

of 9/11. How would you characterize the gravity of the situation for
Native Americans in which it is important to grant them more rights,
but now there appears to be a pulling back out of fear and misunder-
standing on the part of the dominant culture? What are the chances that
native people can win back their religious rights in the current cli-
mate—and what does it say about the times that this is an issue at all?

Smith: Granting rights? Yes, well, we should never forget the principle
on which this nation was founded, which was liberty. What sense
does that make of our nation if we do not grant them liberty in this
component that they value—and I'll go so far as to say, has kept
them alive? So, that's the reason for doing it.

Now for the *pulling back* because of the *bad* name that terrorism
has given to religion, that's where we have to have clear thinking,
and ask ourselves, "What is the true cause of terrorism?"

To answer "religious differences" is to give us an excuse from
examining our own record as to what concrete political action we
have taken that has reduced the Muslim world from its great pride.
In the fifteenth century Islam was the most flourishing and advanced civilization in the world. Progressively, beginning with
colonialism, we have reduced them to a condition of poverty,
relative to the rest of the world, and despair. The failure to draw
that distinction and to see what the cause *really* was over—as again
using religion as an excuse for not looking at the *real* cause. If we get
stuck in that, I have very dim hopes for the future.

Cousineau: For a long time now, I have been strangely moved by the way
you have phrased the question you seem to feel is of the utmost impor-
tance to ask of ourselves: "Is there anything more important than the
way things really are?" Is there?

Smith: I don't think so.

Cousineau: Of course, it's possible to know how things may be for us, but is
it possible to know in a definitive way how things really are?

Smith: Yes. Psychiatrists, therapists, counselors have come out on this
subject. One of the greatest has said it very succinctly, that from
the innumerable hours spent talking with disturbed people, it

comes to view that deeper than the craving for possession, deeper than the outreach for sexual satisfaction, there is an even more fundamental craving in the human makeup. *It is the craving for right orientation.*

I mean, these people are confused. They don't know which way to go. They don't know what to do. They have that need for the sense that says "Yes, I am on the right track." Now, this calls for a sense of the lay of the land. How can you be oriented if you do not know the territory? And that's *where the way things are* kicks in to give us what we need.

Cousineau: And yet, we live in a postmodernist time in which the Zeitgeist tells us that everything is relative, so that it is almost impossible to see through the scrim of things to this ultimate reality, as you might say. Isn't it the task of "seers" to see through the illusions of the times? So what would you suggest that people do to help them see through the mistakes of our times?

Smith: Take a closer look at the history of the modern world that ushered in our mistakes. At the tail end of the Middle Ages, Europe had stagnated, thinking that its outlook was close to the way things actually are. The Renaissance helped to get Europe out of that rut, which was good, but then the Enlightenment took over and overrated the powers of reason. It thought that reason, working hand-in-glove with technology, was opening the gates to unending progress. Postmodernism smashed that idea, but it has come up with nothing constructive to replace it with, and as Alfred North Whitehead put the point vividly, if man cannot live by bread alone, still less can he live by disinfectants. Without something we truly believe in we are left with relativism, and relativism is an unlivable philosophy that is in constant danger of spiraling into cynicism and despair. Moreover, absolute relativism isn't even a coherent outlook, for in turning relativism into an absolute it has an internal contradiction built into it.

There's another way to come at this issue. Deconstructionism is almost a synonym for postmodernism, and some things do need to be torn down—demolition squads have their uses. But to set out to deconstruct everything?—which (as far as one can make out from its unreadable prose) is what postmodernism seems to be bent on accomplishing. At minimum, postmodernists are out to tear down the Great Traditions of the various civilizations, beginning with that of the West. We need to remember that it's a lot harder to create than to destroy. It can take months to make a beautiful vase, but it can be smashed in an instant.

Now to the other part of your question, How have I been able to escape this postmodern malaise? Well, I was lucky. It's public knowledge that I was born to missionaries, in China, and while their outlook was parochial in many ways, what came through to me through my parents wasn't dogmatism—we've got the truth and everybody else is going to hell, or moralisms like don't do this, that, and the other thing. What really came through to me was this: *We're in good hands and in gratitude for that fact it would be good if we bore one another's burdens.* With all my gallivanting around the world, I have yet to come upon a simple formula that surpasses that one, and it shielded me from relativism. Later, I came to realize that my own tradition, Protestant Christianity, was not the only one, and I caught glimpses of the treasures—"in them thar hills"—as prospectors for gold used to say. Following up on those leads opened the world's traditions to me, so, as I say, I've been very fortunate.

When I started looking around I was amazed. The first foreign tradition that came to me was the Vedanta, the philosophic branch of Hinduism. In a way I won't go into here, I didn't so much seek it out as that it came my way. And when it did that it felt like a huge tidal wave of truth was breaking over me. It took me about a decade to get on top of Vedanta, and then the tidal waves of other traditions scrambled me in much the same way.

What kept me going was the marvelous, marvelous truths that kept coming my way. On my own I could never have gotten to come upon them. Having then practiced Zen Buddhism with Daisetz Suzuki and the "Dharma Bums," what struck me most was the *sublime unanimity* behind all of these traditions. Independently, they all came to the same basic conclusions as to *the way things are.* The great reward of my career has been the opportunity it has given me to delve ever more deeply into these traditions which surfaced in this sublime unanimity.

Cousineau: How do you respond to the criticism that your concern about scientism is a "straw dog"?

Smith: With hysterical laughter! I mean, how blind can people be? It's just that we get used to this culture that we are in, and it comes to seem like common sense. But we had to be strong-armed into the scientistic worldview. As I was saying a few moments ago, to become aware of one's conditioning is a bit like trying to step out of your own shoes while you're walking. Aldous Huxley has been one of my heroes; I was very fortunate that he was very generous to me and accepted me as a friend. I just read a new biography of him, which includes his one subversive limerick, and it goes like this:

Damn. I find that I am
A creature that struts
In predestined ruts—
I'm not even a bus, I'm a tram!

And that says it beautifully! We just get into these cultural ruts and find it difficult to get out of them, scientific reductionism being one of the deepest ruts today. Okay, I'm just giving you metaphors, and unloading some of my anger at this obtuseness. But to come back to religion, one of our problems is that on religion our society is polarized between the intellectual elite that controls the medium and the rest of the population. For the hoi polloi (if I may use that phrase not condescendingly), the conflict between science and religion is no big deal. They go to their doctors, they go to church on Sundays. It is no problem. The problem is with "the chattering class," which is the British phrase for intellectuals. After dinner, the hoi polloi turns on TV while the chattering class sits around talking about ideas, like we're doing here. And the chattering class? It doesn't give religion its due.

Consider one clear instance of this. The *New York Review of Books,* which in my mind is something like a house organ for intellectuals, has never reviewed a religious book. Once in a while it will review books *about* religion, typically landing hard on its sins, negative aspects of religion like sex scandals, divisiveness, ethnic conflicts, and the like. But books by authors who really believe that transcendence is true? Never. It has never reviewed one. The one exception is John Polkinghorn, who they couldn't completely ignore because he is also a world-class scientist. And even in his case they praised his science and trivialized his theology. If you look at the publishing business, why, religion probably tops the whole class. More books on religion are published each year than any other single subject, and in truth the house organ of the chattering class gives them a zero rating. Behind all this of course stands the university, which puts the finishing touches on the minds that go out to rule our country.

Now, the university is an interesting case study because colleges were initially founded in this country to train Protestant ministers, and their dominant ethos was Protestant Christianity. Okay, after a century or so that model was inadequate and was rightly retired. Ditched. But that left colleges and universities needing a model, and one was waiting in the wings: the German research university. These were the best in the world at that time, and the United States imported the model. It brought many good things, especially as technology was becoming increasingly important. That's the good side of the story.

The downside is that those German universities were dedicated to the Positivism of the French philosopher Auguste Comte, who divided history into three stages: religious, metaphysical, and scientific. Religion was what the old boys thought way back in the childhood of the human race. Metaphysical was better because it brought reason to the picture. The future, though, belonged to science. Okay: religion, metaphysics, then science. It was progress all the way! Progress would never end.

Now, a passing, parenthetical thought. I thought the tragic events of 9/11 would cause us to see through the myth of progress via ever-advancing technology. But I am not sure we have taken that message to heart.

Anyway, there is not a philosopher or an intellectual historian today who will defend Positivism as a philosophy. But the university is still stuck with it and considers religion passé. So the religious point of view is absent. There are departments of religious studies, but they use social science methodology to bring out facts and figures about religious history, almost never defending its truth claims. A philosopher in nearby U.C. Berkeley recently wrote, again from the *New York Review of Books:* "Most philosophers of mind are materialists because they see that as the only position that is compatible with modern science." Look at who's king! It's modern science that tells us *the way things are*—and that shelves all human sensibilities other than reason working with what our physical senses report. This reduces the stature of the human self. The higher reaches of humanity are beheaded, you might say, by a single stroke of the scientistic sword. And that is the view that goes out to the nation through our educational system.

So people who say scientism is a straw dog are just out of it. They are living in *deep* illusion. They haven't a clue as to what's going on.

Cousineau: Very powerful words. Now I'd like to move to a subject that's close to my heart. First, what relationship does art have with religion? It appears that every religious system has used art as a support of some kind—from icons to architecture—to convey its message. Second, is there any connection for you between what some art critics have called the banishment of beauty, sending Venus into exile, and the banishment of religious belief from the modern world?

Smith: You referred to art supporting religion, cathedrals, icons and all of that. I would go further and say that all great, ennobling art is religious because it transports us to a higher part of ourselves. This realization first came to me a number of years ago when I was in India. As I walked through the temples and gazed at its images sculpted from mountain hillsides, and listened to their *ragas*, it dawned on me that in India art is religion and religion is art. Over the years, I have come to expand that point to cover religion in general, provided the art is great.

Let me put it this way. What I realized in India was that at the time when this art was created most of the people were still illiterate. I forget, but how old is writing? Literacy? I don't know the exact date, but surely several millennia. I am not speaking about language, which goes back to when it became human. Writing only goes back a few millennia. Before then, and still in large parts of the world where people are illiterate, their texts are not books—Bibles and the Koran, et cetera. They were dance, music, painting, drama, storytelling, and sculpture. In other words, it was art that conveyed sublime ideas. And because most of the art of all illiterate peoples is sacred, it pointed upward to higher worlds, and was able to elevate their spirit.

A little anecdote. The one empirical discovery of my career was to be the first Westerner to come upon a unique form of chanting that the Tibetans developed, which has introduced a new term to the lexicography of musicology—multiphonic chanting in which a tonic chord issues from a single throat. This ability fascinated my friend Mickey Hart of the Grateful Dead, who is also a first-rate musicologist, and he put the infrastructure of Grateful Dead behind a concert tour of those specially trained and gifted monks. He has gone on to mount six such coast-to-coast tours, and they have all been sell-outs. The first time he hired those halls, I thought, *Tibetan Monks? Who is going to put out any money to go out for an evening to see them?* On the first round nobody was turned on by the thought of spending an evening with the monks, so Mickey had to drum up an audience. Well, Mickey can get on any talk show he wants to, and so he really did the circuit before this first tour, and he dragged me along to give it a little historical credibility. I remember one of those programs especially. The talk show host had been talking with us for about an hour, and toward the close of the program he said, "Well, Mickey, this has been very interesting, but there's one more question I want to ask you and I'm going to give it to you right between the eyes: 'Professor Smith is no problem, he teaches this stuff. But what is a member of the Grateful Dead doing with Tibetan Monks?'"

Without batting an eye, Mickey said, "We're both in the transportation business." That's brilliant! Rightly heard it comes close to saying it all about the relation between great art and religion.

Cousineau: Does this tie in with what I was saying about the decline of beauty and sublimity in current art?

Smith: Very definitely. Among artists those qualities are no longer even respected. They used to be the supreme heights artists would aim for, but now they aren't even honored. Why this change? If art is to be authentic it has to be *real,* otherwise it's the opposite of real, which is phony. But if there's no transcendental realm that great art can transport us to—and as I keep saying, scientism has induced today's intellectuals to dismiss those realms—efforts to transport us to them are dishonest. Left with nothing but our everyday world to work with, artists are reduced to trying to get us to see that world in a new, not better, way. So they aim for novelty and shock value. What we desperately need is to recapture Plotinus's wise dictum "Those who behold beauty become themselves beautiful."

Cousineau: Beautiful answer, Huston. Now I know you have long been drawn to the Sufi order in Islam. Do you have any thoughts about the growing interest in the poet Rumi in recent years? Does it have something to do with the revival of interest in the perennial philosophy—or is it something in Rumi and Sufism that we need right now?

Smith: The phenomenal interest in Rumi begins with the fact that in the West today we are spiritually starved. A number of factors converge to account for the current Rumi craze.

One is an excessive materialism that has taken over, spin-off technological advances of science, which are incredible in their own right, and deserving of great respect. But nevertheless they concern the material world and the material aspects of life, and that has taken us over into thinking this is all there is. But there is something else in the human spirit that eludes science—that doesn't rule out its existence, though science doesn't cover the whole field. And because this deep-lying component of ourselves has been suppressed or stifled in the last several centuries, it wants out. There is something in the human spirit that resists being caged this way. So when a voice comes along that tells us that there's more to life than physical satisfactions and fleeting pleasures, we respond.

His Holiness the Dalai Lama joins Rumi in reminding us time

and again that a stomach holds only so much. To think that binge-ing would increase our satisfaction would be like strapping sand-wiches to our abdomens and hoping they will nourish us. It's a metaphor for the blandness of our consumerist society.

We are ready to listen to somebody who tells us that there is more. But why Rumi? Why is he so convincing in making life's "more" seem real? Well, it's a combination of things. He is both a superb poet, which means he has access to our souls, and a great mystic, *mystic* being defined here as someone whose whole being is rooted in an alternate, a wider, a more inclusive reality. Connect these qualities to our starvation, and something is going to happen. We're reaching out for more, and here comes a poet who persuades us that there *is* an alternate reality that transcends, exceeds, and surpasses in every way this mundane mode of existence.

Cousineau: What is it about Rumi's spiritual friend, his relationship with Shams, that is so provocative and appeaing to modern audiences?
Smith: His spiritual friend, this mysterious Shams of Tabriz, is a bit of a mystery. We keep circling the mystery of their deep friendship. What was the secret of his power over Rumi? I'm not sure the enigma will ever be resolved. But that doesn't keep their friendship from impacting us, because we find the mystery intriguing.

One thing is clear, however. There was a powerful *bhakti,* or love component, in their friendship. Human love is an analogue of the soul's love for the divine. Rumi's profound human love affair seemed to catalyze his love for Allah and is a powerful metaphor for the ultimate love affair of the finite with the infinite.

Cousineau: I have always been interested in the power of the translator. But I know that translation is a controversial area of discussion not only in literature, but also in religious history. Do you have any thoughts about translators or even translation itself—the mystery of why works have to be translated anew for every generation for new life to be infused into them? Do you think translation can be an authentic spiritual practice?
Smith: There are innumerable translations of Rumi's poetry now. This is a mixed blessing. On the one hand, it's a blessing because it widens

his readership. The downside is that translators differ markedly in quality. Back to the good side. Translators have ears for different sides of a poet's work. Coleman Barks, Rumi's foremost translator today, has a special ear for the erotic in Rumi's poetry. He catches Rumi's use of the erotic to intensify our love of Allah and not let it dribble out in titillation.

Other translators have a great affection or delight in the trickster, which is another important side of Rumi, too. Translators may exaggerate one side or another of Rumi, but never mind. Every genius is multifaceted. No translator can capture the full glory of a great poet in his own voice, so it's good that we have many.

Cousineau: Perhaps inspired by Rumi, many people want to join Sufi groups and participate in their music and dance rituals. I recall that you have danced with the whirling dervishes. What role have they played in the history of Sufism—and does the popularity of Sufi dancing today signify anything about our modern need for ritual?

Smith: It says a lot. Our individualistic society doesn't realize how much ritual contributes to life, for when we sink ourselves in its repetitive rhythms time stands still and we tap into eternity. Sufi dancing turns on circling.

Why this circling motion? Well, there is something magical about a circle. For one thing, geometrically it encompasses more space than any other shape. But this is just a mathematical beginning. The circle is also profoundly symbolic, for a circle travels without leave-taking. So it combines journeying with returning. It's powerful in bringing the two together. And there's more. The circle dance of the Mevlevi order that Rumi founded includes a head jerk. This motion throws blood to the brain in such a way that it facilitates trance. This brings the experience of transcendence directly into this world.

We are so inundated by the everyday, the matter-of-fact, the pitter-patter of existence, and so grounded in the everyday that the notion of an altered state of consciousness with a wider and more intense purview is attractive. It is alluring, it entices us, it mystifies us, it intrigues us. And here they are, the dervishes doing it right here into our presence.

Cousineau: Wonderful. It seems to me that great poetry ultimately leads us back to the still point, back to silence. What do you think it is about poetry—and especially sacred poetry—that touches the spirit? Is there something about the religious dimension of poetry that you would like to talk about?

Smith: Yes, what is the power of poetry *over* our lives? Poetry, music, the visual arts, dance—art comes at us from different directions, through our different physical senses, and it's beyond my powers to differentiate the subtle differences in the way they impact us. But they all converge on the central point. At their best they all transport us to a higher plane of existence. On a deeper level of our own senses, if you prefer psychology to metaphysics, inward to outbound imagery. I can't tell you *how* it does this. It is truly magical. But when it happens we know that something different is happening. And *what* happens is identical with authentic religious experience, so as we were saying earlier, in the end, art is religion, religion is art. But *transport* is what is greater, more beautiful, more powerful, and mysterious than we are.

Cousineau: Now, I know this may be a difficult question, but I'll ask it anyway. Our dear friend Gary Rhine, and one of your ex-students, James Botsford, and I were talking recently about your work and speculating on what your greatest contribution might be as a writer and scholar. James said he felt that it was your willingness to study, participate in, and write about the great world religions in a way that allowed the general American public to see religions that they had not encountered as bona fide spiritual paths. On this front, at least, this has made us a more tolerant and compassionate people than we were. At least two million people have read your work, and your warm and all-encompassing treatment of other religions and cultures has given people permission to be more tolerant. Do you agree with that? Huston, what do you think your legacy will be?

Smith: Wow, listening to that downpour of accolades, I thought, Hey, what nice things to say. As to their applicability, I am too close to them to judge. I also remember the admonition of the Tao Te Ching, "The axe falls first on the tallest tree," so don't build me up too much. I also think of what Indians say: "The amount of difference that any one human being makes to history is like putting your finger in a glass of water and then taking it out." I am not sure that that is altogether right—think of Gandhi, his Holiness the Dalai Lama, and the great seers of the past, Plato high among them. I don't think that's saying it altogether right, but it is a nice counsel against developing big heads.

Cousineau: But if you were to address the possibility that you have a modicum of influence, made some contribution—

Smith: All right. If you are not going to let me off the hook, I would dip back into my formative years in China, and side with Confucius, saying, "I am not an original thinker, I am simply a lover of the ancients." Of course, the ancients had their foibles too. They weren't admirable in every way, but they honored—more precisely revered—transcendence. Confucius again put it succinctly: "Heaven and earth. Only Heaven is great." It's the ancients' right-minded regard for transcendence that I love, and I have tried to use the ounces of my strength to get it to the general public, to share that love. This, in our times, isn't easy in a generation that, as one intellectual historian has put it, has reproached its past more than any other in history. I think that's a tragedy, so I have stood up for the saints, the seers, the prophets that I think have brought humanity to whatever nobility it has achieved. There's still a lot of that nobility around in our world, and it needs to be protected.

Cousineau: Finally, you are fond of the phrase "winnowing the wisdom of the world." What is the wisest wisdom you have winnowed? I asked our old friend Joseph Campbell if he had a favorite line or quotation or nugget of wisdom that he had picked up from his readings in mythology and religion that had given him some heart's consolation. And he said immediately that there was a line by the Buddha that had given him a great deal of solace over the years. The Buddha said that the most important task in life is to "participate with joy in the sorrows of the world." Do you have an equivalent nugget of wisdom that has given you comfort over the years, given you joy?

Smith: That's wonderful! Well, I can't top Joe's favorite, but what comes to mind is the answer my *roshi* gave me at the close of my farewell with him when I asked him what Zen came down to for him.

He said, "Infinite gratitude to all things past. Infinite service to all things present. Infinite responsibility to all things future."

And with that he bowed with his palms together in *gassho,* a bow signifying deep respect.

My soul is a Mosque for Muslims,
a Temple for Hindus,
an Altar for Zoroastrians,
a Church for Christians,
a Synagogue for Jews,
and a Pasture for gazelles.

—IBN ARABI

REFERENCES

Anderson, Walter Truett. *Reality Isn't What It Used To Be: Theatrical Politics, Ready-To-Wear Religion, Global Myths, Primitive Chic, and Other Wonders of the Postmodern World.* San Francisco: HarperCollins, 1992.

Appleyard, Bryan. *Understanding the Present: Science and the Soul of Modern Man.* New York: Doubleday, 1993.

Armstrong, Karen. *The Battle for God.* New York: Ballantine Books, 2000.

Bellah, Robert. *Habits of the Heart: Individualism and Commitment in American Life.* Updated ed. Berkeley and Los Angeles: University of California Press, 1996.

Blofeld, John, trans. *The Zen Teachings of Huang Po: On the Transmission of Mind.* New York: Grove Press, 1959.

Bohm, David. *On Dialogue.* London and New York: Routledge, 1996.

Burke, T. Patrick. *The Fragile Universe: An Essay on the Philosophy of Religions.* London: Macmillan, 1979.

Burtt, Edwin A. *The Metaphysical Foundations of Modern Physical Science.* Rev. ed. Atlantic Highlands, N.J.: Humanities Press, 1980.

Campbell, Joseph. *The Hero with a Thousand Faces.* Princeton: Princeton University Press, 1949.

———. *The Inner Reaches of Outer Space.* Novato: New World Library, 2001.

Carter, Stephen. *The Culture of Disbelief: How American Law and Politics Trivialize Religious Devotion.* New York: Basic Books, 1993.

Cousineau, Phil. *The Art of Pilgrimage: Making Travel Sacred.* Berkeley: Conari Press, 1998.

———. *The Hero's Journey: Joseph Campbell on His Life and Work.* San Francisco: HarperCollins, 1990.

———. *Soul: An Archaeology: Readings from Socrates to Ray Charles.* San Francisco: HarperCollins, 1995.

Cox, Harvey. *Fire from Heaven: The Rise of Pentecostal Spirituality and the Reshaping of Religion in the Twenty-first Century.* Reading, Mass.: Addison-Wesley, 1995.

———. *Religion in the Secular City: Toward a Postmodern Theology.* New York: Simon & Schuster, 1984.

Coyote, Peter. *Sleeping Where I Fall: A Chronicle.* Washington, D.C.: Counterpoint Press, 1999.

Dante Alighieri. *The Divine Comedy.* Translated by Allen Mandelbaum. Introduction by Eugenio Montale. New York: Knopf, 1995.

Dunne, John S. *The Way of All the Earth: Experiments in Truth and Religion.* Notre Dame, Ind.: University of Notre Dame Press, 1978.

Eliade, Mircea. *The Sacred and the Profane: The Nature of Religion.* Translated by Willard R. Trask. New York: Harcourt Brace, 1959.

Fingarette, Herbert. *Confucius: The Secular as Sacred.* New York: Harper & Row, 1972.

Guénon, René. *Reign of Quantity and the Signs of the Times.* Translated by Lord Northbourne. 4th ed. Paris: Sophia et Universalis, 2001.

Heard, Gerald. *Pain, Sex, and Time: A New Outlook on Evolution and the Future of Man.* New York and London: Harper & Brothers, 1939.

Heiler, Friedrich. "The History of Religions as a Preparation for the Cooperation of Religions." In *The History of Religions: Essays on the Problem of Understanding,* edited by Joseph M. Kitagawa. University of Chicago Press, 1967.

Hillman, James. *Re-Visioning Psychology.* New York: Harper & Row, 1975.

Hui Hai. *The Zen Teaching of Instantaneous Awakening.* Totnes, England: Buddhist Publishing Group, 1972.

Huxley, Aldous. *Brave New World.* New York: Harper & Row, 1963.

———. *The Perennial Philosophy.* New York: HarperCollins, 1990.

James, William. "The Moral Equivalent of War." In *Annotated Biography of William James,* edited by Ralph Barton Perry. New York: Longman, 1965.

———. *The Varieties of Religious Experience.* New York: Touchstone Books, 1997.

Kerényi, Karl. *Eleusis: Archetypal Image of Mother and Daughter.* Translated by Ralph Manheim. Princeton: Princeton University Press, 1991.

Lao-tzu. *The Tao Te Ching: A New English Version.* Translated by Stephen Mitchell. New York: Harper Perennial, 1992.

Lewis, C. S. *The Screwtape Letters.* San Francisco: HarperCollins, 2001.

Lings, Martin. *What Is Sufism?* London: Unwin Hyman, 1975.

Lovejoy, Arthur O. *The Great Chain of Being: A Study of the History of An Idea.* Cambridge: Harvard University Press, 1970.

Mascaro, Juan, trans. *Upanishads.* New York: Penguin Books, 1962.

McGinn, Colin. *The Mysterious Flame: Conscious Minds in a Material World.* New York: Basic Books, 1999.

Miller, David. *The New Polytheism.* Dallas: Spring Publications, 1981.

Mitchell, Stephen, trans. *Bhagavad Gita: A New Translation.* New York: Harmony Books, 2000.

Nasr, Seyyed Hossein. *Knowledge and the Sacred.* Albany: State University of New York Press, 1990.

Needleman, Jacob, ed. *The Sword of Gnosis: Metaphysics, Cosmology, Tradition, Symbolism.* Baltimore: Penguin Books, 1974.

Padma Sambhava. *The Tibetan Book of the Dead.* Translated by Robert A. F. Thurman. Boston: Shambhala, 1994.

Pepper, Stephen. *World Hypotheses.* Berkeley and Los Angeles: University of California Press, 1970.

Prince, Raymond, and D. H. Salman, eds. *Do Psychedelics Have Religious Implications?* Montreal: R. M. Bucke Society, 1967.

Rumi, Jelaluddin. *The Essential Rumi.* Translated by Coleman Barks. San Francisco: HarperCollins, 1995.

Russell, Bertrand. *A Free Man's Worship, and Other Essays.* London: Unwin Hyman, 1976.

Santayana, George. *Skepticism and Animal Faith.* New York: Dover Publications, 1955.

Schuon, Frithjof. *Language of the Self.* Bloomington, Ind.: World Wisdom Books, 1999.

———. *The Transcendent Unity of Religions.* Wheaton, Ill.: Quest Books, 1984.

———. *Treasures of Buddhism.* Bloomington, Ind.: World Wisdom Books, 1993.

———. *Understanding Islam.* Bloomington, Ind.: World Wisdom Books, 1994.

Shah, Idries. *The Sufis.* Introduction by Robert Graves. New York: Anchor Books, 1971.

Smith, Huston. *Beyond the Post-Modern Mind.* 2nd ed. Wheaton, Ill.: Theosophical Publishing House, 1989.

———. *Cleansing the Doors of Perception: The Religious Significance of Entheogenic Plants and Chemicals.* New York: Jeremy P. Tarcher/Putnam, 2000.

———. *Essays on World Religion.* Edited by M. Darrol Bryant. New York: Paragon House, 1992.

———. *Forgotten Truth: The Primordial Tradition.* New York: Harper & Row, 1976.

———. *The Wisdom of Faith.* Videorecording. With Bill Moyers. New York: Public Affairs Television, 1996.

———. *The World's Religions.* Revised and updated edition of *The Religions of Man.* San Francisco: HarperCollins, 1991.

Smith, Huston, and David Ray Griffin. *Primordial Truth and Postmodern Theology.* Albany: State University of New York Press, 1989.

Smith, Huston, and Reuben Snake, comps. and eds. *One Nation Under God: The Triumph of the Native American Church.* Santa Fe: Clear Light Publishers, 1996.

Smith, Page. *Killing the Spirit: Higher Education in America.* New York: Viking, 1990.

Stace, Walter T. *Mysticism and Philosophy.* New York: Macmillan, 1960.

Suzuki, Daisetz Teitaro. *Manual of Zen Buddhism.* New York: Grove Press, 1987.

Tillich, Paul. *Systematic Theology.* 3 vols. Chicago: The University of Chicago Press, 1951–1963.

Trungpa, Chogyam. *Cutting Through Spiritual Materialism.* Boston: Shambhala, 1987.

Wach, Joachim. "Master and Disciple." In *Essays in the History of Religions*, edited by Joseph M. Kitagawa and Gregory D. Alles. New York: Macmillan, 1988.

Wallace, B. Alan. *Choosing Reality: A Contemplative View of Physics and the Mind.* Boston: New Science Library, 1989.

Walsh, Roger. *The Spirit of Shamanism.* Los Angeles: Jeremy P. Tarcher, 1990.

Weinberg, Steven. *The First Three Minutes: A Modern View of the Origin of the Universe.* New York: Basic Books, 1977.

Wilber, Ken. *The Essential Ken Wilber: An Introductory Reader.* Boston: Shambhala, 1998.

ACKNOWLEDGMENTS

First and foremost, I want to thank Huston Smith for his cooperation in helping me create a book of interviews that best represents his life and work, especially his revisioning of philosophy and religion over the last half-century. His passion for philosophical discourse and spiritual ideas made selecting material for and editing this collection a deeply rewarding project for me. My most ardent hope is that the book demonstrates not only Huston's considerable scholarship but also his genuine humility and exemplary empathy for the religious beliefs of people everywhere. I am proud to call him both friend and colleague.

I would also like to express my gratitude to my editor, Reed Malcolm, at the University of California Press, who had the inspired idea of creating a book of Huston's selected interviews. I have deeply appreciated his faith in me as the editor of the project, his exuberance for the book, and his editorial advice, which was always in the interest of clarifying the ideas and opening the book up to the widest possible audience. I also want to express my appreciation to Jacqueline Volin for her spirited guidance through the book's production; to my Argus-eyed copyeditor, Mimi Kusch, whose devotion to the most infinitesimal details in the manuscript was an inspiration; and to Lance Shows for his radiant portrait of Huston.

Many thanks, too, to Tom Grady, the agent I share with Huston

Smith. His personal understanding of the depths of the religious life and his confidence in my work made him the perfect advisor for the creation of this book. I also want to express my incalculable gratitude to my late friend Trish O'Rielly, with whom I had numerous and numinous conversations over the years about Huston's vital role in healing the rifts between the world's various spiritual communities. Her keen insight into Huston's unique blend of inner and outer work, wisdom and practice, was key to my understanding of his worldwide appeal. I would also like to express my genuine thanks to my soul brothers, Gary Rhine and James Botsford, with whom I have shared incisive conversations on three continents about Huston's impact on their important work in support of religious freedom. I would like to acknowledge the support and suggestions of Vine Deloria Jr., Oren Lyons, Winona LaDuke, Robert A. Johnson, the Reverend Alan Jones, R. B. Morris, Fiona Queen, Edwin Bernbaum, John Keating, Maureen Gilbert, Steven Musser, and the late Jamake Highwater, who encouraged me to carry on his work of finding parallels between the world's primal religions, while also respecting each of their distinctive gifts to world culture. My deepest thanks and boundless gratitude go out to my companion, Jo Beaton, for her patience, faith, and encouragement. She thought it would do me good to work with Huston on such a project, knowing in her heart of hearts that it would help me understand the way things are in the wisdom garden of everyday life.

Finally, I would like to express my appreciation to the writers and their publications for permission to include in this volume their interviews with Huston Smith. Their enthusiastic response to my requests to reprint their interviews is living testimony to their affection and admiration for Huston Smith as well as their desire to contribute to further understanding between the world's religious traditions. For those interested in more extensive publishing information about the interviews, it is included in the footnotes found on the first page of each chapter.

dervishes, whirling, xiv, 274
despair: from materialism, 260;
  Muslim world, 265; relativist,
  266; wiser than, 147
Dharamsala, 71
dharma (path of right living), 129;
  Eternal Dharma, 63
Dharma Bums, 267
dialectics, 49
dialogues, xi
Dickens, Charles, 73
Dionysius, 20–21
discrete atomism, shift to field
  theory, 159
disease, visionary states, 226,
  233–34, 235
divine madness, 227
divine within, 216–18
DNA, reincarnation and, 71
"Do Drugs Have Religious Import?"
  (Smith), 229, 230
Dōgen, 201, 210
dogma, scientific, 184, 241
dogmatism, religious, 20, 151–52,
  267
The Doors of Perception (Huxley),
  214, 215
doors of perception, cleansing, 192,
  193, 198, 222–27
*Do Psychedelics Have Religious
  Implications?* (Prince and Salman),
  233
double-slit experiment, 178
Dow Chemical, 109
downward causation, 198–99
dream, group, 183
Dreaming/Dreamtime, Australian
  aborigine, 51, 218–19
drugs, entheogens, xiv, 189, 213–16,
  222–42

Dunne, John, 41–42
Durkheim, Émile, 217–18

Earth Might Be Fair (Smith), 109
Easterbrook, Greg, 184
Eastern religions. *See* Asian philosophy
Eckhart, Meister, 20–21, 28,
  153–54, 201
ecology: ecological crisis, 92, 109,
  157, 210; of mind, 217
economics: education based on, 123;
  problems, 74, 205–6. *See also*
  materialism; poverty
ecstasy: dangers of excess, 45; ecstatic
  technologies, 189, 235–37; and
  entheogens, xiv, 189, 213–16,
  222–42; and fasting, 226,
  233–34, 235, 236; higher
  madness, 169; NDEs, 234–35
ecumenism, 57
education, 108, 189, 192–206; cave
  allegory and, 262; economic
  purposes, 123; enchanted garden,
  169; meditation in, 202–3; new
  paradigm, 197; rote learning, 197.
  See also child-rearing; guru-pupil
  tradition; humanities; literacy;
  method in education; religious
  studies; science; university
egoism, 68, 97, 205
Einstein, A., 23–24
Eleusinian Mysteries, 226–27, 229
Eleventh Amendment, 239
The Eleventh Hour (Lings), 157
Eliade, Mircea, 43, 51, 76, 153
Eliot, T. S., ix, 29–30, 118
El Salvador, 180
Emerson, Ralph Waldo, xi, 193, 196
emotions, absolute perfection
  unclear through, 25

greed, poison, 206
Greeks, 40; Aristotle, 78, 96;
Eleusinian Mysteries, 226–27,
229; India and, 109; *jnanic*
knowledge, 96; Olympics, 174;
Temple of Apollo, xiv; *theoria,* 96,
241. See also Plato
Griffin, David, xv, 2
group dream, 183
group mind, 217
Guatemala, 180
Guénon, René, 5, 156–57
guru-pupil tradition, xx, 65–66,
75–82. See also *roshi* (Zen master)
Guthrie, Woody, 209
Gyutu Monastery, near Dalhousie, 168

Habits of the Heart (Bellah), 122
Haeckel, Ernest, 66
Half-Dipper Bridge, Kyoto, 210
happiness, 146–48
hara, 33
Harman, Willis, 89
Hart, Mickey, 271
Harvard University: "Bermuda
Triangle" of Harvard/
Princeton/Cornell, 4; Leary, xiv,
214, 224–25
Hassidic stories, 203
hatred, poison, 206
Hawking, Stephen, 138
Heard, Gerald, 4, 5–6, 80–84
heaven, 216
Heidegger, Martin, 200
Heiler, Friedrich, 39
hero's journey, of scientists, 128–29
The Hero's Journey (Cousineau), xviii,
178–79
Heywood, John, 207

hierarchies, 155, 167, 260
Highwater, Jamake, 174
Hillman, James, 43
Hinduism, 17–18, 20; death, 28;
divine within, 218; Eternal
Dharma, 63; eternity, 28; India, v,
xiv, 6; *jivanmukta,* 6, 25, 254; *The
Psychedelic Experience* and, 213;
Ramakrishna, 28, 66, 77–78;
reincarnation, 28, 93; in *The
Religions of Man/ The World's
Religions,* 86, 87; Sanskrit chant,
148; Sri Lanka conflict with
Buddhists, 130. See also *swamis;*
Vedanta; yogas
Historical Atlas (Campbell), 177
The History of Religions (University of
Chicago), 39
Holistic Education Review, 191
Holocaust, 24, 259
hope, 172
Huang Po, 62, 86
Huichol Indians, Mexico, xiv,
60–61, 229
Hui Hai (Blofeld translation), 86
human intelligence, 195. *See also*
mind
humanism, 47, 108, 159
humanistic psychology, 63–64
humanities: Gifford Lectures, 195;
interdisciplinary, 109; sacrifice of,
123; science and, 109, 110, 114,
118, 123–24. *See also* philosophy
human origin, 135–36, 165–67,
199. *See also* evolution
human potential movement, 80,
159
humility, virtue, 206
Huxley, Aldous, 5–6, 68, 80–84,

Huxley, Aldous *(continued)*
268; *Brave New World,* 4, 80; *The
Doors of Perception,* 214, 215; dying
of cancer, 25; and egoism, 97, 205;
Heard influence, 4, 80–82;
mescaline, 214, 224, 227; MIT,
214–15, 224; mysticism, x, 80, 83;
The Perennial Philosophy, 4, 80–81,
84, 88, 153; Smith in remembrance of *(Los Angeles Times Book
Review),* 142; in Smith's *Cleansing
the Doors of Perception,* 224

Ibn Arabi, 53, 279
I Ching, 161
idealism, religious, 16
illusions, 9–10, 266, 270
implicate order, 170
implicate wholeness, 124–25
India, xix, 168–69; art, 270–71;
Auroville, 79–80; Buddhism, 64;
Hinduism, xiv, 6; the infinite, 40;
personality types delineated,
109–10; poverty, 70; "Spiritual
Summit Conference," 68–69;
Tibetans, xiv, 4, 68, 71, 168; way
of the cat/way of the monkey, 44,
236. *See also* Hinduism
Indians. *See* India; Native Americans
infinity, 40, 77–78, 119–20, 134;
everyday as, 192; in four levels of
reality, 171; God as, 138–39;
satchitananda, 16, 58, 153–54. *See
also* eternity; formlessness;
timelessness
The Inner Reaches of Outer Space
(Campbell), 177
insight and delirium, difference
between, 226–27
Insight Meditation Society, 129

instincts, 205–6
intellectuals, 181, 268–69. *See also*
university
intellectus, 7–8, 105. See also
gnosis/Gnostics
intelligence: human, 195. *See also*
mind
intelligent design theory, 150–51
In the Tracks of Buddhism (Schuon),
xix
intuition, 105, 108; satori (intuitive
illumination), 31, 49, 105–6, 231.
See also mysticism
invisible: primordial tradition and,
153; science and, 137–38, 164,
248
Iran: hostage crisis, 93; and Schuon
book, xix–xx; Sufism, xiv, 4,
52–53
Ireland, 196, 235, 264
Iroquois nations, 175
Isa, Sheikh, 5–6
Islam, xix–xx, 4, 20, 53; *barakah,* 47;
Bosnia, 24, 258; death/afterlife,
28; and esoteric, 48, 53; and folk
religion, 60; fundamentalist, 89,
158; great jihad, 157; Koran, 20,
53; last great tradition, 57;
Muhammad, 39, 140, 236;
physical universe, 260; prayers,
xiv, 4, 17–19; in *The Religions of
Man/ The World's Religions,* 53, 87;
Western philosophical lineage, 78;
Western political effect on, 265.
See also Sufism
Italy, Christianity, 61

Jainism, 87
James, Henry, 27
James, William: best things are the

department, 103, 104–7; quantum physics, 242; religious studies, 108; Reuys, xv, 101; Smith leaving, 103–8
"Master and Disciple" (Wach), 76
materialism, 31; bankruptcy of, 241–42; as belief starving for ideas, 260; and mind, 101–2, 115; mirror, 171; of modern world, 121–22, 150, 260–61; Native Americans and, 263; new physics and, 30, 169–70; of philosophers, 270; and Rumi craze, 272–73; scientific/gross, 181, 260–61; spiritual/material poverty, 70; value lacking in, 116. *See also* matter; naturalism
matriarchy, 155–56
matter: and consciousness, 160; etherealization of, 159; fundamental in universe, 101; and meaning, 164; only thing that matters, 240. *See also* materialism
May, Rollo, 217
Mazatecs, Mexico, 229
meaning, 254–55; God as, 138; India, 168–69; primordial tradition and, 167; science and, 116–17, 128–29, 137, 164, 241–42. *See also* value
mechanical causation, 166–67
mechanics, quantum. *See* quantum mechanics
mechanistic causation, 166–67
media: on mistakes of religion, 162, 180. *See also* television
medical technology, 141
meditation: in children's education, 202–3; daily practice, 210; and entheogens, 224–25; Insight

Meditation Society, 129; Vipassana, 4, 129, 130, 132; yoga of (raja), 19, 21, 77, 96, 237; Zen, 32, 231
Melville, Herman, 256
Merton, Thomas, 49, 53, 68–69
mescaline, 214, 223, 224–25, 227
Messianism, 87
metanarrative, 159
"Metaphysical Foundations of Contextualistic Philosophy of Religion" (Smith), 3
The Metaphysical Foundations of Modern Scientists (Burt), 198
metaphysics, xiii, 15; Comte stage of history, 269; depth of, 171; materialistic, 116; philosophy's demotion of, 115; in science, 160; science deserted in favor of, 165; scientific method in, 164
metaxy, Plato's, 29
method in education: vs. content, 195, 197–99; religious studies, 162, 270; university rooted in, 11, 114, 123–24, 183. *See also* science
Methodism, xiv, 20, 22; Central Methodist College, xii, 2, 76; missionary work during Smith's youth in China, xii, 2, 20, 55, 60, 83, 267
Metzner, Ralph, 213
Mexico: Huichol Indians, xiv, 60–61, 229; Mazatecs, 229; prayer meetings, xviii
microbiology, 200
Middle Ages, 78, 105, 126, 266
mid-life crisis, 146
Miller, David L., 43
mind, 149–52; group, 217; higher

mind *(continued)*
  madness, 169; holographic model,
    170; human intelligence, 195;
    materialism and, 101–2, 115;
    Mind-at-Large, 101–2; One, 62;
    paradox has last word, 160;
    reaching out, 217–18. *See also*
    mind-set
mind-altering entheogens, xiv, 189,
    213–16, 222–42
mind-set: aboriginal, 210; modern
    Western, 198
minorities, rights of, 142, 157, 180
"Miracle of Marsh Chapel," 229–30,
    231
Mishlove, Jeffrey, 101, 111–20, 189,
    212–21
missionary work: religious studies
    and, 253; Smith's youth in China,
    xii, 2, 20, 55, 60, 83, 267; value
    of, 55–56
Mitchell, Stephen, 76
models, teachers as, 206
modern world, 6, 158–59, 164;
    awry, 107; banishment of religious
    belief from, 270; and fundamen-
    talism, 158; history that ushered
    in mistakes of, 266; materialism/
    naturalism, 121–22, 150, 260–
    61; pessimism about, 156–57;
    reductionism, 263; seculari-
    zation, 158, 239–41, 246; Western
    mind-set, 198; and wisdom
    traditions, 63, 89, 91–92. *See
    also* postmodernism; science
monasticism, 69, 132
mondo (question-and-answer
    teaching system), Zen, 49
monkeys: man from, 136; way of the
    cat/way of the monkey, 44, 236

Monod, Jacques, 116
monotheism, 26, 43, 61–62, 171.
    See also God
Moody, Raymond, 234
Moore, Marianne, 110
"The Moral Equivalent of War" (W.
    James), 92
moralism, 20, 151–52
morality, xiii–xiv, 204–6
Moses, 236, 261
the Mother, 79
Mother Theresa, 70, 201, 222
Mount Sinai, Moses on, 261
Moyers, Bill, xxiii, 189, 243–56
Mozart, Wolfgang Amadeus, 249,
    250
Muhammad, 39, 140, 236
Muller, Steven, 114, 124
multiplicity, unity and, 205
Murphy, Michael, 80
mushrooms: *Amanita muscaria*,
    228–29; psilocybin, 214, 230,
    231; sacred, 229; *teonanacatl*
    (God's flesh), 229
musicology, 271. *See also* chanting
Muslim religion. *See* Islam
mystery: afterlife, 93; Eleusinian
    Mysteries, 226–27, 229; God as,
    97; vs. ignorance, 30; Ineffable,
    154, 171; personal relationship
    with, 95; Rumi and Shams of
    Tabriz, 273
mysticism, xiii, 16, 83–84, 108, 171,
    189; and absolute perfection,
    23–24; Buddha, 63; Christian,
    68–69, 137; empirical, x, 63;
    encounter with God, 97; en-
    theogenic, 189, 214–15, 224–27,
    228–42; esoterics and, 47;
    everyday, 264; Godhead, 171;

Heard, 4, 80–81, 83; Huxley, x,
80, 83; infinite abyss of God, 154;
New Age and, 171; perennialism,
80; and physics, 215, 242;
reduction to feeling, 105; Rumi,
273; singular at the top and plural
at the bottom, 264; spiritual
personality type, 26, 61–62, 170;
symbols seen by, 170; transcendental realities, xvii. *See also*
revelation
Mysticism and Logic (Russell), 105
Mysticism and Philosophy (Stace), 230
myth, 23, 183–84, 202, 240–41;
Campbell and, xviii, 23, 127–28,
177–79, 183; defined, 178–79,
183–84; of progress, 183, 269;
and religion, xviii, 23, 178; and
science, 127–29; timeless aspect
of, 262–63

Nagarjuna, 201
Nasr, Seyyed Hossein, 5, 195
National Association of Biology
Teachers, 241
National Education Television
(NET), 84–85
Native American Church (NAC):
freedom of religion, 4–5, 22–23,
237–40, 265; Huichol Indians,
xiv, 60–61, 229; peyote meetings,
xiv, xviii, 225, 229, 238, 240;
Reuben Snake, v, 4–5, 22–23,
263; sweat lodge ceremonies, xiv,
240
Native Americans, xiv, xix, 20;
American Indian Religious
Freedom Act Amendments
(AIRFA), 237–38; and animals,
177; archaic tradition, 43; Black

Elk, 51; Chief Seattle, 180; Lakota
Sioux, 51, 237; materialism never
adopted by, 263; Onondaga
Indians, 86, 174–75, 176; primal
religion, 4–5, 174–77, 182–83,
263–64; Religious Freedom
Restoration Act (RFRA), 237–39;
shamans with NDEs, 234–35;
speech over writing, 79; Vine
Deloria Jr., xxiv, 182; Winnebago,
263; Winona LaDuke, xxi, 184;
World Parliament of Religions
(1999), xx–xxi, 173–74, 184
naturalism, 3–4, 11, 76, 80–81, 150,
158. *See also* materialism
natural philosophy, 124–25. *See also*
physics
natural selection, 135, 166
nature: not the whole of reality, 140;
science as knowledge of, 111–12,
126, 137, 248; unification of, 170;
virgin, 193. *See also* naturalism;
physical universe
NBC, *Wisdom* series, 95–96
near-death experiences (NDEs),
234–35
Needleman, Jacob, 5, 9
Nepal, 69–70
New Age, 89–90, 151–52, 154, 158,
164, 171
new colonialism, 158
New Dimensions interests, 125
Newman, Cardinal John Henry,
232–33, 234
Newman, Marsha, 102, 163–72
new paradigms, 158, 159, 170, 197
new physics, 169–70. *See also*
quantum mechanics
The New Polytheism (Miller), 43
New Realities, 164

Perfect Dirt, 208, 210, 211
perfection: absolute, 23–28;
 infinitude, 192; source, 250;
 transcendence as, 244
Perls, Fritz, 50
personal God, 61–62, 95–97,
 109–10, 147–48, 154
personal-growth programs, 44
personality types: delineated in India,
 109–10; spiritual, 26, 61–62, 170.
 See also spiritual temperaments
pessimism, 156–57
peyote, xiv, xviii, 222, 225, 229,
 238
The Peyote Road (Smith, Rhine, and
 Cousineau), xviii
phenomenology, 105, 162
philosophy, xii; ad hominem
 arguments, 30–31; analytic,
 104–7; "Bermuda Triangle" of
 Harvard/Princeton/Cornell, 4;
 debatable assumptions, 101;
 demotion of metaphysics and
 ontology, 115; fundamental
 questions, xv; future of religion
 and, 133; logical fallacies, 30–31;
 medieval, 105; natural, 124–25;
 religion distinguished from,
 xii–xiii; science and, 104–7;
 Socratic definition, 27. *See also*
 Asian philosophy; metaphysics;
 Perennialists; religious studies
philosophy departments, 103, 104–7
physical exhaustion, visionary states,
 226, 233–34, 235
physical universe: in Abrahamic
 traditions, 260; expansion of
 knowledge of, 111, 140; humans
 superior to, 112–13; only in your
 mind, 217; science limited to,

144, 150, 160, 189; sequence of
 evolution of, 160. *See also* nature
physics, 124–25, 199, 215, 242. *See
 also* quantum mechanics
Plantinga, Alvin, 241
Plato, xiii–xiv, 27, 28, 78, 96, 201,
 276; *Apology*, 1; beauty as splendor
 of the true, 193; cave allegory, xvii,
 78, 189, 222, 260–62; Eleusinian
 Mysteries, 226–27; eye of the soul,
 145; higher madness, 169; *metaxy*,
 29; on myths, 178; *The Republic*,
 xvii, 262. *See also* Socrates
Plotinus, 40, 78, 201, 272
pluralism, religious, 9, 42, 43, 57
poetry, 246, 275; Jeffers, 256; Rumi,
 263, 272–74; truth, 196
poisons, three, 206
Pokhara, trek to, 69
Polaroid inventor, 128
political action, 73, 110, 152;
 Buddhist monks, 130; churches
 involved with, 180; reducing
 Muslim world, 265; violence bred
 by differences in, 93. *See also* war
The Politics of Experience (Laing),
 115
Polkinghorn, John, 150, 269
polyphonic chanting, xiv, 51, 56–57,
 168, 271
polytheism, 26, 43, 61–62, 171
positivism, 115, 169, 270; Comte,
 269; and education, 197, 199;
 logical, 104
possession, craving for, 265–66
postmodernism, 12, 91, 134,
 158–59, 266–67; *Primordial
 Truth and Postmodern Theology*
 (Smith and Griffin), xv–xvi, 2. See
 also *Beyond the Post-Modern Mind*

poverty: monastic, 69; Muslim world, 265; self-image, 199; social problem, 72; spiritual/material, 70
Power, God as, 97, 138
powers: paranormal, 126, 218–20. *See also* empowerment
practice. *See* spiritual practice
pragmatism, 3, 26, 67
prajna, 7–8. See also *jnana* (knowledge) yoga
pratiyasammutpada, 7
prayers, xiv, 4, 17–19, 210; favorite, 148; Native American, xviii, 176, 229
present, responsibility to, 207
Pribram, Karl, 170
primal religions, 4–5, 34; Native American, 4–5, 174–77, 182–83, 263–64; in *The Religions of Man/ The World's Religions,* 87. *See also* aborigines; Native American Church
primordial tradition, xiii, xvi, 15, 37–58, 102, 155; defined, 15, 37–38, 54, 153; polarizing sacred and profane, 153, 155, 175; recent scientific findings analogous with, 160; return to, 167, 172. *See also* Traditionalists; wisdom traditions
Primordial Truth and Postmodern Theology (Smith and Griffin), xv–xvi, 2
Prince, Raymond, 233, 234, 235
privatism, 110
Procrustean view, 10, 63–64
profane, sacred and, 153, 155, 175
progress, 111, 141–42, 176–77, 183, 269
progressive religion, 201

prophesy, 164. *See also* futurism
prophetic faith, and ontological faith, 109
Prophets, Judaism, 39, 78
Protestantism, 96, 267; colleges founded to train ministers for, 269; and mysticism, 81; salvation as gift of divine grace, 236; splintered, 91. *See also* Methodism
psilocybin mushrooms, 214, 230, 231
The Psychedelic Experience (Leary, Metzner, and Alpert), 213, 216
psychedelics, xiv, 213, 215–16, 228–42
psychic abilities, 219–20
psychologizing, 30–31
psychology: on anger, 70; Freudian, 30–31, 63, 68; humanistic, 63–64; parapsychology, 219–20; of religious experience, 213; transpersonal, 63–64. *See also* Jung, Carl
psychotropics (soul-turning), 189. *See also* entheogens
Ptolemies, ix
publishing, religious books, 269
purpose: science and, 116–17, 137. *See also* meaning
Pythagoras, 78, 226

Quakers, xii
quality: religious studies, 162; science and, 117
quality of life, religious dimension, 215–16, 231
quantum mechanics, 23–24, 160, 169–70, 247; mystical, 242; other worlds, 30, 177–78, 184–85, 247
Quine, Willard, 106, 115

religion *(continued)*
traditions, 42; truth in, xv–xvi, 6,
22–27, 137–38, 248–49; unity-
in-diversity, 88–91; varieties of
explorations, 212–21; violence/
war linked with, 93, 130, 220–21;
world, 91. *See also* Asian philosophy; Christianity; churches; Islam;
Judaism; mysticism; Native
Americans; primal religions;
primordial tradition; religious
studies; revelation; wisdom
traditions
religion-science relationship, 10–12,
150–51, 179–85; Dalai Lama and,
71–72; hoi polloi unconcerned
with conflict in, 268; humanistic
and transpersonal psychology and,
63–64; intellectuals seeing conflict
in, 181, 268–69; limited worldview of science, 101–2, 111–51,
158–60, 163–65, 172, 181, 183,
189, 197, 241–42, 248; mutual
rejection, 240–41; no conflict,
xvi–xvii, 101, 108; as partnership,
143–48, 180; primordial tradition
and, 10–11, 102; reconciliation
unsuccessful, xii, xiii, 3, 189;
science king in, 270; unbalanced,
xvi–xvii, 101–2, 108; university
and, 247–48, 269, 270. *See also*
evolution; scientism
*The Religions of Man/ The World's
Religions* (Smith), xiii, 43, 45, 77,
83–88, 164, 207; art, 193; Bellah
epigraph, 90; Islam, 53, 87;
revised elements, 85–88, 176–77;
sales figures, 151; sins of religions,
xvi; voices of religions, xxi

religious freedom, 4–5, 22–23,
237–40, 264–65
Religious Freedom Restoration Act
(RFRA), 237–39
Religious Olympics, 174
religious pluralism, 9, 42, 43, 57
religious studies, xii, 50–52, 77,
161–62, 212–13, 246–47; cross-
cultural, xiv–xvi; importance of,
45–46; MIT, 108; objectivity in,
162, 252–53; scientific method in,
162, 270; and truth, 162, 252,
270. *See also* philosophy
Renaissance, 266
The Republic (Plato), xvii, 262
Reuys, Steve, xv, xvi, 101, 103–10
revelation, 8–9, 63, 231; by direct
discernment, 237; diseases/fast-
ing/physical exhaustion and, 226,
233–37; "distributive revelation,"
89–90; entheogenic, 222–26,
231–33; from inside, 250; in
NDEs, 234; science replacing,
126–27. *See also* mysticism; vision
Rhine, Gary, xxi, 263, 275
rights: minority, 142, 157, 180;
religious, 5, 22–23, 237–40,
264–65. *See also* freedom
Rig Veda, 228–29
rituals, 201–2, 237, 274
"The Rock" (Eliot), ix
Rogers, Carl, 217
Rolling Stones, 133
Romans, 183. *See also* Plotinus
romantic love, 193–94, 255
roots, importance of, 133
Rorschach blot, life as, 26, 31
roshi (Zen master), 31–34, 132,
146–47, 277; Dōgen, 201, 210;

Goto Zunigan, 5–6, 76–77;
Huang Po, 62, 86
Rosicrucianism, 155
rote learning, 197
Rumi, 263, 272–74
Russell, Bertrand, 29–30, 51, 105
Russia: atheist Soviet Union, 259;
czarina and St. John Chrysostom,
146
ruts, cultural, 268
Ryoanji temple complex, 76–77

sacred: art, 167–68, 193, 270–75;
children's education in, 192–93;
everything, 191–206; and profane,
153, 155, 175
sadhana (spiritual quest), 43
Sagan, Carl, *Cosmos*, 113
Saguna Brahman, 77
St. Louis, 81, 82; Committee on
Racial Equality (CORE), 22;
Swami Satprakashananda, 5–6,
55, 84; Washington University,
xii, 4, 84, 85
saints: Augustine, 20–21, 161, 201,
250, 251; early Irish, 235; Francis,
145–46; Italian, 61; John
Chrysostom, 146; Paul, 97, 152;
"Saint Ego," 68; Thomas, 160–61
Salins, Marshall, 115, 199
salvation, 27–28, 157, 236
Salzburg Seminar on American
Studies (1972), 233–34
samadhi, 48, 105
samsara, 72–73, 260
sanctity, 41–42
sangha (spiritual community), 129
sannyasin (homeless renunciates), 73
Santayana, George, 133, 149

sat (infinite being), 16
satchitananda (infinite being, infinite
awareness, infinite bliss), 16, 58,
153–54
satori (intuitive illumination), 31,
49, 105–6, 231
Satprakashananda, Swami, 5–6, 55,
82, 84
savants, 196–97; spiritual, 154–55
Scheinin, Richard, 189, 222–27
schizophrenia, 134–35, 165–66
Schumacher, E.{ths}F., 88
Schuon, Frithjof, xv–xvi, xix–xx, 6,
157; esoteric/exoteric distinction,
40–41, 52; *In the Tracks of
Buddhism*, xix; *Language of the
Self,* xix; Traditionalist, 5, 156;
Transcendent Unity of Religions, 9,
37, 88; *Understanding Islam,*
xix–xx
science: animate/inanimate objects,
199–200; balanced, 107–9, 110;
Cartesian, 170; Comte stage of
history, 269; and control, 107–8,
113–14, 125, 200; culture and,
179, 268; dogma, 184, 241;
emergence of modern, 121–22;
humanities and, 109, 110, 114,
118, 123–24; and impoverished
self-image, 199; interdisciplinary,
109; and invisible, 137–38, 164,
248; and knowledge, 101–6,
111–20, 126, 137, 164, 248;
limited worldview, 101–2,
111–51, 158–60, 163–65, 172,
181, 183, 189, 197, 241–42, 248;
on matter and consciousness, 160;
metaphysics in, 160; modern
distinguished from generic, 125;

science *(continued)*
   new colonialism, 158; Newtonian,
   125, 163–64, 169, 170; as oracle
   of our age, 121, 125–33; paradigm shifts, 158, 159, 170;
   philosophy and, 104–7; place of,
   103–10; pure, 165; as religion,
   126–27, 181; religious studies
   using method of, 162, 270; spirit
   connected to, 200; and transcendence, 102, 125–26, 164–66,
   169–70; and truth, 101, 116, 117,
   169, 172, 198, 241, 247–48;
   unification of nature, 170;
   university rooted in method of,
   11, 114, 123–24, 183; upward
   causation, 198–99; West different
   because of, 54–55; white heat in
   quest of, 128–29; and wisdom
   traditions, 62, 72. *See also*
   evolution; physics; religion-science
   relationship
scientism, x, 10–12, 55, 101, 108,
   118, 165; vs. collective outlooks,
   55; countering, 163–72; defined,
   127; and fundamentalism, 158;
   human potential movement and,
   159; new physics and, 170; primal
   religions and, 182–83; primordial
   tradition and, 167; reducing
   stature of human self, 270; and
   secularization, 158, 240–41; straw
   dog, 268, 270; waning/not
   waning, 151, 158
Scopes "Monkey Trial," 136
The Screwtape Letters (Lewis), 192
Seattle, Chief, 180
secularization, 158, 239–41, 246
seeing, 96, 266. *See also* eye; vision
seers, 39, 266

self: Atman, 218; *hara* as center of,
   33; human divine, 15–16;
   scientism reducing stature of, 270;
   Western view of, 134–35
self-effort *(jiriki)*, 236
self-image, 134–35, 199
self-realization, *samadhi*, 48
separation of church and state, 202,
   239
September 11 (2001), xxi, 257–59,
   264–65, 269
Serengeti Plain, 34–36
Sermon on the Mount, 152
sex, 69, 205–6, 255, 266. *See also*
   gender issues
Shakespeare, William, 194
shamanism, 29, 61, 220, 234–36
Shams of Tabriz, 273
Shankara, 201
shape-shifting, 127
Shaw, G. B., 21
sheikhs (spiritual masters), Sufi, 4,
   5–6
Sheldon, William, 109
Shenandoah, Chief, 175
Shield, Benjamin, 95
Shinto, xix, 87, 88
Shultes, R. E., 229
siddhis, 219–20
Sikhism, 87
silence, inner, 202, 203, 275
Simon, Mayo, 85
Skepticism and Animal Faith
   (Santayana), 149
Smith, Huston (personal): on
   autobiography, 1, 5, 83; Berkeley
   home, xxi, 4, 175; daughters, xiv,
   20, 24–26, 140–41, 146–48;
   granddaughter, 208–9; Isaiah
   (grandson), 20; retired, xii; youth,

spirituality: Creation, 160–61; India, 169; offbeat, 154–55; religion and, 151–52, 182
spiritual/material poverty, 70
Spiritual Olympics, 174
spiritual personality types, 26, 61–62, 170. *See also* spiritual temperaments
spiritual practice, 50–51; daily, xiv, 4, 17–20, 22, 210–11; demystifying, 207–11
spiritual savants, 154–55
"Spiritual Summit Conference," Calcutta, 68–69
spiritual temperaments, 41, 44, 77, 96–97. *See also* spiritual personality types
spiritual wholeness, 6
spoken word: over writing, 79, 196; problem area in human life, 205–6; Tao, 77, 153–54. *See also* oral traditions
Sri Lanka: Buddhist-Hindu conflict, 130; Theravada Buddhism, 131
Stace, Walter T., 230
state, separation of church and, 202, 239
state religion, 239–40
"Steady State," 71
Steiner, Rudolf, 154–55, 192–93, 200
subjectivity, 105, 108, 114, 162
Su Ch'e, v
suffering, 145–48
Sufism, 45, 52–53; certainty lore, 47; esoteric, 45, 48, 53; exoteric, 48; eye of the heart, xviii, 145; al-Ghazzali, 44–45, 53; Ibn Arabi, 53, 279; Mevlevi order, 274; prayers, xiv, 4, 17–19; in *The*

Religions of Man/ The World's Religions, 86, 87; Rumi, 263, 272–74; sheikhs (spiritual masters), 4, 5–6; three ways to understand fire, 251; whirling dervishes, xiv, 274
sun, salute to, 263
Sunim, Soen, 76
supernatural, 11, 140
Supreme Court decisions, on Native American religion, 5, 22–23, 237–40
surrender, 108
Suzuki, Daisetz T., 31, 95–96, 267
swamis: Ramakrishna Order, 4; Satprakashananda, 5–6, 55, 82, 84
sweat lodge ceremonies, xiv, 240
Swedenborg, Emanuel, 28–29, 154–55, 200
The Sword of Gnosis (Needleman), 5
symbolic dimension: biblical, 137; capacity to see, 167–68, 170; of overtones, 168
symbolic logic, 105
synchronicity, xix–xx
Syracuse University, xii, 4, 103–4; Bohm visit, 170; near Onondaga Reservation, 86, 174–75

tai chi, xiv
A Tale of Two Cities (Dickens), 73
tantric tradition, 56–57, 220
Tanzania, Masai warriors, 34–36
Tao, 249; ecological crisis and, 109; spoken/unspoken, 77, 153–54. *See also* Tao Te Ching
Taoism, 86–87, 248, 249; China, xiv, 60, 78–79. *See also* Tao
Tao Te Ching, 20, 275
tariki (other effort), 236

teachers, as examples, 206
"Teaching Science with Awareness of Its Limitations" conference, 183
technology: computer analogue to education, 197; destructive, 157; medical, 141; myth of progress, 269; and Rumi craze, 272–73; upward causation and, 198. *See also* ecstatic technologies
telepathy, 219
television: birth of NET/PBS, 84–85; *Cosmos* (Sagan), 113; "The Wisdom of Faith" (PBS), xxiii, 243–56; *Wisdom* series (NBC), 95–96
Temple of Apollo, Delphi, xiv
Tensin, Osel, 64
terrorism: September 11 (2001), xxi, 257–59, 264–65
Thailand, Theravada Buddhism, 131
"That Strong Mercy," 1
theoria, 96, 241
Theravada (southern) Buddhism, 131–32
thin places, 264
third eye, 145
Thomas, Lewis, 183
Thomas, St., 160–61
Thomists, 192
Thompson, April, 143–48
A Thoughtful Soul, 155
Tibetan Buddhism, 22, 68, 130, 132, 168; America, 64, 65, 68; *bardos,* 28, 157; and China, 130, 131; India, xiv, 4, 68, 71, 168; Kagyupa school, 65; literature, 132–33; monks with Grateful Dead, 271; polyphonic chanting, xiv, 51, 56–57, 168, 271; *puja* (worship ceremony), 168;

reincarnation, 93; in *The Religions of Man/ The World's Religions,* 85–86, 87; third eye, 145; U.S., 132–33. *See also* Dalai Lama
Tillich, Paul, 41, 109
time: entheogenic visions, 223; eternity as beyond, 185; in preaxial religion, 204; religious institutions taking, 21; religious/scientific view of, 91–92; for retreats, 129–30. *See also* death; future; past; present
timelessness, 184, 262–63, 264. *See also* eternity; infinity
Toms, Michael, 101, 102, 121–33
Traditionalists, xiii, 5, 9–11, 156–57. *See also* Perennialists; primordial tradition
transcendence, xiii, 243–44, 246, 276; art, 272; defined, 244; mystical, xvii; myth as language of, 178–79; Native Americans and, 263; new physics and, 170; religious institutions and, 15–16, 122, 165–66, 201; restoration of, 167; science and, 102, 125–26, 164–66, 169–70; Sufi dancing, 274
Transcendent Unity of Religions (Schuon), 9, 37, 88
translations: Blofeld, 86; Rumi, 273–74
transpersonal aspects, of God, 109–10
transpersonal psychology, 63–64
transport: by art, 270, 271–72, 275; by Eastern philosophies, 168
transportability, of religious traditions, 42
tribal peoples, 34, 193, 204. *See also* aborigines; Native Americans

Trungpa Rinpoche, Chogyam, 64,
65, 68, 143
truth: dogmatic, 151–52; God as,
96–97; *jnanic* knowledge, 96;
literal, 137; myths as, 178–79;
new paradigms and, 159; objective, 105; one, 248; ontological,
162; poetry telling, 196; proving,
248–49; quest for, xiii, xv–xvi; in
religions, xv–xvi, 6, 22–27,
137–38, 248–49; religious studies
and, 162, 252, 270; rituals as
containers for, 237; science and,
101, 116, 117, 169, 172, 198,
241, 247–48; subjective, 105;
timeless, 184. *See also* reality; the
way things really are

Understanding Islam (Schuon), xix–xx
Understanding the Present (Appleyard), 12, 158, 199
Unitarians, 202
unity, 125, 205. *See also* universalism
unity-in-diversity, religions, 88–91
universalism, 9, 59–60; of primordial
tradition, 54; salvation, 27–28;
world religion, 91; in world's
religions, 205–6. *See also* unity
university: Cardinal Newman and,
232; enchanted garden, 169;
German research university, 269;
and indigenous religions, 174;
religion passé at, 270; religion-
science relationship, 247–48, 269;
rooted in scientific method, 11,
114, 123–24, 183. *See also*
humanities; philosophy departments; religious studies; science
University of California at Berkeley,
xii, 3, 4; Good Society Conference

(1992), 12; Leary, 214; library, ix;
materialism of philosophers, 270;
quantum physics, 242
University of California at Los
Angeles (UCLA): Dalai Lama, 70;
Smith lecture, xxii–xxiii; "Soul
and Spirit" seminar, xviii
University of Chicago, 85; Divinity
School, xii, 3, 76; *The History of
Religions*, 39
Unmoved Mover, 96
Upanishads, 40, 48; Katha, 82; seers,
39. *See also* Vedanta
upaya, 39
Updike, John, 252
upward causation, 198–99

value: Asian philosophy, 108–10;
infinite, 119–20, 138–39; lost,
142; other world, 247; primordial
tradition and, 167; relative/ab-
solute truths, 138; science and,
113, 116, 117, 119. *See also*
meaning; morality; worth
The Varieties of Religious Experience
(W. James), 136–37, 213
Vatican II, 165
Vedanta, xix, 4, 20, 77, 79–80,
109–10, 267; Vedanta Society, 84.
See also Upanishads; Vedas
Vedas, xvi, 80; Rig Veda, 228–29.
See also Vedanta
veracity: virtue, 206. *See also* truth
violence: object of knowledge, 164;
problem area in human life,
205–6; religions linked with, 93,
130, 220–21. *See also* war
Vipassana meditation, 4, 129, 130,
132
virtues, 206, 244. *See also* goodness

vision: binocular, 102; Buddhism as a total civilization, 131–32; Newman's, 232–33, 234; religious, 145–46; religious institutions losing, 121–22; of whole, 250–51. *See also* invisible; revelation; seeing; transcendence

vision quests, 236

Wach, Joachim, 76
Wakan Tanka, 264. *See also* Great Spirit
Wallace, Allan, 160
Walsh, Roger, 29
war, 92; religion and, 130, 220–21; "There never was a war that wasn't inward" (Moore), 110; World War II, 3
Washington University, St. Louis, xii, 4, 84, 85
Wasson, R. Gordon, 228–29
"The Waste Land" (Eliot), 118
Watts, Alan, 217
way of the cat/way of the monkey, 44, 236
the way things really are, ix–xxiv, 265–68, 270. *See also* reality; truth
wealth, problem area in human life, 205–6
Weber, Max, 163
Weinberg, Steven, x, 117, 129
Wells, H. G., 177, 243
West: appeal of Asian philosophy/ Eastern religions, 122, 161, 168–69; Asian philosophy as unconscious of, 108–9; difference because of science, 54–55; knowledge as impersonal and detached, 195; modern mind-set, 198; and progress, 177; value of Asian

philosophy, 108–10; virtues, 206. *See also* university
What Is Sufism? (Lings), 46–47
whirling dervishes, xiv, 274
White, Timothy, 189, 228–42
Whitehead, Alfred North, xii, 180, 240, 266
whole, view of, 250–51
wholeness, 6, 124–25
Why Religion Matters (Smith), xiii, 144, 151, 177–82, 258
Wieman, Henry Nelson, 3, 76
Wilde, Oscar, 43
Wilhelm, Richard, 161
Wilson, E. O., 67, 150–51, 179–80, 181, 183
wisdom, 27; in Christianity, 141; of faith, xxiii, 243–56; two-sided, xiv; "winnowing the wisdom of the world," 276–77; wiser than despair, 147. *See also* wisdom traditions
"The Wisdom of Faith" (PBS), xxiii, 243–56
Wisdom series (NBC), 95–96
wisdom traditions, 59–74, 88–92, 171, 189; downward causation, 199; other worlds of, 247, 260; in religious studies, 253; singular at the top and plural at the bottom, 264; sublime unanimity of, 267–68; and whole, 251. *See also* mysticism; primordial tradition; religion
Wittgenstein, Ludwig, 106
World Hypotheses (Pepper), 3
World Parliament of Religions (1999), Cape Town, South Africa, xx–xxi, 173–74, 184
world religion, 91

worlds, other, 101, 153–54, 223,
224, 244, 260; different languages, 178; divides in, 153–54;
physics, 30, 177–78, 184–85,
247; students learning, 246–47
*The World's Religions. See The
Religions of Man/ The World's
Religions* (Smith)
World War II, 3. *See also* Holocaust
worth, 138, 247. *See also* value
Wovoka (shaman), 234
writing: academic, 124; beginning
of, 271; detached, 195–96; spoken
word over, 79, 196. *See also*
literature
Wuthering Heights (Brontë), 255
wu wei (nonaction), 79, 87

yogas, xiv, 21, 54; *bhakti* (love), 21,
77, 96; four (knowledge, love,
work, and meditation), 21, 77, 96;
hatha, 17, 19, 79, 210; *jnana*
(knowledge) yoga, 7–8, 21, 27,
77, 79–80, 90, 96–97; karma

(service), xxiii, 21, 77, 96; raja
(meditation), 19, 21, 77, 96, 237
Young, Jack, 134–42
Youth Seminar, 175–76

zazen (seated meditation), Zen, 231
Zen, xiv, 4, 31–34, 52, 130; American,
42; Blofeld translations, 86; China,
60; Christianity compared with, 52;
Dharma Bums, 267; esoteric, 48;
finger pointing at the moon, 194;
"He stinks of Zen," 256; Japan, xiv,
4, 31–34, 84; *joriki*, 231; koans,
31–34; Korea, 76; Mahayana form,
132; *mondo* (question-and-answer
teaching system), 49; Rinzai, 31–34;
satori, 31, 49, 105–6, 231; sleep
deprivation, 32; Soen Sunim, 76;
Suzuki, 31, 95–96, 267; *zazen*
(seated meditation), 231. See also
roshi (Zen master)
The Zen Teachings of Huang Po
(Blofeld translation), 86
Zoroastrianism, 87

HUSTON SMITH is widely regarded as the most eloquent and accessible contemporary authority on the history of religions. A leading figure in the comparative philosophy of religion, he has taught at Washington University, MIT, Syracuse University, and at the University of California, Berkeley.

PHIL COUSINEAU is a best-selling author, an editor, a photographer, an award-winning filmmaker, and an independent scholar who lectures around the world on a wide range of topics, from mythology to mentorship to soul. His recent books include *Once and Future Myths, The Art of Pilgrimage, The Book of Roads,* and the forthcoming *The Olympic Odyssey.* He lives in the North Beach neighborhood of San Francisco, California.

Compositor:	Binghamton Valley Composition, LLC
Text:	11/14 Garamond
Display:	Akzidenz Grotesk
Printer and Binder:	Maple-Vail Manufacturing Group
Index:	Barbara Roos